WHO'S BURIED WHERE IN LONDON

Peter Matthews

BLOOMSBURY
SHIRE

Published in Great Britain in 2017 by Bloomsbury Shire
(part of Bloomsbury Publishing Plc), PO Box 883,
Oxford, OX1 9PL, UK.

1385 Broadway, 5th Floor New York, NY 10018, USA.

E-mail: shireeditorial@ospreypublishing.com
www.shirebooks.co.uk

Bloomsbury Shire is a trademark of Bloomsbury
Publishing Plc.

A CIP catalogue record for this book is available from the
British Library.

Shire Library no. 770. ISBN-13: 978 0 74781 296 8

PDF e-book ISBN: 978 1 78442 202 8

ePub ISBN: 978 1 78442 201 1

Peter Matthews has asserted his right under the Copyright,
Designs and Patents Act, 1988, to be identified as the
author of this book.

Index by Zoe Ross.

Typeset in Perpetua, Adobe Garamond Pro and
Gill Sans Std.

Printed in China through World Print Ltd.

17 18 19 20 21 10 9 8 7 6 5 4 3 2 1

COVER IMAGE
A picturesque row of graves at Highgate Cemetery
(Alamy).

TITLE PAGE IMAGE
A general view of Kensal Green Cemetery, illustrating
the great variety of tomb types and designs.

ACKNOWLEDGEMENTS
All images are the author's own photographs except
for the following:

Alamy, cover image; © Martin Colloms, page 156 (right);
Friends of Kensal Green Cemetery, pages 103 (inset) and
112 (inset); The London Metropolitan Archives, page 92
(right); The Music Hall Guild of Great Britain & America,
pages 194 and 250; St Paul's Cathedral © Graham
Lacdao, pages 18 and 27; Westminster Abbey © The Dean
& Chapter of Westminster, pages 42–57.

I would also like to thank Fr Paul Reece, rector of
St Lawrence, Little Stanmore, for permission to publish
my photograph of the Chandos mausoleum on page 69.

Shire Publications is supporting the Woodland Trust, the UK's leading woodland conservation charity, by funding the dedication of trees.

CONTENTS

INTRODUCTION

MANY IMPORTANT PEOPLE have been buried in London, in its churches, graveyards and cemeteries. This book is a detailed guide to the last resting places of famous people, individuals who deserve to be better known, as well as a few eccentrics and some infamous criminals. The book comprises over 1,000 people, and I have tried to include a wide range of people who were important in their chosen profession, including soldiers, scientists, writers, actors, artists, sculptors, architects, sportsmen and engineers. I have tried to include as many people as possible, especially those who have left a legacy in London, whether it be buildings or bridges they built, institutions they founded, or collections they bequeathed to London's museums. When I began my research I already had an idea about many of the people I would feature, but I soon found many lesser-known individuals who deserved to be included, and I hope you will enjoy making their acquaintance as much as I did. I have concentrated on the people, not the monuments, so the book doesn't always include the most impressive tombs (though you will pass many of those when you walk round any of the cemeteries). It will become clear very quickly that some of the most important people have quite modest memorials. I am sure I will be criticised for the people I have featured as well as for those I have left out, but I make no apologies, as this is my own personal selection.

As well as cemeteries, I have included parish churches and their graveyards, as well as St Paul's Cathedral and Westminster Abbey. I have spent over three years researching the book, and have walked round all the cemeteries and almost all the churches. I have not just listed the people buried in each location, but tell you where to find their graves. The only exceptions are a few of the central churches, where the graveyards and vaults have been cleared, and often there are no memorials; in these instances, even if there is nothing to see, I list the important people who were buried there.

There is a growing interest in visiting cemeteries, something the Victorians would recognise, as their cemeteries were designed and landscaped to be visited, not only by bereaved families, but also by the general public. The major cemeteries are full of interesting architecture, and contain a variety of different types of tomb, covered in a fascinating range of Victorian symbolism. They are an open-air sculpture

Some impressive tombs in West Norwood Cemetery.

gallery, offering the work of some of our finest sculptors. Most cemeteries are also now important wildlife sites, with a great variety of flora and fauna, and many are maintained so as to allow birds, butterflies and mammals to thrive.

Cemeteries are usually open daily, but their visiting hours change throughout the year. Details can be checked on their websites, where you can also learn about tours and events. Please note that the Jewish cemeteries are closed on Saturdays, and also close early on Fridays; they also do not usually allow photography. Some churches are open for limited hours, and in many cases their opening hours, or a telephone number, can be found online, so you should check before travelling to avoid disappointment. In researching this book I have received a lot of help from the staff of churches and cemeteries, to whom I am hugely grateful. In particular I would like to thank Henry Vivian-Neal at Kensal Green Cemetery, Robert Stephenson at Brompton Cemetery, Colin Fenn at West Norwood Cemetery, Ian Dungavell at Highgate Cemetery, Eric Willis at Golders Green Crematorium, Ed Holmes at St Paul's Cathedral and Tony Trowles at Westminster Abbey.

Books I have consulted are listed in Further Reading. In addition I have made regular use of the online *Oxford Dictionary of National Biography*, as well as the 'Find a Grave' website which, though very useful, is not always reliable.

A BRIEF HISTORY OF BURIAL IN LONDON

THE ROMANS DID not allow burials in their cities, so the dead were buried in cemeteries located outside the city boundaries. From the Middle Ages, Londoners were buried in their parish church, the wealthy in the vaults and the others in the graveyard. The Romans had often cremated their dead, but this was no longer allowed, as for Christians the body had to remain whole to be resurrected. After the Reformation, dissenters opened up their own unconsecrated burial grounds, such as Bunhill Fields. As time went on the graveyards and vaults of the city's churches became full to overflowing, and by the nineteenth century they were becoming a serious health risk. They were also a target for the body-snatchers, who supplied fresh bodies to the hospitals for dissection. During the 1830s, while the government discussed what could be done to improve the situation, a number of private cemeteries were developed in London's countryside, offering more salubrious surroundings, beautiful landscaping, and high walls to deter the resurrection men. The first was Kensal Green, which opened in 1833, and was soon followed by others,

The central avenue at Brompton Cemetery, leading to its classical chapel.

The ruined Gothic chapel at Nunhead Cemetery.

usually referred to as the Magnificent Seven; West Norwood opened in 1837, Highgate in 1839, Abney Park, Brompton and Nunhead in 1840, and Tower Hamlets in 1841. After much discussion and procrastination, and many reports of the scandalous treatment of the dead, in 1852 the government finally banned burials in central London, and the parishes began to create their own cemeteries further out, such as St Marylebone Cemetery in Finchley.

Towards the end of the nineteenth century, with an increase in secularism, cremation began to be discussed seriously, though at first there was much resistance. The first crematorium opened in Woking in 1885, and London's first dedicated crematorium opened in Golders Green in 1902. Several of the existing cemeteries soon began to offer cremation, and it is now the most popular form of funeral. By the middle of the twentieth century, some of the private cemeteries found it hard to keep afloat, and Highgate and Nunhead both closed down. Nunhead is now operated by Southwark Council and Highgate is run by the Friends of Highgate Cemetery.

The story now seems to have come full circle, as burial space in London is again in short supply, so that some cemeteries have had to find ways of creating new burial plots, including making use of what were once paths, and one cemetery is planning to re-use old graves.

CITY OF LONDON

MOST OF THE City's churches are open regularly, though it is best to check opening hours on their websites or the website of the Friends of the City Churches, www.london-city-churches.org.uk.

The ancient Temple Church lies south of Fleet Street and is accessible via Middle Temple Lane. On the north side of the graveyard is the modest ledger stone marking the grave of **Oliver Goldsmith** (1728–74), the Irish-born playwright, poet and novelist whose last home was in Brick Court, Middle Temple. His most important works are the novel *The Vicar of Wakefield*, the poem *The Deserted Village* and the classic comedy *She Stoops to Conquer*. Buried in the church itself, but with no monument, is the Elizabethan playwright **John Marston** (1576–1634), whose most important play was *The Malcontent*.

In the nineteenth-century church of St Dunstan-in-the-West in Fleet Street a number of memorials remain from the earlier church, including one to **Sir Richard Hoare** (1648–1719), who

The modest tomb of playwright and novelist Oliver Goldsmith in the graveyard of Temple church.

founded Hoare's Bank, which still operates in Fleet Street. It is the oldest private bank in Britain and is still owned by the family. He was buried in the family vault, and his memorial, a baroque cartouche, is on the east wall. Also buried here, but with no memorials, are the poets **Thomas Campion** (1567–1620) and **Thomas Carew** (1594/5–1640).

Until the 1980s most national newspapers were printed in Fleet Street, and St Bride's church, at its eastern end, is still referred to as the 'journalists' church'. The street's printing history goes back to the time of **Wynkyn de Worde** (d. 1534/5), who trained with William Caxton, and took on his business when he died, later moving to Fleet Street. He was

Opposite: Sir Henry Wood conducting at the Proms in a stained glass window above his grave in St Sepulchre without Newgate, where he learnt to play the organ, (see page 11).

The modern wall plaque to the printer Wynkyn de Worde in St Bride's in Fleet Street.

buried in St Bride's, though his grave has been lost, but there is a modern plaque to him at the back of the church. Also buried here was the organist and composer **Thomas Weelkes** (1576–1623), who is best known for his madrigals. The site of his grave is not known, but in the crypt is a plaque erected in 1923 to commemorate him. On the exterior wall at the east end of the north aisle is the badly weathered gravestone of **Samuel Richardson** (1689–1761), who is considered to be the father of the English novel. His epistolary novel *Pamela* was a huge success and inspired many imitations. There is also a commemorative brass plaque in the crypt, which was erected on the two hundredth anniversary of his birth by the Stationers'

Company. Although the crypt was cleared of coffins in the 1950s, Richardson's lead coffin was unexpectedly found there in 1992, so he still remains there, in body as well as in spirit. Also buried in St Bride's, but without a memorial, are **Mary Frith** (1584–1659), the notorious cross-dressing thief known as Moll Cutpurse, **Richard Lovelace** (1617–57), the cavalier poet, and **Thomas Hansard** (1776–1833) who, like his father before him, was the publisher of parliamentary debates.

Off Playhouse Yard in Blackfriars Lane EC4 are Ireland Yard and Church Entry, where you can see all that is left of the churchyard of St Ann Blackfriars, which was destroyed in the Great Fire of 1666, though burials continued until 1849. Buried here was the lutenist **John Dowland** (1563–1626), who is best known for his tune *Lachrimae*. Also interred here was the famous painter of miniatures **Isaac Oliver** (*c.* 1565–1617), who was a pupil of Nicholas Hilliard. He was limner to Anne of Denmark and her son, Prince Henry, and some of his portraits are still in the Royal Collection.

At the west end of St Andrew's Holborn, under the organ, is the tomb of **Thomas Coram** (*c.* 1668–1751), the sea captain who established the Foundling Hospital in Bloomsbury to house and educate abandoned children. Coram was buried in the hospital's chapel, but when it closed in 1926 his body was moved to the chapel of the new site in Berkhamsted before being re-interred in St Andrew's in 1961. The distinguished sculptor **Francis Bird** (1667–1731) was buried in a vault in the church, but there is now no memorial. When the crypt was cleared in 2002–03

The Foundling Hospital coat of arms is prominent on the tomb of its founder, Thomas Coram, in St Andrew's Holborn.

his body, with many others, was removed to the City of London Cemetery in Ilford. Bird is most famous for his sculpture of St Paul's conversion on the west pediment of St Paul's Cathedral.

On Holborn Viaduct is the church of St Sepulchre without Newgate. Its north aisle is the Musicians' Chapel, where the famous conductor **Sir Henry Wood** (1869–1944) is buried. He is celebrated as the founder of the Promenade Concerts, which continue to fill the Royal Albert Hall every summer. His ashes are buried under the St Cecilia window, which has two scenes of him at work, playing the organ of St Sepulchre's and conducting a Promenade concert (see page 8). Also buried here is **John Smith** (1580–1631), the founder of Jamestown and first governor of Virginia. He was, famously, saved from the local Indian tribes by Pocahontas. There is a bronze plaque in the south aisle, marking the approximate site of his grave, and nearby is a memorial window to him.

The baroque wall memorial to banker Sir Richard Hoare in St Dunstan-in-the-West church in Fleet Street.

11

The grand tomb of Rahere, founder of St Bart's, London's oldest hospital, in St Bartholomew the Great in Smithfield.

Wren's Christ Church Newgate Street is now just an empty shell, and is laid out as a garden. It stands on the site of the church of Greyfriars monastery, and buried in the medieval church were **Isabella of France** (1295–1358), the wife of Edward II, and **Sir Thomas Malory** (1415–71), the author of the *Morte d'Arthur*, the inspiration for all future books on the Arthurian legend.

St Bartholomew the Great, by Smithfield Market, is all that is left of the church of the priory founded in 1123 by **Rahere** (d. 1143). Legend has it that Rahere, a courtier of Henry I, fell ill while on a pilgrimage to Rome, and promised God he would build a monastery if he recovered. Rahere was the first prior, and was buried in the church, but the impressive monument, on the north side of the sanctuary, was not erected until 1405. His recumbent figure is dressed in the Augustinian habit, with an angel at his feet. St Bartholomew's Hospital, which was an important part of the priory, is the oldest hospital in London.

St Giles Cripplegate, at the heart of the Barbican, has been sympathetically restored after being badly damaged in the Blitz, and still contains memorials of several major figures who were buried here. The most important burial is that of the poet **John Milton** (1608–74), whose *Paradise Lost* is considered to be one of the greatest poems in the English language. He spent his last years in Cripplegate, and is buried next to his father before the altar, the spot now marked by an inscribed stone. In 1790 his grave was opened and for a while visitors could view the body for a small fee. At the western end of the south aisle is a memorial to him with a bust by John Bacon the Elder, which was erected in 1793. Also in the south aisle is a bronze statue of Milton by Horace Montford, which used to stand outside the west end of the church, but was brought inside after it was damaged in the war. Next to the statue is a wall memorial to the cartographer **John Speed** (1551/2–1629), who produced the earliest set of county maps as well as plans of many English towns. Damaged in the Blitz, his bust has been restored and placed in a replica of the original monument. Next to it is a modern memorial to **Sir Martin Frobisher** (1535–94), the explorer and privateer, who worked with Drake in the West Indies, and again in defeating the

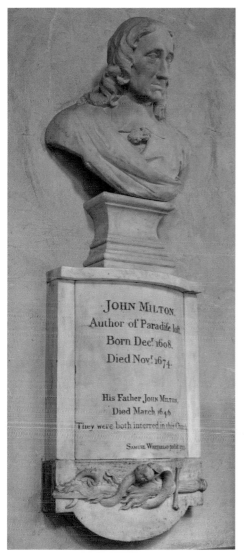

Spanish Armada of 1588, after which he was knighted. He died in battle in France and his entrails were buried in Plymouth, but his body was brought to London, where it was buried in the south aisle of the church. Also buried here, but with no memorial, are **John Foxe** (1516/7–87), author of a history of Protestant martyrs commonly known as *Foxe's Book of Martyrs*, and the composer **Giles Farnaby** (d. 1640), best known for his madrigals.

The medieval St Mary Aldermanbury church, next to the Guildhall, was destroyed in the Great Fire of 1666, and Wren's replacement was badly damaged in the Blitz. The church has been rebuilt in Fulton, Missouri, as a memorial to Winston Churchill, and the foundations and churchyard have now been laid out as

Above: John Bacon's wall memorial to John Milton in St Giles Cripplegate, with its symbolism of a fiery sword and a serpent.

Right: The restored memorial to the important cartographer John Speed in St Giles Cripplegate.

Memorial to Heminges and Condell, who published the First Folio of Shakespeare's plays, in the churchyard of St Mary Aldermanbury.

a garden. There is a monument to **John Heminges** (1566–1630) and **Henry Condell** (1576–1627), who were both members, with Shakespeare, of the Chamberlain's Men, and were buried in the church. They compiled the First Folio of Shakespeare's plays, without which 18 of the Bard's plays would probably have been lost to us. Buried under the chancel of Wren's church was the infamous judge **George Jeffreys** (1645–89), who got caught up in the religious politics of the

day, and is known as 'The Hanging Judge'. He gained his reputation when he had many of the supporters of the Duke of Monmouth hanged after the rebellion in the West Country.

St Mary Aldermary in Queen Victoria Street is one of Wren's few Gothic churches. At the eastern end of the south wall is a memorial to the celebrated physician **Percivall Pott** (1714–88), who worked for most of his life at St Bartholomew's Hospital, where he was senior surgeon from 1765. He is best known for 'Pott's disease' (a condition of the spine) and 'Pott's fracture', which he described after sustaining the injury when he fell off his horse. Both terms are still used in surgical language today.

St Mary Woolnoth in Lombard Street is one of Hawksmoor's most unusual churches. It is here that **Edward Lloyd** (c. 1648–1713) was buried. In 1892, because of the smell coming from the vault, all the coffins were cleared out and taken to the City of London Cemetery in Ilford. Lloyd ran a coffee house where ship-owners and underwriters met to hear the latest maritime news, and which later became the Corporation of Lloyds, which still operates in Richard Rogers' modern building in Lime Street.

In the church of St Benet, Paul's Wharf, was buried the great architect and theatre designer **Inigo Jones** (1573–1652). He was Surveyor of the King's Works for 27 years and introduced the classical style of architecture to England, his major works being the Queen's House in Greenwich, the Banqueting House in Whitehall and Covent Garden piazza. He also designed spectacular sets and costumes for court masques written by Ben Jonson. His tomb, which carried reliefs of the Banqueting House and a portrait bust, was destroyed in the Great Fire of 1666, but a copy of the inscription has been placed over the site of the family vault where he was buried, to the right of the altar.

In College Street is St Michael Paternoster Royal, where the famous Lord Mayor **Richard (Dick) Whittington** (*c.* 1350–1423) was buried. He lived next door to the church, worshipped there, and paid for it to be rebuilt. He once had a fine monument, but the church was destroyed in the Great Fire of 1666, and in Wren's new church a plaque marks the spot where the monument once stood, to the right of the altar. He is also commemorated by a modern window.

The plaque in St Stephen Walbrook to Nathaniel Hodges, who heroically remained in London to treat the sick during the Great Plague of 1665.

Sir John Vanbrugh (1664–1726), the playwright and architect, is buried in his family's vault in the south aisle of the church of St Stephen Walbrook, though he has no memorial. His first play, which took him only six weeks to write, was *The Relapse*, which is still performed, but he is best known today as the architect of Castle Howard and Blenheim Palace. Also buried here was **John Dunstable** (d. 1453), the composer of motets and other religious music. His grave and memorial were destroyed in the Great Fire, but a new memorial was placed on the south wall of the church in 1904. On the north wall is the memorial to **Nathaniel Hodges** (1629–88), a doctor who lived in Walbrook, and is revered for having remained in London during the Great Plague of 1665, treating anyone who asked for his help.

Miles Coverdale (1488–1569), the religious reformer, and the first person to translate the whole of the Bible into English, is buried in St Magnus the Martyr in Lower Thames Street. He lived in turbulent times, and spent many years in exile. Towards the end of his life he was rector of St Magnus for a short time. He was buried in St Bartholomew by the Exchange, but when it was demolished in 1840 his body was re-interred in a vault in the south-east corner of St Magnus, and there is a memorial to him on the east wall of the south aisle. In the earlier church was buried **Henry Yevele** (d. 1400), the most important master mason of his time. He worked for three kings, and was responsible for building the nave of Westminster Abbey.

St Olave Hart Street was the parish church attended by **Samuel Pepys** (1633–1703), the famous diarist and official

The Victorian wall memorial to the diarist Samuel Pepys in St Olave's church, where he worshipped.

The monument to the historian John Stow in St Andrew Undershaft. Stow holds a real quill, which is replaced every three years.

at the Navy Office. He lived above the office nearby and helped to save the church during the Great Fire by demolishing buildings to create a fire-break. His eyewitness accounts of the Restoration, Great Plague and Great Fire are invaluable sources of information. He died in Clapham, but was buried here, in the chancel, though no monument was erected at the time. The present monument on the south wall was put up in 1883, above where Pepys would have sat in the Navy Office pew. His wife, **Elizabeth Pepys** (1640–69), has a fine memorial on the north wall of the chancel, which Pepys commissioned from John Bushnell.

In St Andrew Undershaft in Leadenhall Street is the tomb of **John Stow** (1524/5– 1605), the antiquarian and historian, who is best known for his book, *A Survey of London*, which gives a detailed description of the city and its buildings. It is an invaluable source of information about the London of his time, and is still in print four hundred years after his death. His wife put up the marble and alabaster monument at the east end of the north aisle, showing Stow writing at a desk with a real quill pen. Every three years, on a day near the anniversary of his death, the pen is replaced by the Master of the Worshipful Company of Merchant

The elaborate tomb of Sir Thomas Gresham, founder of the Royal Exchange, in St Helen's Bishopsgate.

Taylors, which had given Stow its freedom in 1547.

In the church of St Helen's Bishopsgate, at the east end of the north nave, is the fine chest tomb to **Sir Thomas Gresham** (c. 1518–79), the successful merchant who founded the Royal Exchange. He also left money to create an educational establishment, and Gresham College still continues to give free lectures to this day. His tomb is splendidly carved with classical imagery and his coat of arms. The great polymath **Robert Hooke** (1635–1703)

was also buried in the church. For many years he was curator of experiments at the newly formed Royal Society and was also professor of geometry at Gresham College. After the Great Fire of 1666 he was one of the official surveyors, and was involved in a number of building projects, including the Monument. He was buried in the south nave of the church, but the only memorial is a plaque on the exterior south wall. His remains were among those removed in 1891 to the City of London Cemetery in Ilford.

ST PAUL'S CATHEDRAL

O LD St Paul's contained many magnificent tombs to the great and the good, but they were nearly all destroyed during the Great Fire of 1666. Some of the fragments are displayed in the crypt of Wren's church, but the most important surviving memorial is that to **John Donne** (1572–1631), the poet who was also dean of St Paul's. It is now in the south choir aisle and shows him in his burial shroud with an urn at his feet. He posed in a shroud for the portrait, and the sculpture is the work of Nicholas Stone. Nearby is a modern wall memorial to **John Colet** (1467–1519), who was dean of St Paul's and founded St Paul's School.

All the burials in Wren's building are in the crypt, which can be accessed via the south transept, through a door marked by skulls carved on the lintel. Turn right at the bottom of the stairs and in the first bay, on the right, is the ledger stone to **Robert Mylne** (1733–1811), the architect of the first Blackfriars Bridge, who was later appointed surveyor to St Paul's Cathedral. In the next bay is the raised red granite

ledger marking the grave of the great engineer **John Rennie** (1761–1821). The inscription lists some of his most important works, including Plymouth Breakwater, Sheerness Docks and three London bridges,

Opposite: The tomb of Horatio Nelson, the great admiral, is located directly beneath the centre of the dome (see pages 26–27).

John Donne's shroud memorial remains from the old cathedral, complete with scorch marks from the Great Fire of 1666.

The wall memorial to the popular Victorian painter Landseer includes a relief of one of his most celebrated works.

The fine brass to the artist Alma-Tadema.

which have now all been replaced by more modern crossings. Next to him is the eminent Greek Revival architect **Charles Robert Cockerell** (1788–1863), who was married to Rennie's daughter, Anna. His most important buildings are the Ashmolean Museum in Oxford and St George's Hall in Liverpool. He succeeded Sir John Soane as architect to the Bank of England, and was also surveyor of St Paul's Cathedral. On the wall above them is a memorial to **Sir Edwin Landseer** (1802–1873), the acclaimed animal painter who designed the lions at the base of Nelson's Column in Trafalgar Square. The

memorial, installed in 1882, is the work of Thomas Woolner, and features a portrait of the artist and a pair of lions with, below, a relief of one of Landseer's best-known paintings, *The Old Shepherd's Chief Mourner.* He is buried near Wren's tomb further east. On the inner eastern wall is a beautifully cut plaque to the writer **Walter de la Mare** (1873–1956), who wrote poetry and fiction, including many stories for children, and is best remembered for his poem *The Listeners.* He was a chorister in the St Paul's Cathedral choir school. A floor tile inscribed W. De La M. marks the spot where his ashes are interred.

Sir Christopher Wren's simple tomb is surrounded by the graves of great nineteenth-century artists.

Further east is the grave of the artist **Sir Lawrence Alma-Tadema** (1836–1912), a black marble slab with a fine brass relief and inscription. Dutch-born, he came to London in his thirties and became an acclaimed, and very rich, painter, concentrating on scenes of the ancient Roman world, populated by beautiful people. Next to him is the grave of the illustrious portrait painter **Sir Thomas Lawrence** (1769–1830). He was painter to George III and was later patronised by the Prince Regent, of whom he painted a number of flattering swagger portraits. He was later commissioned to paint a series of portraits to celebrate the defeat of Napoleon, which hang in the Waterloo Chamber at Windsor Castle. In 1820 he was elected president of the Royal Academy.

In the next bay is the simple tomb of **Sir Christopher Wren** (1632–1723), the architect of the cathedral and so much else in London following the Great Fire of 1666. As well as supervising the rebuilding of 51 of the City churches, he built the Royal Hospital, Chelsea and the Royal Naval Hospital in Greenwich, as well as substantial additions to Kensington and Hampton Court Palaces. His grave is marked by a massive black marble ledger, and above it on the wall is a white marble plaque with a Latin inscription, which ends with the appropriate line '*Lector, si monumentum requiris, circumspice*' (Reader, if you seek his monument, look around you).

Around Wren's tomb is a remarkable collection of graves of artists, architects and sculptors, including several presidents of

In the north aisle of the church is Sir Thomas Brock's impressive memorial to Lord Leighton, who is buried in the crypt.

the Royal Academy, and it is often referred to as Artists' Corner. It is usually difficult to see all the graves, as there are often chairs on top of them, which are needed for regular services. Alongside Wren's grave is the brass to **Frederic Leighton, Baron Leighton** (1830–96), the hugely successful artist and sculptor, whose house in Kensington is now a museum. He was elected president of the Royal Academy, and shortly before his death he was made a peer, the first artist to receive the honour. The brass ledger, designed by Richard Norman Shaw, includes his coat of arms and a branch of weeping willow. Leighton also has a splendid memorial in the north aisle of the main church, the work of Sir Thomas Brock. Next to him, going north, is **Benjamin West** (1738–1820), the American-born history painter who was one of the founders of the Royal Academy, and later became its president. Next is **George Dance the Younger** (1741–1825), the Neo-Classical architect who designed Newgate Prison, and added the curious Indian-style façade to the Guildhall. Alongside him is the grave of **Henry Fuseli** (1741–1825), the Swiss artist who specialised in literary subjects, including Shakespeare, as well as more sensational subjects, such as his best-known painting *The Nightmare*, which made him a celebrity. Next is the grave of **George Dawe** (1781–1829), the portrait artist whose greatest success came when he was invited to be court painter to the Russian tsar, producing over 300 portraits of generals who fought against Napoleon. Last in this line is the grave of **Sir Edwin Landseer** (1802–73), whose wall memorial is described above.

The first grave in the next row, alongside Leighton, is that of **Sir John Everett Millais** 1829–96), one of the founders of the Pre-Raphaelite Brotherhood. He later became a successful society artist, painting more traditional pictures, including many portraits. He was elected president of the Royal Academy on the death of Lord Leighton, whose funeral he attended only five months before his own death. His splendid gravestone, of marble and brass, was designed by Richard Norman Shaw. Alongside Millais is the plain stone slab of the grave of **Joseph Mallord William Turner** (1775–1851), who is generally considered to be the greatest British artist of all time. Born in Covent Garden, and largely self-taught, his unconventional style and personal eccentricity made him many enemies, but his landscapes and seascapes were highly regarded in his lifetime. He died in Chelsea, where he lived with a widow, Mrs Booth, and he was known locally as Admiral Booth. In 1862 a statue of him by Patrick McDowell was erected upstairs in the south transept. Next is the history painter, **James Barry** (1741–1806), whose most important works are the six large murals he painted in the Great Room of the Royal Society of Arts in John Adam Street, telling the ambitious story of *The Progress of Human Culture*. He had a persecution complex and regularly insulted his fellow artists, and he is the only member of the Royal Academy to have been expelled. There is a Coade stone bust of him on the wall above Wren's tomb, which was added in 1810. Alongside Barry is the ledger stone of **Sir Joshua Reynolds** (1723–92), the most celebrated and successful portrait painter of his time. Born in the village of Plympton in Devon, he rose to become the first president of the Royal Academy. He painted some of the most important members of Georgian society, many of whom he could call friends, and the pallbearers at his funeral were all members of the aristocracy. Next is the grave of the artist **John Opie** (1761–1807), best known for his historical paintings and portraits. The last in the row is the

Turner, who is buried in the crypt, has a statue in the south transept, the work of Patrick McDowell.

magnificent brass ledger to the sculptor **Sir Edgar Boehm** (1834–90). Austrian born, he settled in London, where his realistic style of portraiture proved popular, and he received many royal commissions. He has a number of statues in London, including that of Thomas Carlyle in Chelsea, as well as the memorial to General Gordon in the north aisle of the cathedral.

Further east is the grave of the Pre-Raphaelite painter **William Holman Hunt** (1827–1910), whose *Light of the World* is in the north transept of the cathedral. He was the most spiritual member of the group, and several of

HERE lie the Remains of
Sʳ JOSHUA REYNOLDS Kᴺᵗ
PRESIDENT of the
ROYAL ACADEMY
OF
PAINTING SCULPTURE
and ARCHITECTURE.
He was Born at
PLYMPTON in DEVONSHIRE
the 16ᵗʰ of July 1723
And died at LONDON
the 23ʳᵈ of Feb 1792

The grave of the great portrait painter, Sir Joshua Reynolds, who was the first president of the Royal Academy.

his pictures contain overt religious or moralistic symbolism. He specifically asked to be cremated, a very early example of it in this country, although his full-length ledger would suggest otherwise. In St Martin's Chapel, at the east end of this aisle, is the grave of the sculptor **John Henry Foley** (1818–74), marked by a simple brass plaque. Although less well known than some of his contemporaries, two of his best works are in very prominent positions in London, his sensitive statue of Lord Herbert in Waterloo Place and the monumental gilded figure of Prince Albert on the Albert Memorial in Kensington Gardens. Nearby is a modern memorial to **Sir Anthony Van Dyck** (1599–1641), the renowned Flemish artist who is so closely associated with the court of Charles I, and whose portraits made the royal family and their courtiers look elegant and glamorous. He was buried in the choir of old St Paul's in a tomb erected by the king, but it was destroyed in the Great Fire. The present memorial, in an appropriate Baroque style, was erected in 1928, the work of Henry Poole.

The central part of the crypt is known as St Faith's chapel, but is also the Chapel of the Most Excellent Order of the British Empire. In the south-east corner of the chapel is the marble and brass ledger to the artist **Sir John Poynter** (1836–1919), who was renowned for his large-scale, archaeologically accurate, paintings of classical antiquity. He was also a noted arts administrator, as director of the National Gallery and president of the

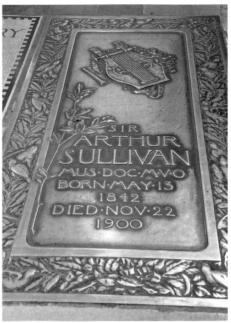

A modern baroque wall memorial to the great portrait painter, Sir Anthony Van Dyck.

The brass marking the grave of Sir Arthur Sullivan, the composer of the Savoy operas.

Royal Academy. On the nearby south wall is a memorial to **Sir Henry Maximilian (Max) Beerbohm** (1872–1956), the writer and caricaturist. He worked as a theatre critic and essayist, and wrote the acclaimed novel *Zuleika Dobson*, but he is best known for his witty caricatures of writers, artists and politicians. Nearby, on the same wall, is a memorial to the influential architect **Sir Edwin Landseer Lutyens** (1869–1944). He made his name designing country houses in the Arts and Crafts style, but later built a number of major public buildings in London, many in the classical style, including the Midland Bank in Poultry and Britannic House in Moorgate. On the way to St Paul's his coffin passed his most famous work, the Cenotaph

in Whitehall. Floor tiles marked MB and ELL mark where Beerbohm's and Lutyens' ashes are buried.

On the north side of the chapel is a small musicians' corner. A black and white mosaic plaque marks the grave of **Sir Hubert Parry** (1848–1918), the composer best known for his choral pieces, including *I Was Glad*, written for Edward VII's coronation, and his setting of Blake's *Jerusalem*, which is sung every year at the Last Night of the Proms. Next to him is the splendid brass tombstone of **Sir Arthur Sullivan** (1842–1900), the composer of songs such as *The Lost Chord* and the hymn *Onward Christian Soldiers*, but who is most famous for the music he wrote for the Savoy operas in collaboration with W. S. Gilbert. He had

The wall memorial to the celebrated horse painter Sir Alfred Munnings.

planned to be buried in his family plot at Brompton Cemetery, but Queen Victoria expressed her wish for him to buried in St Paul's. Alongside is the plain stone ledger marking the grave of the eighteenth-century composer **William Boyce** (1711–79), who was a chorister at St Paul's and rose to become the Master of the King's Musick, writing music for royal occasions. His best-known song is *Heart of Oak*, which is the official march of the Royal Navy.

On the east wall of the next bay to the west is a wall memorial to **Sir Alfred James Munnings** (1878–1959), an artist best known for his paintings of horses, though he also painted many fine landscapes. He was an eccentric president

of the Royal Academy, and resigned after making a controversial speech in which he attacked modern art. The memorial includes a portrait medallion, and is placed close to a memorial to John Constable who, like Munnings, was born in Suffolk. Further west, on the inner wall, is an elegant marble plaque to **Sir Alexander Fleming** (1881–1955), who discovered penicillin while working at St Mary's Hospital in Paddington, for which he was awarded the Nobel Prize for physiology.

Pass through the central door to the large space that houses the impressive sarcophagus of **Arthur Wellesley, Duke of Wellington** (1769–1852), the great army commander who drove the French from Spain during the Peninsular War, and defeated Napoleon at Waterloo in 1815. He died at Walmer Castle, and his body remained there for several weeks while his state funeral was arranged. Around one and a half million people watched the spectacular procession to St Paul's, and owners of houses along the route rented out seats for the occasion. After the funeral the coffin was lowered into the crypt, where it was suspended above Nelson's tomb until his own was ready in 1858. The classical sarcophagus is of polished red porphyry from Cornwall, and it stands on a granite plinth with lions at each corner. There is a colossal monument to Wellington, by Alfred Stevens, under the north arcade of the nave of the cathedral, which took over 50 years to complete.

Continue westwards to the area directly under the cathedral's dome where, amid a forest of columns (see page 18), lies the body of **Horatio Nelson, Viscount Nelson** (1758–1805), Britain's most celebrated naval commander. He fought many

The magnificent tomb of the Duke of Wellington, the great army leader.

successful battles against the French, and died a hero's death at the battle of Trafalgar. His body, preserved in a 'cask of spirits', was brought back to London, where he lay in state in the Painted Hall at Greenwich Hospital. Accompanied by a flotilla of boats and barges, he was taken upriver to spend the night at the Admiralty before the funeral procession to St Paul's, with huge crowds lining the route. After the service under the dome, the coffin was lowered through a specially created hole in the floor into the crypt. The black marble sarcophagus was originally made by the Italian sculptor Benedetto da Rovezzano for Cardinal Wolsey, but never used, and it had been stored at Windsor Castle and forgotten. Nelson's coronet was placed on top of it, replacing Wolsey's cardinal's cap. Nelson has a memorial upstairs in the church, a fine work by John Flaxman, in the south transept.

In the bays surrounding Nelson are several more heroes, both naval and military. In the south-east bay are buried **John Rushworth Jellicoe, first Earl Jellicoe** (1859–1935) and **David Beatty, first Earl Beatty** (1871–1936), two naval heroes from the First World War. Jellicoe's grave is marked by a raised ledger with well-cut lettering and his coat of arms. Beatty's was the last body to be buried in the cathedral – all future burials were of ashes. Moving clockwise, the next bay contains the tomb chest of **Cuthbert Collingwood, Baron Collingwood** (1748–1810), who was Nelson's second-in-command at the battle of Trafalgar and assumed command after Nelson's death. He continued in the fight against Napoleon and died on board his ship at Menorca. Collingwood also has a monument in the south transept, by Richard Westmacott. In the next bay is the grey marble tomb of **Robert Cornelis Napier, Baron Napier of Magdala** (1810–90), the celebrated soldier who served in India, China and Abyssinia. On the back wall is a memorial with a relief portrait by Frederick Woodington.

In the last bay on the north side, there are ledger stones to two field marshals, **Garnet Joseph Wolseley, Viscount Wolseley** (1833–1913) and **Frederick Sleigh Roberts, Earl Roberts** (1832–1914). Wolseley fought in the Crimean War and the Chinese War, and led the expedition that arrived in Khartoum too late to rescue General Gordon. Roberts fought in India, Afghanistan and the Boer War.

Take the exit to the right and turn left and left again to find the head and torso of

Sir Nicholas Bacon (1510–79), all that is left of his grand monument, which stood in the choir of the old cathedral. Bacon was a lawyer who rose to high office under Elizabeth I, who relied on his expert advice in legal matters. On the wall next to him is a modern memorial to the soldier-poet **Sir Philip Sidney** (1554–86), who was buried in the old cathedral, but never given a monument. He was a respected courtier, but is best known as a poet, though none of his work was published in his lifetime. He died fighting in the Netherlands.

Further west, turn left to find the simple but striking ledger slab, of red, white and black marble, to the artist **George Cruikshank** (1792–1878). He was probably the greatest caricaturist of

The modern memorial to the soldier-poet Sir Philip Sidney, and all that remains of the original tomb of Sir Nicholas Bacon.

The simple but striking gravestone of the great artist George Cruikshank.

his age, producing biting political satires as well as illustrations for novels by Thackeray and Dickens. The modest inscription simply gives his name and the year he died. Originally there was also a wall memorial with a bust by John Adams-Acton, but this has now been relegated to the triforium.

Just before the exit from the crypt, on the right, is a double memorial to **Sir George Williams** (1821–1905), one of the founders of the Young Men's Christian Association (YMCA). A devout evangelical Christian, he joined fellow workers at a draper's in St Paul's Churchyard in organising prayer meetings; this was the beginning of an organisation that quickly

The monument to Sir George Williams, founder of the YMCA.

spread across the globe. On the wall is a fine marble monument by Sir George Frampton, with a portrait bust, and on the floor is a splendid brass ledger marking his grave.

CITY OF WESTMINSTER

COVENT GARDEN WAS developed in the seventeenth century, attracting many aristocratic residents, but by the eighteenth century it was at the heart of London's theatreland, and the area became home to many artists, writers and, of course, actors. St Paul's church is, therefore, the last resting place of many well-known names of Georgian art and literature, and is often referred to as the Actors' Church. On the north wall of the church is the memorial to **Thomas Arne** (1710–78), the composer who is best known for the song *Rule, Britannia*, though he also composed settings for many of Shakespeare's songs, some of which are still used today. On the south wall is a memorial to **Charles Macklin** (*c*. 1699–1797), one of the finest actors of his day, with an acting style more natural than was usual at the time. He was both a friend and rival of David Garrick, his greatest role being that of Shylock, which he performed for 50 years.

Further east on the same wall is a black marble tabernacle containing a silver casket

with the ashes of **Dame Ellen Terry** (1847–1928), the finest actress of her generation, who performed for 24 years with Sir Henry Irving at the Lyceum. She was a particularly fine Shakespearean actress, especially in the comedies, and both Barrie and Shaw wrote parts for her. The birth date on the monument was originally given as 1848, and the correction is still visible. Nearby is a plaque to another great actress, **Dame Edith Evans** (1888–1976), whose

The wall memorial to Thomas Arne, the composer of *Rule, Britannia*, in St Paul's Covent Garden.

Opposite: The Wesley family memorial in the garden in Marylebone High Street, the site of the previous St Marylebone church, in whose graveyard they were buried (see page 37).

Sacred to the Memory
of CHARLES MACKLIN, Comedian:
This Tablet is Erected
(with the Aid of Public Patronage)
by his affectionate Widow ELIZABETH MACKLIN,
Obiit 11ᵗʰ July 1797. Ætatis 107.

MACKLIN ! the Father of the modern Stage.
Renown'd alike for Talents and for Age.
Whose Years a Century and longer ran.
Who liv'd and dy'd as may become a Man.
This lasting Tribute to thy Worth receive.
'Tis all a grateful Public now can give.
Their loudest Plaudits now no more can move.
Yet hear ! thy Widow's still small Voice of Love.

The memorial to the great eighteenth-century actor, Charles Macklin, in St Paul's Covent Garden, has a curious emblem of a dagger piercing the eye of a mask.

ashes are interred here. She is now most associated with the role of Lady Bracknell in Oscar Wilde's *The Importance of Being Earnest*, but in a long career she played a great variety of roles. She was a versatile actress with a unique and unforgettable voice.

The graveyard was rearranged in the nineteenth century, and some remains were moved to Brookwood, while others were placed in the vault. All the gravestones have now been removed, but many important people were once buried here or in the church vault. They include the poet and satirist **Samuel Butler** (1613–80), best known for the mock heroic poem *Hudibras*, and **William Wycherley** (1641–1716),

the Restoration rake and wit who was the author of *The Country Wife*. Several important artists were buried here, including the celebrated watercolourist **Thomas Girtin** (1775–1802) and the great caricaturist **Thomas Rowlandson** (1757–1827), as well as the Dutch-born portrait painter **Sir Peter Lely** (1618–80), the most successful artist of the Restoration. His monument was destroyed in the fire of 1795. It was the work of **Grinling Gibbons** (1648–1721), who was also buried here. Gibbons is considered to be the finest woodcarver who ever lived, and his work can be found in many London buildings, including Hampton Court and St Paul's Cathedral.

Among the actors buried here are **Edward Kynaston** (1643–1712), who began his career playing female parts and went on to become a versatile leading player, and **Susanna Centlivre** (1669?–1723), who started out playing breeches roles before becoming the successful author of a number of witty comedies. Also buried here is the celebrated Irish tenor **Michael Kelly** (1762–1826), who performed for many years at the Theatre Royal, Drury

Memorials to two great actresses, Dame Edith Evans and Dame Ellen Terry, in the Actors' Church, St Paul's Covent Garden.

The modern gravestone of the writer William Hazlitt in the churchyard of St Anne's Soho.

Lane, often in operas by Stephen Storace. In recent years the ashes of several actors have been interred in the churchyard, including the great stage and screen actor **Sir Michael Redgrave** (1908–85).

All that remains of St Anne's church in Wardour Street, Soho, is the curious tower and the churchyard, the rest having being destroyed in the Blitz. By the north wall is the grave of **William Hazlitt** (1778–1830), an artist and writer best known for his essays, though he was also a journalist and theatre critic. He died in poverty in a house in Frith Street, which is now a hotel bearing his name. The original tombstone was replaced in 1870 by a simpler headstone, which now stands against the tower, and in 2003 a new gravestone was unveiled, bearing the original inscription in full. Under the floor of the tower are buried the ashes of the author **Dorothy L. Sayers** (1893–1957), who was churchwarden here. She is best known for her detective novels featuring Lord Peter Wimsey. Earlier in her career she had worked as a copywriter in an advertising agency, where she created slogans such as 'My goodness,

my Guinness!' Also buried here, but with no memorial, is the artist **Francis Hayman** (1707–76), who started out painting theatre scenery, and later specialised in painting conversation pieces and small-scale portraits. Also here, in unmarked graves, are **Paul de Lamerie** (1688–1751), the celebrated silversmith, and the actress **Mary (Moll) Davis** (c. 1651–1708), who became one of Charles II's mistresses, and bore him a daughter.

Grosvenor Chapel in South Audley Street opened in 1731 to cater for the residents of the new Grosvenor Square estate. The most famous of its permanent residents is the politician and journalist **John Wilkes** (1725–97), who suffered persecution and imprisonment for his radical views. He later became Lord Mayor, returned to parliament, and continued to fight for the freedom of the press. He is buried in the vault and his simple memorial, by John Flaxman, is on the east wall of the north gallery. Also buried here, but without a memorial, is the writer and traveller **Lady Mary Wortley Montagu** (1689–1762), a celebrated society hostess

The memorial to the influential Dutch painters, Willem van de Velde, father and son, in St James Piccadilly.

who was a friend to many of the intellectual elite. She is probably most famous for introducing inoculation against smallpox to Europe, something she had seen in Turkey, where it was common.

St James Piccadilly was built by Sir Christopher Wren as part of a new estate developed by Henry Jermyn. The parish soon attracted many distinguished literary and artistic figures, several of whom were buried here. The churchyard was always very small, and it has now been covered over, with only a few headstones round the walls. During the week there is a busy market in the forecourt, but on Sundays it is clear, and it is possible to see, to the left of the gate, the eroded modern replica of the tombstone of the great caricaturist **James Gillray** (1756–1815). At his best, Gillray's satirical prints were inventive, baroque, witty and bawdy, and are much reworked by today's political cartoonists. His main targets were politicians, and later Napoleon (whom he dubbed *Little Boney*), but he also parodied the Prince Regent and other members of the royal family, which no one had dared to do before. He suffered severe mental illness during his last five years in a room in St James's Street, where he died.

Just inside the north vestibule of the church are two floor plaques marking the graves of artist and designer **Robert Anning Bell** (1863–1933) and the architect **William Curtis Green** (1875–1960). Anning Bell was a book illustrator and mosaicist, working in the Arts and Crafts style, his most important work being the tympanum over the west door of Westminster Cathedral and the mosaic on the façade of the Horniman Museum. Curtis Green designed a number of London buildings, including the Dorchester Hotel in Park Lane. In the lobby under the tower is a wall plaque to the famous Dutch marine artists, father and son **Willem van de Velde the Elder** (1611–93) and **Willem van de Velde the Younger** (1633–1707). From 1673 they worked in London, based in Greenwich, where Charles II provided them with a studio in Queen's House. Their work inspired many English artists, and a number of their works can be seen in the National Gallery and the National Maritime Museum.

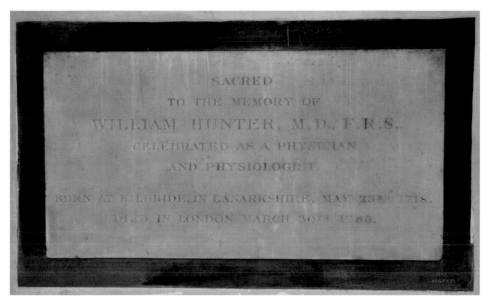

SACRED
TO THE MEMORY OF
WILLIAM HUNTER, M.D., F.R.S.,
CELEBRATED AS A PHYSICIAN
AND PHYSIOLOGIST.
BORN AT KILBRIDE, IN LANARKSHIRE, MAY 23RD 1718,
DIED IN LONDON MARCH 30TH 1783.

The modest wall memorial to the great surgeon, William Hunter, in St James Piccadilly.

In the south aisle of the church is a simple stone plaque to the great Scottish surgeon **William Hunter** (1718–83). Like his brother, John, he spent much of his professional life in London, where he lectured and gave anatomy courses. He became Queen Charlotte's royal physician, and was professor of anatomy at the newly founded Royal Academy of Art. He formed a vast collection of books, coins, shells and curiosities, which are now in the Hunterian Museum in Glasgow. Under a window in the north aisle is a modern memorial to **Mary Beale** (1633–99), who was, unusually for her time, a successful professional portrait painter, with a studio in Pall Mall. Her style was influenced by that of Sir Peter Lely, who was a personal friend, but her informal portraits have a unique charm of their own.

Also buried here, but with no memorial, are **Thomas Sheraton** (1751–1806), the influential furniture designer, the Swedish-born portrait painter **Michael Dahl** (1659–1743), the landscape artist **Alexander Cozens** (1717–86), **John Arbuthnot** (1667–1735), the physician who was also a celebrated satirist, the famous landscape gardener **Charles Bridgeman** (d. 1738) and **Francis White** (d. 1711), the Italian-born founder of White's Chocolate House in St James's, the precursor of today's prestigious White's Club.

St Martin-in-the-Fields is one of London's most famous churches, standing prominently overlooking Trafalgar Square. The churchyard was once extensive, but it has now mostly been built over. It is a royal parish church and has attracted many important people, some of whom were buried here, but there are no memorials to them in the church. Probably the most

The grave of the great actress Sarah Siddons in the churchyard of St Mary's Paddington.

famous was **Eleanor (Nell) Gwyn** (1651–87), the actress who became Charles II's favourite mistress. Many artists were buried here, including **Nicholas Hilliard** (1547–1619), the famous miniature painter who painted Elizabeth I many times, **Paul Somer** (1577–1621), who painted portraits of James I and his family, **William Dobson** (1611–46), who painted Charles I and his courtiers in Oxford during the Civil War, and **John Michael Wright** (1617–94), best known for his striking state portrait of Charles II. Others interred here were architects **James (Athenian) Stuart** (1713–88) and **Sir Robert Taylor** (1714–88), the playwright **George Farquhar** (1676–1707), best known for his comedy *The Recruiting Officer*, and the poet **John Taylor** (1578–1653), who was known as the 'Water Poet', as he worked as a waterman on the Thames. Also buried here were the renowned physicist and chemist **Robert Boyle** (1627–91), the celebrated French sculptor **Louis François Roubiliac** (1702–62), the eminent English sculptor

Nicholas Stone (1585–1647), the famous cabinet-maker **Thomas Chippendale** (1718–79) and the notorious thief **John (Jack) Sheppard** (1702–24), who was famous for his audacious escapes from Newgate Prison.

St Marylebone Parish Church, on Marylebone Road NW1, is the fourth one to serve the parish. The first was on Oxford Street, and the second and third were on Marylebone High Street, where the site is now marked by a garden. In response to the growing population, today's much larger church was built by Thomas Hardwick and opened in 1817. The crypt was cleared in the 1980s and the remains were removed to Brookwood Cemetery. Parts of the churchyard were also cleared and the remains re-interred in the East London Cemetery. In the eighteenth century Marylebone was very fashionable, and many artists lived and were buried here. In the garden in Marylebone High Street are some headstones and a plaque with a list of some of the celebrated people who were buried there. Artists include the great horse painter **George Stubbs** (1724–1806), the Scottish portrait painter **Allan Ramsay** (1713–84), the miniaturist **Richard Cosway** (1742–1821), the history painter **James Northcote** (1746–1831), and **John Wootton** (1681–1764), who specialised in hunting and sporting pictures. The opera composer **Stephen Storace** (1762–96) was buried here, as were the celebrated sculptor **(John) Michael Rysbrack** (1694–1770) and the architect **James Gibbs** (1682–1754), whose most famous London building is St Martin-in-the-Fields church. Also buried here were **Charles Wesley** (1707–88), one of the founders of Methodism and author of many popular hymns, and his son **Samuel Wesley** (1766–1837), who was a child prodigy, known as the 'English Mozart', and a fine organist and composer. The Wesley family monument (see page 30) in the form of an obelisk can be seen in the garden in Marylebone High Street.

Alongside the busy Westway is St Mary's church on Paddington Green. In the adjacent gardens is a statue to **Sarah Siddons** (1755–1831), the great Shakespearean actress, and her grave can be found at the far end of what was once an extension to the churchyard, and is now a park. What was originally a simple ledger was later given a finely wrought canopy, and it is now protected by ugly modern railings. She was the greatest tragedienne of her age, so famous that she was painted by artists such as Reynolds and Gainsborough. Nearby is the grave, also protected by an unsightly iron cage, of **Benjamin Haydon** (1786–1846), the history painter who, despite his great talent, was always short of money, and was imprisoned four times for debt. His grand style went out of fashion during his later years, and he suffered disappointment and paranoia before committing suicide.

Also buried in the churchyard, but with no grave markers, are the sculptor **Thomas Banks** (1735–1805), some of whose best work can be seen in Westminster Abbey and St Paul's Cathedral, **John Bushnell** (1636–1701), the sculptor Samuel Pepys commissioned to make his wife's memorial for St Olave's in the City, the distinguished portrait painter, **Sir William Beechey** (1753–1839), who painted many royal portraits, the portrait painter **Thomas Phillips** (1770–1845), who depicted many

The monument to Joseph Nollekens in the chancel of St Mary's Paddington includes a version of one of his own monuments.

of the greatest men of the age, and **Joseph Bramah** (1749–1814), the inventor who designed a thief-proof lock. The sculptor **Joseph Nollekens** (1737–1823) is buried in the church vault, and there is a memorial to him on the south chancel wall by William Behnes, with a relief of one of Nollekens' finest monuments.

St John's Wood Burial Ground, in Wellington Street WC2, opened in 1814, as the graveyard of St Marylebone church was full. It closed in 1855 when the St Marylebone cemetery in East Finchley opened, and it is now a public garden.

The grave of artist John Sell Cotman in St John's Wood Burial Ground.

The tomb of Cardinal Vaughan in Westminster Cathedral.

There are still many graves here, including that of **John Sell Cotman** (1782–1842), which is in the western part of the garden and is clearly marked. Cotman, who was an original member of the Norwich School of artists, was one of the finest painters of his generation, celebrated for his landscapes of Wales, Yorkshire and Normandy.

In Westminster Cathedral, in Victoria Street SW1, are buried a number of cardinals. In the chapel of St Joseph, in the north aisle, is the grave of **Cardinal Hinsley** (1865–1943), who was made archbishop of Westminster at the age of 70. A blunt Yorkshireman, he was much loved, especially for his popular broadcasts during the Second World War. In the chapel of St Thomas of Canterbury, further along the aisle, is the tomb of **Cardinal Vaughan** (1832–1903), with a fine marble effigy. Vaughan was responsible for the construction of Westminster Cathedral, commissioning John Francis Bentley to design it in the Byzantine style. His requiem was held in the unfinished cathedral and he was buried in St Joseph's College in Mill Hill, which he founded in 1866. The

college has now closed, and his body was re-interred here in 2005. In the chapel of St Gregory and St Augustine, in the south aisle, is the grave of **Cardinal Hume** (1923–99), whose appointment in 1976 was a surprise, as he had been a monk rather than a clergyman. He was, however, a popular choice. A humble man, with great warmth and a sense of humour, he was highly respected by all, not just Catholics. Also in the chapel is the grave of **Bishop Challoner** (1691–1781), who was a bishop during difficult times for Catholics. He escaped injury during the anti-Catholic Gordon Riots, but died shortly afterwards. He was originally buried in Milton, Berkshire, but he was re-buried here in 1946. Buried under Eric Gill's twelfth Station of the Cross is **Cardinal Heenan** (1905–75), who was a rather conservative archbishop, but a fine communicator on radio and television.

Four more cardinals are buried in the chapel of St Edmund of Canterbury in the crypt, which is not usually open to the public. Here are the tombs, both with fine effigies, of the first two archbishops of Westminster,

Cardinal Wiseman (1802–65), and **Cardinal Manning** (1808–92). They were both originally buried in St Mary's Roman Catholic Cemetery in Kensal Green, and their remains were brought here in 1907. Nearby are the graves of two less well-known archbishops, **Cardinal Godfrey** (1889–1963) and **Cardinal Griffin** (1899–1956).

Further along Victoria Street, at the junction with Broadway, are Christchurch Gardens, all that is left of the substantial graveyard of Broadway Chapel, which was destroyed by a bomb in 1941. Buried here with much ceremony was **Sir William Waller** (1598–1668), the parliamentary soldier who won many victories in the early years of the Civil War, but later changed sides and was imprisoned in the Tower for his royalist sympathies. Also buried here was **Ignatius Sancho** (1729?–80), a slave who worked for the Montagu family, who recognised his great intelligence and encouraged him to learn to read. He moved in literary and artistic circles, and was painted by Gainsborough. The letters he wrote to many influential people were published after his death. **Colonel Thomas Blood** (1617–80), the notorious Irish spy and adventurer, was also buried here. He is famous for his attempt to steal the Crown Jewels from the Tower. He managed to steal the crown, but was arrested and imprisoned, though Charles II later pardoned him. When he was buried, it was thought to be yet another trick, so the body was exhumed to prove it really was him.

In the shadow of Westminster Abbey is St Margaret's church, founded in the twelfth century for the local population so that the monks could carry out their devotions undisturbed. It is now known as the parish church of the House of Commons, and is administered by Westminster Abbey. Several important people were buried in the extensive graveyard, but the graves were all cleared in 1853, and the bones were interred in the vault or sent to Brookwood Cemetery. The church contains several interesting memorials. On the west wall is a fine monument to **Patrick Colquhoun** (1745–1820), the magistrate who founded the Thames Police in 1798 to prevent crime on the river, the first police force to be set up in London. On the top of his memorial

The wall memorial to Patrick Colquhoun, who created the Thames Police, London's first police force, in St Margaret's Westminster.

are various symbols, such as a beehive for industry, a ship, scales for justice, and books. In the north aisle is a modern oval plaque to **Wenceslaus Hollar** (1607–77) the Bohemian etcher who produced many detailed views and panoramas of London before and after the Great Fire of 1666, and it is through his work that we know what seventeenth-century London looked like.

At the east end of the south aisle, by the east door, is a plaque to **Sir Walter Ralegh** (1554–1618), the famous explorer and writer. He was a favourite of Elizabeth I, though he regularly fell out of favour. Under James I he was imprisoned for treason in the Tower, where he wrote *The History of the World*. He was executed at Westminster, and his widow took away his head in a bag. His body was buried in St Margaret's, and tradition has it that when his son was buried in the grave, Ralegh's head was buried with him. To the right of the east door is a memorial to **William Caxton** (d. 1492), erected in 1820. Caxton introduced the printing press to England, setting up his business near the east end of Westminster Abbey. As well as many historical and religious books, he published the first edition of Chaucer's *The Canterbury Tales*. Buried in front of the high altar, but with no monument, is the clergyman and poet **John Skelton** (*c.* 1460–1529). He was tutor to the future Henry VIII and later rector of Diss in Norfolk. He wrote allegorical and satirical poems, including one attacking Cardinal Wolsey, for which he took sanctuary in the monastery at Westminster. On the external west wall of the church is a modern plaque, erected by the Cromwell Association, listing the names of the Parliamentarians who had

The memorial to Sir Walter Ralegh in St Margaret's Westminster, where his body, minus his head, was buried after his execution.

been buried in Westminster Abbey, but whose remains were removed after the Restoration and buried anonymously in the graveyard of St Margaret's. These include **Robert Blake** (1598–1657), one of the country's greatest admirals, **John Pym** (1584–1643), a radical politician who was one of the 'five members' Charles I tried to arrest in the House of Commons in 1642, and several signatories of Charles I's death warrant.

The Queen's Chapel of the Savoy, on Savoy Hill, south of the Strand, dates from the sixteenth century, but its history goes back much further. In the small graveyard to the east was once the tomb of two artists, **Peter de Wint** (1784–1849) and his wife's brother, **William Hilton** (1786–1839). There was also a monument in the chapel, but this was destroyed in a fire in 1864, and the elaborately carved font was subsequently presented by Harriet de Wint in memory of her husband and brother. Hilton was a painter of historical subjects, often on vast canvases, but De Wint was the more significant artist, best known for his watercolour landscapes and still lives.

The graveyard of St Clement Danes in the Strand disappeared a long time ago, and in 1901, after the Strand was widened, 4,000 bodies were exhumed and re-buried at Brookwood Cemetery in Surrey. The church itself was bombed in 1941, but it has been restored, and is now the official church of the Royal Air Force. The vaults have been cleared to make room for a chapel, and the bodies were cremated and have been buried under the south stairs. Although there are no memorials to them, among the distinguished people buried in the vault or graveyard were **George Gower** (d. 1596), the official painter to Elizabeth I, **Thomas Otway** (1652–85), the Restoration playwright whose most famous play is *Venice Preserv'd*, and **Rudolph Ackermann** (1764–1834), the publisher, based in the Strand, who produced beautiful hand-coloured prints of London by artists such as Thomas Rowlandson. Under the main altar is a small crypt where the ashes of RAF personnel are kept, including those of the famous World War Two hero **Sir Douglas Bader** (1910–82), who lost both legs in an air crash in 1931, but, with artificial legs, went on to play an important role in the Battle of Britain before being shot down and imprisoned in Colditz. Also here are the ashes of **Arthur William Tedder, 1st Baron Tedder** (1890–1967)

The font in the Savoy Chapel is the memorial to artists Peter de Wint and William Hilton, who are buried there.

and **Sir William Sholto Douglas** (1893–1969), high-ranking RAF officers who played key roles in the military operations of the Second World War. As a special honour, the ashes of a civilian, **Sir Archibald McIndoe** (1900–60), are also here. McIndoe was a plastic surgeon who was employed by the RAF at a hospital in East Grinstead to treat airmen who had suffered severe burns.

TO THE MEMORY OF
DAVID GARRICK,
WHO DIED IN THE YEAR 1779,
AT THE AGE OF 63.

TO PAINT FAIR NATURE, BY DIVINE COMMAND,
HER MAGIC PENCIL IN HIS GLOWING HAND,
A SHAKSPEARE ROSE, THEN TO EXPAND HIS FAME
WIDE O'ER THIS BREATHING WORLD, A GARRICK CAME
THOUGH SUNK IN DEATH THE FORMS THE POET DREW

WESTMINSTER ABBEY

WESTMINSTER ABBEY IS probably the most famous church in Britain, as it is the place of coronations, royal weddings and the last resting place of many kings and queens. About 3,000 people have been buried there over the centuries, including politicians, writers, scientists, architects and musicians, and there are also many monuments to important people who are buried elsewhere, which can confuse visitors. I have only included people who are buried there. The description follows the visitor route in operation at the time of writing, though occasionally some areas are not accessible.

The entrance is via the North Door, which leads you into the North Transept, known as Statesmen's Aisle, because of the many politicians buried there. The first thing you see, as it is next to the ticket desk, is the impressive monument by John Flaxman to **William Murray, Earl of Mansfield** (1705–93), the famous judge. Lord Mansfield was Lord Chief Justice for over 30 years, and he played a major part in the abolition of slavery. His effigy, based on a portrait by Sir Joshua Reynolds, is

Opposite: The great actor, David Garrick, takes his final bow with great swagger (see page 56).

flanked by figures of Wisdom and Justice. In the central aisle is a statue of **Henry John Temple, Viscount Palmerston** (1784–1865), and close by is his gravestone, designed by Sir George Gilbert Scott. Palmerston was prime minister twice, taking office for the first time at the age of seventy. His last words were said to be 'Die, my dear doctor? That's the last thing I shall do!' Next to him is the massive marble monument by John Bacon to **William Pitt, Earl of Chatham** (1708–78), usually referred to as Pitt the Elder. Pitt was prime minister twice, and during his time in office the country was at war with the French. The inscription suggests he led the country to 'prosperity and glory', which is echoed in the symbolism on the monument. His son, **William Pitt** (1759–1806), known as Pitt the Younger, is also buried here, though his monument is over the west door of the nave. Pitt became prime minister at the amazingly young age of 24, and remained in power for most of his short life. In front of the Pitt monument is the gravestone of **Charles James Fox** (1749–1806), the celebrated liberal politician, and bitter rival of Pitt. His monument was moved to the west end of the nave (see below). Directly opposite, against the first column

The imposing marble monument to the Earl of Chatham, in the north transept, the work of John Bacon.

on the east side, is the statue, by Sir Francis Chantrey, of another prime minister, **George Canning** (1770–1827). He held several posts under Pitt the Younger, and was an outspoken critic of the slave trade, but he died four months after becoming prime minister. Canning's gravestone is close by, and next to it is the grave of the famous anti-slavery campaigner **William**

Wilberforce (1759–1833), whose statue can be seen in the north choir aisle. Further south is the grave of **William Ewart Gladstone** (1809–98), with a statue by Thomas Brock. Gladstone was leader of the Liberal Party and prime minister four times. He was a fine speaker, but Queen Victoria claimed he spoke to her as if she were a public meeting.

The north choir aisle is so full of memorials to composers that it is often referred to as Musicians' Aisle. On the north wall is a cartouche to **John Blow** (c. 1648–1708), who was organist here. He resigned to allow his pupil Purcell to have the post, and returned after the latter's early death. On the next pillar on the south side is a cartouche to **Henry Purcell** (1659–95), and his gravestone is close by. Purcell is considered to be the greatest composer of his age and is best known for his opera *Dido and Aeneas*. As organist at the Abbey, he produced many odes and anthems for royal occasions. He was buried near the organ, which used to be here.

A little way along this wall is the statue of **William Wilberforce**, on a tall plinth, showing him looking relaxed, if a little awkward, in a chair. He is buried in the north transept. In front of him is the white gravestone of **Sir William Sterndale Bennett** (1816–75), the celebrated pianist, composer and conductor of the early nineteenth century. Next there is a group of three stones marking where the ashes of three great composers are interred. **Sir Charles Villiers Stanford** (1852–1924) was an eminent composer whose music was sadly neglected until fairly recently. He was also an inspiring teacher, and two of his pupils are buried close to

Left: The baroque cartouche to composer Henry Purcell in the north choir aisle, near where he used to play the organ.

Below: The statue of William Wilberforce, the great abolitionist, in the north choir aisle.

him, **Herbert Howells** (1892–1983), who is best known for his choral music, and **Ralph Vaughan Williams** (1872–1958), who produced a great variety of music, including nine symphonies and works inspired by folk music.

Charles Darwin (1809–82), author of the ground-breaking book *The Origin of Species*, has a bust on the wall here, but he is buried just the other side of the gates, in the nave, in what is known as Scientists' Corner. The first scientist to be buried here was **Sir Isaac Newton** (1642–1727), one of the greatest of all mathematicians, who made many discoveries, and is famous for formulating the laws of gravity. He

H. S. E.
ISAACVS NEWTON Eques Auratus,
Qui animi vi prope divinâ,
Planetarum Motus, Figuras,
Cometarum Semitas, Oceanique Æstus.
Suâ Mathesi facem praferente
Primus demonstravit:
Radiorum Lucis dissimilitudines,
Colorumque inde nascentium proprietates,
Quas nemo antea vel suspicatus erat, pervestigavit.
Naturæ, Antiquitatis, S. Scripturæ,
Sedulus, sagax, fidus Interpres.
Dei O. M. Majestatem Philosophiâ asseruit,
Evangelij Simplicitatem Moribus expressit.

CHARLES JAMES FOX
B: 24. JAN. 1749. N.S.
D: 13. SEPT: 1806

Charles James Fox's monument in the north aisle, with a mourning slave in recognition of his support for the abolition of slavery

has a splendid monument on the choir screen, which contains references to his many inventions and discoveries. It was designed by William Kent and executed by Rysbrack. Also here are **Sir Joseph John Thomson** (1856–1940), the physicist who won the 1906 Nobel Prize, **William Thomson, Baron Kelvin** (1824–1907), the first scientist to be given a

Opposite: Sir Isaac Newton's splendid monument stands against the choir screen. It contains many symbolic references to his scientific discoveries.

peerage, and **Ernest Rutherford, Baron Rutherford** (1871–1937), another Nobel Prize-winner for physics. Rutherford's grave cannot usually be seen, as it is under the altar platform.

Further down the north aisle of the nave is the lozenge to **Sir Ninian Comper** (1864–1960), the architect and restorer of many churches. His ashes are buried close to a series of eight stained glass windows he designed, featuring images of kings. A little further on, low down on the north wall, is a simple stone marking the grave of the famous playwright **Benjamin (Ben) Jonson** (1572–1637), whose surname is mis-spelled. Jonson died in poverty and could not afford a normal grave, so he was buried standing up. Close by is an elaborate brass to **John Hunter** (1728–93), the great surgeon. He was originally buried in St Martin-in-the-Fields, but his remains were moved here when the crypt was cleared in 1859. The memorial was installed by the Royal College of Surgeons.

At the west end of the north aisle is the impressive monument to **Charles James Fox** (1749–1806), the distinguished Whig politician, who was in constant opposition to **William Pitt** (1759–1806), whose statue stands over the west door. Both are buried close together in the north transept (see above) and both monuments are by Sir Richard Westmacott. Pitt is shown in full oratorical flow, while Fox reclines in the arms of Liberty, with a bereaved slave kneeling at his feet, alluding to Fox's opposition to the slave trade. In front of Fox are buried the ashes of several important socialists: **Clement Attlee** (1883–1967), the post-war Labour prime minister who created the National Health Service; **Ernest Bevin** (1881–1951), the great trade unionist; and **Sidney Webb** (1859–1947) and **Beatrice Webb** (1858–1943), leading members of the Fabian Society, who founded the London School of Economics.

Right in the centre of the nave is the grave of **David Livingstone** (1813–73), the famous explorer and missionary. He died in the heart of Africa, and his embalmed body was brought back to Britain by his native followers. Alongside is the grave of **Thomas Tompion** (1639–1713), the finest watch-and clock-maker of his time. Buried in the same grave is his partner **George Graham** (1673–1751), who inherited the business and continued producing fine pieces, including astronomical instruments for the Royal Observatory in Greenwich. Nearby are the graves of two great engineers, **Thomas Telford** (1757–1834) and **Robert Stephenson** (1803–59). Telford is best known for his many canals and bridges, as well as the St Katherine Docks in London. Stephenson was an important railway engineer, who designed many railway bridges. His brass was designed by Sir George Gilbert Scott.

Nearby is a group of graves of eminent architects, which are usually covered by chairs, and are rather difficult to see. **George Edmund Street** (1824–81) has a fine brass memorial, showing him kneeling in front of a cross. He designed many churches, but his best-known work is the Royal Courts of Justice in the Strand. Behind him is **Sir George Gilbert Scott** (1811–78), with a brass designed by Street. Scott was the most prolific Gothic Revival architect, designing and restoring many churches, but his most famous London structures are the Albert Memorial and the Grand Midland Hotel at St Pancras. He was surveyor to Westminster Abbey, as was **John Loughborough Pearson** (1817–97), whose brass memorial is alongside Scott's. Pearson designed many churches, including St Augustine's in Kilburn, but his most important work is Truro Cathedral. To his right is the grave of **Sir Herbert Baker** (1862–1946), marked by a simple tablet. Baker was the architect who rebuilt the Bank of England, but most of his work was designing government buildings in the colonies, in particular India and South Africa. Behind is the brass to **Sir Charles Barry** (1795–1860), the architect of the Houses of Parliament, and the Victoria Tower and ground plan of the building feature on his memorial.

Alongside the grave of Gilbert Scott is a white slab marking the grave of **Thomas Cochrane, Earl of Dundonald** (1775–1860), the brilliant naval officer who, after making enemies in Britain, went on to help Chile, Perú and Brazil gain their independence. The Chilean Navy lays a wreath on his grave every May. By the second pillar before the choir screen, to the right, are stones marking the graves of two prime ministers, **Neville Chamberlain**

Charles Barry's brass in the nave includes depictions of his most important building, the Houses of Parliament.

(1869–1940), who was premier when war was declared in 1939, and **Andrew Bonar Law** (1858–1923), who was in post for only 209 days.

In the south choir aisle, which is not always open, is the tombstone of **Dame Sybil Thorndike** (1882–1976), the great actress, for whom Shaw created *Saint Joan*. The epitaph was penned by J. B. Priestley. On the south wall is the elaborate memorial, by Grinling Gibbons, to the wonderfully named **Sir Cloudesley Shovell** (1650–1707), the celebrated admiral who died in a shipwreck off the Scillies.

In the sanctuary, to the right under a side altar, is the low tomb of **Anne of Cleves** (1515–57), the fourth wife of Henry VIII, who annulled the marriage within six months, having rejected her as a 'Flanders mare'.

The north ambulatory takes you to the royal heart of the abbey, the shrine of the Saxon king, **Edward the Confessor** (1003–66), who built the new abbey church

MEMORIÆ ÆTERNÆ

ELIZABETHÆ ANGLIÆ, FRANCIÆ, ET HIBERNIÆ
REGINÆ, R HENRICI VIII FILIÆ, R HEN VII NEPTI R
ED IIII PRONEPTI, PATRIÆ PARENTI RELIGIONIS
ET BONARVM ARTIVM ALTRICI, PLVRIMARVM
LINGVARVM PERITIA PRÆCLARIS TVM ANIMI
TVM CORPORIS DOTIBVS, REGISQ VIRTVTIBVS
SVPRA SEXVM PRINCIPI
INCOMPARABILI

IACOBVS MAGNÆ BRITANNIÆ, FRANCIÆ, ET
HIBERNIÆ REX, VIRTVTVM, ET REGNORVM
HÆRES, BENE MERENTI PIE
POSVIT.

The magnificent tomb of Elizabeth I in the north aisle
of Henry VII's Chapel also contains the remains of
her half-sister Mary I.

and was buried before its high altar. He was canonised in 1161 and his grave became a place of pilgrimage. Henry III rebuilt the Abbey and made a magnificent new shrine for the saint, which stood at the heart of his new church. At the Reformation the shrine was badly damaged, but it still contains his remains, though it cannot now be visited. **Henry III** (1207–72) was devoted to the saint and was buried on the north side of his shrine, in a splendid tomb of Purbeck marble, covered in Cosmati mosaic, and with a gilt bronze effigy. To his right and left are the tombs of his son **Edward I** (1239–1307) and his wife **Eleanor of Castile** (1241–90). Edward was known as 'Longshanks' because of his height, and also as 'Hammer of the Scots', as he carried out a long war against them. His tomb has no effigy, but Eleanor's has a fine gilt bronze effigy. Opposite her tomb is the Chapel of St Paul. **Sir Rowland Hill** (1795–1879), who reformed the postal service and introduced the penny post, is buried here, and his grave is marked by a black lozenge. He also has a marble bust on the wall, which looks rather out of place among the grand Tudor tombs. At the foot of the steps leading to Henry VII's chapel is the gravestone of **Edward Hyde, Earl of Clarendon** (1609–74), the powerful politician who became lord chancellor and Charles II's right hand man. He was later impeached after criticising the king, and went into exile. Opposite the steps is the tomb of **Henry V** (1386–1422), under a chantry chapel where his wife **Catherine de Valois** (1401–37) is buried. Henry's head was originally made of silver, and the body was covered in silver plates, but these were all stolen in 1546, and the head is now a resin copy.

Go up the steps and turn left into the north aisle of Henry VII's Chapel. Just inside is the grave of **Joseph Addison** (1672–1719), the satirical writer who, with Richard Steele, founded the *Spectator*. His most famous creation was the slightly ridiculous country squire Sir Roger de Coverley. Nearby is the vault of **George Monck** (1608–70), the Parliamentarian general who changed sides and arranged for Charles II to reclaim the throne. In the centre of the chapel is the magnificent tomb of **Elizabeth I** (1533–1603), the work of Maximilian Colt. Elizabeth's jewels and the orb and sceptre are modern replicas, as the originals were stolen a long time ago. Her half-sister, **Mary I** (1516–58), known as Bloody Mary, is buried with her. At the far end of the chapel is what is known as Innocents' Corner, where, in the centre, are the supposed remains of **Edward V** (1470–83) and his brother **Richard, Duke of York** (1473–83), the so-called 'Princes in the Tower'. The bones were discovered at the Tower in the seventeenth century and assumed to be the young princes. On either side are the tombs of two of James I's daughters, both of whom died young.

Just inside the entrance to the nave of Henry VII's Chapel, on the left, is the grave of the **Duke of Cumberland** (1721–65), the army leader known as the 'butcher of Culloden'. The vault is marked by an inscribed lozenge in the floor. In front of the first steps on the left are stones marking the graves of his brother **Frederick Louis, Prince of Wales** (1707–51) and his wife, **Princess Augusta of Saxe-Gotha** (1719–72), the parents of George III. Frederick was not much missed, and legend has it that his death was caused by a blow to the head by a cricket ball. They are buried in the vault of **George II** (1683–1760) and his wife **Caroline of Ansbach** (1683–1737), whose markers are in the centre of the chapel. The king asked for the sides of the coffins to be removed so that their dust could intermingle. He was the last monarch to be buried in the Abbey; all later sovereigns are buried at Windsor. **Edward VI** (1537–53) was buried under the altar of the chapel, with no memorial, but there is now a stone marking the location, installed in 1966 by Christ's Hospital, which he founded. Behind the present altar is the spectacular Renaissance tomb of **Henry VII** (1457–1509) and his wife **Elizabeth of York** (1465–1503), designed by the Italian sculptor Pietro Torrigiano who, it is said, was forced to flee Florence after breaking Michelangelo's nose. Their gilt bronze effigies lie on a chest tomb surrounded by a beautiful grille. Lying next to them in the same vault is **James I** (1566–1625), who never had his own monument.

Filling the first apsidal chapel on the left is the large monument to **George Villiers, Duke of Buckingham** (1592–1628), the work of Hubert le Sueur, with four obelisks resting on skulls. Buckingham was the favourite of James I and Charles I, which made him very unpopular, and he was assassinated by a disgruntled army officer. In the next chapel, now under an organ, is a modern stone marking the grave of James I's queen, **Anne of Denmark** (1574–1619). Partly visible to the left of the organ is the stone marking the grave of **Anne Mowbray, Duchess of York** (1472–81), who was married to the five-year-old Richard, Duke of York, one of the princes murdered in the Tower. She died

aged eight and was buried in the Abbey, but, when Henry VII's chapel was built, her remains were moved to the church of the Minoresses of St Clare in Stepney. Her coffin was found by archaeologists in 1964 and she was re-buried here a year later.

At the east end is the RAF Chapel, dedicated to men who died in the Battle of Britain. Buried here are the ashes of **Hugh Trenchard, Viscount Trenchard** (1873–1956), who was known as the 'Father of the RAF', and **Hugh Dowding, Baron Dowding** (1882–1970), who commanded RAF Fighter Command during the Battle of Britain. A stone marks the vault where the regicides **Oliver Cromwell** (1599–1658), **John Bradshaw** (1602–59) and **Henry Ireton** (1611–51) were originally buried. After the Restoration, their bodies were exhumed and hanged and beheaded at Tyburn, where their bodies were buried. Their heads were stuck on spikes on the roof of Westminster Hall; Cromwell's skull is now said to be at Sidney Sussex College in Cambridge.

Leave the nave of the chapel and turn left into the south aisle. The first tomb is that of **Lady Margaret Douglas, Countess of Lennox** (1515–78), grand-daughter of Henry VII and mother of Henry Darnley, who married Mary, Queen of Scots and was later murdered. On the side of the tomb are weepers of her children, including Darnley, who is the first figure on the south side. Next is the outstanding tomb of **Mary, Queen of Scots** (1542–87), erected by her son James I. Mary was a Catholic and a great threat to Elizabeth I, who had her captured, imprisoned and, eventually, executed. Her tomb is even grander than Elizabeth's. Between the two tombs is a

The impressive tomb of Henry VII and his wife, Elizabeth of York, stands at the heart of the chapel he built.

large stone marking the burials of several royals, including **Henry, Prince of Wales** (1594–1612), James I's eldest son, who died tragically young, and **Elizabeth Stuart, Queen of Bohemia** (1596–1662), who married Frederick, King of Bohemia, and is known as the 'Winter Queen', as their reign lasted only one winter. Also here is her son, **Prince Rupert** (1619–82), who was a commander of the royalist army during the Civil War. The third tomb is that of **Lady Margaret Beaufort** (1443–1509), the mother of Henry VII. Her effigy is the work of Torrigiano, who has modelled her wrinkled hands beautifully. At the end of the aisle are floor plaques marking the vault in which are buried **Charles II** (1630–85), **William III** (1650–1702), his wife

Mary II (1662–94), and **Queen Anne** (1665–1714). The large monument on the left is to **General Monck**, who is buried in the north aisle. Curiously, his name is not mentioned in the inscription, only the names of those who erected the monument.

Leave Henry VII's Chapel and enter the south ambulatory, where there are more royal tombs. First are **Edward III** (1312–77) and his wife **Philippa of Hainault** (1314–69), on separate tombs with fine effigies. Next are **Richard II** (1367–1400) and his first wife, **Anne of Bohemia** (1366–94), lying side by side on the same tomb. In the Chapel of St Edmund opposite is the inscribed slab of **Edward Bulwer Lytton** (1803–73), a very popular novelist in his day, though he is little read today. His novel *Paul Clifford* begins with the famous line 'It was a dark and stormy night'. Back in the ambulatory, by the next column, is a modern plaque to **Anne Neville** (1456–85), the queen of Richard III. She wasn't given a monument, probably because her husband was killed in the same year. The second monument after the gate is to **Richard Busby** (1606–95), the eminent headmaster of Westminster School for 55 years, who is buried in the choir. His teaching was based on the classics, and he was a strict disciplinarian, but he gave the school an enviable reputation. He taught such notables as John Dryden and Christopher Wren. To the left of his memorial is a small inscription marking the back of **Anne of Cleves**' tomb.

The south transept is known as Poets' Corner, as many writers are buried or commemorated there. The first was **Geoffrey Chaucer** (*c.* 1340–1400), the great poet who wrote *The Canterbury Tales*, whose tomb is on the east wall. He lived in a house just outside the east end of the Abbey, which was the reason for his burial here. His Purbeck marble monument was not erected until 1556. Outside the Chapel of St Benedict is the monument to **John Dryden** (1631–1700), who was poet laureate until he converted to Roman Catholicism. To the left of Chaucer is a monument to **Abraham Cowley** (1618–67), who was recognised as an important poet in his day, but is considered very old-fashioned today. In front of the monument is his gravestone, which has the additional names of those buried in the same vault, including the playwright, **Francis Beaumont** (1584–1616), most of whose plays were co-written with John Fletcher, including *The Knight of the Burning Pestle*.

In front of Chaucer's tomb are the gravestones of three great poets, **Robert Browning** (1812–89), **Alfred Lord Tennyson** (1809–92) and **John Masefield** (1878–1967). Browning died in Venice, but the cemetery there was closed, so his body was brought over by train to be buried here. Masefield and Tennyson were both poets laureate. There is a bust of Tennyson by Thomas Woolner on an adjacent pillar. On the south wall is a simple marble monument to **Edmund Spenser** (1552?–99), the author of *The Faerie Queen*. It is said that, at his funeral, his contemporaries, including Shakespeare, dropped elegies into his grave. It was after Spenser's burial close to Chaucer that it became a custom for poets and dramatists to be buried here. On the same wall is a memorial by Rysbrack to the playwright **Ben Jonson**, who is buried in the nave.

The fine tomb of Edward III on the south side of the Confessor's Chapel.

On the adjacent wall is a large memorial, designed by James Gibbs, to **Matthew Prior** (1664–1721), who was both poet and diplomat. On the other side of the pillar, in the west aisle, is a marble statue by William Calder Marshall of the popular Scottish poet **Thomas Campbell** (1777–1844). In front is the grave of **Samuel Johnson** (1709–84), with a bust by Nollekens on the wall above it, installed in 1939. Dr Johnson is best known for his great dictionary and the biography by Boswell, which includes

The monument in the south transept to Geoffrey Chaucer, the first burial in what is now known as Poets' Corner.

so many of his sayings. Johnson came to London in 1737 with **David Garrick** (1717–79), the great Shakespearean actor, who is buried next to him (see page 42). His monument is high up at the north end of the west wall, depicting him taking his final curtain, flanked by the figures of Tragedy and Comedy. Next to Garrick, and in front of the Shakespeare memorial, are the graves of two more celebrated Shakespearean actors, **Sir Henry Irving** (1838–1905) and **Laurence Olivier, Baron Olivier** (1907–89). Irving managed the Lyceum

Theatre for 23 years and was the first actor to receive a knighthood. Olivier was equally successful on stage and screen, and was the first director of the National Theatre. On the south wall are two thirteenth-century wall paintings, which were discovered in 1936, behind the monuments to **John Gay** (1685–1732), author of the phenomenally successful *The Beggar's Opera*, and **Nicholas Rowe** (1674–1718), who was poet laureate. The monuments have been removed to the triforium. Gay's monument, by Rysbrack, carries the epitaph, composed by Gay himself, 'Life is a jest and all things show it; I thought so once, but now I know it'.

In the centre of the aisle are the gravestones of four great writers, **Charles Dickens** (1812–70), **Thomas Hardy** (1840–1928), **Rudyard Kipling** (1865–1936) and **Richard Brinsley Sheridan** (1751–1816). Dickens wished to be buried in Rochester Cathedral, but the authorities decided that Westminster Abbey was a more appropriate place for him to be interred. The funeral was private, with only 12 people attending, and the inscription is simple. Hardy's ashes are buried here, but his heart was buried at Stinsford, Dorset, where his parents are buried. One of the mourners at Hardy's funeral was Rudyard Kipling, who was the first English author to win the Nobel Prize for literature. As well as writing comedies, such as *The Rivals*, Sheridan was a successful theatre manager and politician. By the west wall is the grave of the celebrated composer **George Frideric Handel** (1685–1759), and on the wall above it is a fine monument by Roubiliac, showing the composer holding the score of his most famous composition, *Messiah*. The face is an exact likeness, as it was based on his death mask.

Next to Handel's grave is a statue, by Sir Richard Westmacott, of **Joseph Addison**, whose grave is in the north aisle of Henry VII's Chapel. Below the statue is the grave of **Thomas Babington Macaulay, Baron Macaulay** (1800–59), the eminent historian, whose major work was his *History of England*. Just after the next pillar is the grave of the architect, **James Wyatt** (1746–1813), with a simple classical memorial on the wall. Wyatt designed

GEORGE FREDERICK HANDEL Esq!
born February XXIII. MDCLXXXIV.
died April XIV. MDCCLIX. *L.F.Roubiliac invt.et sct*

Roubiliac's statue of the composer Handel holds a copy of his greatest work, *Messiah*.

many churches and country houses, and was also surveyor to the Abbey. Close by, and side by side, are the gravestones of the architects **Robert Adam** (1728–92) and **Sir William Chambers** (1722–96). Adam was a fashionable architect, whose most important London works include Apsley House, the Admiralty Screen in Whitehall, and the library in Kenwood House. He also designed several monuments in the Abbey. Chambers' most important works in London are Somerset House and the Pagoda in Kew Gardens.

The simple grave of playwright Aphra Behn in the East Cloister.

In the east cloister is the grave of **Aphra Behn** (1640?–89), the Restoration playwright, possibly the first professional female writer in England. Her best-known plays are *The Rover* and *Oroonoko*. A little further on is the gravestone of **Anne Bracegirdle** (1671–1748), the beautiful and popular actress, famous for her parts in Congreve's plays. She acted at Drury Lane Theatre under **Thomas Betterton** (1635–1710), who is buried nearby, with no inscription. As well as running the theatre, he was considered to be the greatest actor of his time, especially in tragedy. His wife, **Mary Betterton** (c. 1637–1712), herself a fine actress, is buried with him.

In the south cloister is the grave of **Muzio Clementi** (1752–1832), the virtuoso pianist and composer, who is referred to as the 'father of the pianoforte'. Next to him is the grave of the composer **William Shield** (1748–1829), who specialised in operas and songs, including *Auld Lang Syne* and *Comin' Thro' the Rye*. Buried in the same grave is the musical impresario **Johann Peter Salomon** (1745–1815), who organised many concerts in London, including two visits by Haydn, who composed a set of 12 symphonies, known as the 'London' or 'Salomon' symphonies. Also buried in the south cloister, but with no memorial, is the neo-Palladian architect **Colen Campbell** (1676–1729). On the wall of the north cloister is a memorial to **Ephraim Chambers** (1680?–1740), who wrote the *Cyclopaedia*, the first proper encyclopaedia.

Return to the nave by the west cloister door. On the south wall of the nave is the monument to **William Congreve** (1670–1729), the playwright best known for the comedy *The Way of the World*.

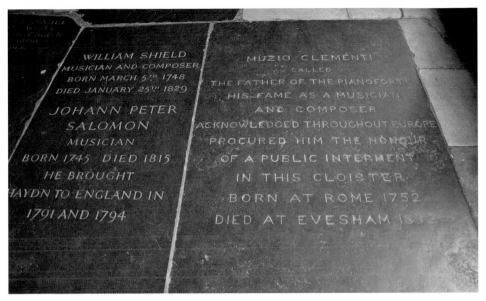

In the south cloister are the adjacent graves of musicians Muzio Clementi and Johann Salomon

The wall memorial in the north cloister to Ephraim Chambers, who produced the first real encyclopaedia.

The memorial has a portrait relief based on the painting by Godfrey Kneller. The epitaph was composed by the Duchess of Marlborough, with whom Congreve had a liaison.

In St George's Chapel at the west end of the nave, where the Coronation Chair is displayed, are stones marking the burials of **Edmund Allenby, Viscount Allenby** (1861–1936) and **Herbert Plumer, Viscount Plumer** (1857–1932), army officers who distinguished themselves in the First World War. Near the west door is the grave, marked by a black lozenge, of the great philanthropist **Angela Georgina Burdett-Coutts** (1814–1906), who inherited a fortune and used it to alleviate poverty and suffering. She was the first woman to be granted the Freedom of the City of London.

WEST LONDON

LONDON BOROUGH OF HOUNSLOW

There are several tombs to important artists in the graveyard of St Nicholas church in Chiswick. The most famous is that of **William Hogarth** (1697–1764), the great painter and satirist, which is on the south side of the church. It carries a relief of the artist's tools and eulogies by Dr Johnson and David Garrick. Hogarth spent his later years at a house in Chiswick, which is now a museum. Further west, and surrounded by elegant railings, is the large tomb of the artist **Philippe de Loutherbourg** (1740–1812), designed by Sir John Soane. De Loutherbourg was a notable landscape artist, who also designed scenery for Garrick and Sheridan at Drury Lane Theatre. Further west, in the centre of the newer part of the cemetery, is the grave of the sculptor **Thomas Thornycroft** (1815–85), which consists of a white marble slab with an inscription, surrounded by a low wall of pink granite. Thornycroft's most famous work in London is the statue of

Opposite: Hogarth's tomb in the St Nicholas graveyard has epitaphs by Dr Johnson and David Garrick as well as symbols of the artist's trade, including a palette with his 'line of beauty'.

Boadicea by Westminster Bridge, which was not installed until 17 years after his death.

Close to the northern wall is the tomb of **James McNeill Whistler** (1834–1903), the American-born artist who spent much of his career working in London. He is best known for his paintings of the Thames, especially views of Battersea and Chelsea. His tomb is of bronze and is Renaissance in style, with Ionic pilasters. The mourners at the four corners are resin copies, as the originals have been stolen. In the lower part of the cemetery, by the northern path, is the grave of **Sir William Blake Richmond** (1842–1921), a painter of mythological scenes and society portraits, but whose most important works are

Whistler's bronze tomb in Chiswick old cemetery is Renaissance in style.

The relief of Hope on the headstone of Sir William Blake Richmond in the old cemetery at Chiswick.

the mosaics in St Paul's Cathedral. His tombstone is double-sided, with striking reliefs of Charity and Hope, the work of one of his pupils. Buried in the church, but with no monument, are **Barbara Palmer, Countess of Castlemaine** (1640–1709), one of Charles II's mistresses, and **William Kent** (1686–1748), the architect and designer, who is buried in the vault of his patron, Lord Burlington.

St Leonard's church in Heston is the last resting place of **Sir Joseph Banks** (1743–1820), the naturalist who accompanied Captain Cook on his first voyage to New Zealand and Australia in 1768–71. He received many honours and was president of the Royal Society for nearly 40 years. His vast collection of specimens is now in the Natural History Museum. He was buried, following his own instructions, without any monument, though there is now a plaque to him in the church.

In the vault of St Lawrence church in Brentford, sadly now derelict, is buried **Thomas Hardwick** (1752–1829), one of an illustrious family of architects. He built several London churches, the most important being St Marylebone parish church. His son Philip Hardwick and grandson Philip Charles Hardwick, also important architects, are buried in Kensal Green Cemetery.

Gunnersbury Cemetery, in Gunnersbury Avenue, opened in 1929 on land that was part of the Rothschilds' estate. Its layout is quite formal and it is neat and well kept. As you enter, in the centre of block A on the left, is the grave of the legendary pianist **John Ogdon** (1937–89). To find it, walk up the central grass path, and it is half way up and four rows to the right. Ogdon became famous after he was joint winner of the Tchaikovsky piano competition in 1962. He had a phenomenal technique and an amazing memory, which allowed him to play some of the most difficult pieces in the repertoire. In his thirties he had a severe nervous breakdown, but after treatment was able to continue his career for a few more years. The grave is of light granite, with stepped sides and a concave headstone. The inscription says, 'Your musical genius brought so much joy to all who heard it'. Go on up the grass path to block B. By the path, to the left, opposite a bench, is the large ledger marking the grave of the artist

The grave of virtuoso pianist John Ogdon in Gunnersbury Cemetery.

Sir Matthew Arnold Bracy Smith (1879–1959). Smith's style was influenced by French artists, including Gauguin, Matisse and the Fauves. He specialised in painting nudes and landscapes, later turning to portraiture, and he always painted using strong colours. On his death, more than 1,000 of his pictures were left to the City of London, and a selection is on display in the Guildhall Art Gallery.

In the middle of block D is the large white ledger to the photographer **Terence Donovan** (1936–96), who was one of the most famous photographers of the 'Swinging Sixties', introducing a working class look to the fashion photography of the

time. He also worked in advertising, made television commercials, and produced portraits of the royal family. In the same block, just past the chapel, on the left, are the unusual squat headstones of the graves of **Sir Carol Reed** (1906–76), the film director, and his wife Penelope. Reed started his career as an actor and stage director before making many successful films. His masterpiece is considered to be *The Third Man*, with Graham Greene as scriptwriter, and he won an Oscar for the musical *Oliver!*

Continue straight on, past the Katyn memorial, which remembers the Polish prisoners of war murdered by the Russians in 1940, to section G, which has a number of simple headstones, with names inscribed on both sides, marking paupers' graves. Looking back towards the chapel, at the far right of row four is one with the names of **Beryl Evans** (1929–49) and her daughter **Geraldine** (1948–49), victims of one of London's most notorious mass murderers, John Christie, of 10 Rillington Place in Notting Hill. Beryl's husband, Timothy Evans, was hanged for the murder of Geraldine, but in 1966 he received a

The unusual gravestone of the film director Sir Carol Reed in Gunnersbury Cemetery.

The tall cross marking the grave of architect Sir Aston Webb in Gunnersbury Cemetery.

The grave of British spy Greville Wynne in Gunnersbury Cemetery bears the Latin motto *Fortiter et virtute* (Boldly and with valour).

posthumous pardon, and he is now buried in St Patrick's Cemetery in Leytonstone. Three more of Christie's victims are buried in Gunnersbury Cemetery.

Walk back down to block J, turn left and then right and, by the path on the left is the grave of **Sydney Lee** (1866–1949), with a relief portrait on the headstone. Lee was an influential but little known artist and print maker, whose work has only recently been re-appraised, with an exhibition at the Royal Academy in 2013. He helped to revive the art of wood engraving, producing many fine landscapes and architectural views. Just beyond is one of the largest memorials in the cemetery, looking rather like a village cross. This is the grave of **Sir Aston Webb** (1849–1930), the architect of the Victoria and Albert Museum, Admiralty Arch and the eastern façade of Buckingham Palace. He and his wife died within a few months of each other, and an inscription says 'They lived and loved and died together'. There is also a carving of his coat of arms, which features a spider in its web.

Take the left fork and carry on down to block OA. Three rows in on the left is the black marble grave of **Greville Maynard Wynne** (1919–90), a businessman who travelled regularly to Russia and worked as a spy for MI6. He was arrested in Budapest in

1962 and sentenced to eight years in prison, but was released in 1964 in exchange for the Russian spy Gordon Lonsdale.

LONDON BOROUGH OF HILLINGDON

In the churchyard of St John the Baptist in Hillingdon is the elaborately carved tomb of **John Rich** (1692–1761), the theatre manager who was the creator of English pantomime. He became rich when he produced John Gay's phenomenally successful *The Beggar's Opera* at his theatre in Lincoln's Inn Fields. It was said that the play made Gay rich and Rich gay. Although he lived in Covent Garden, he bought a country house near Uxbridge, and he chose to be buried here with his wife. The tomb is in the south-east corner of the graveyard.

St Dunstan's in Cranford Park stands beside the M4, and is rather inaccessible. It is usually open on Saturdays from April to September. The easiest way to reach it is via a footpath from Roseville Road under the motorway. On the east wall of the chancel is a cartouche to **Thomas Fuller** (1607–61), who was rector here from 1658, and is buried a few feet in front under a stone which says Fullers Earth. He is best known for his *History of the Worthies of England*, which was the first dictionary of English biographies. At the east end of the graveyard, at the end of a wall, is a memorial to the great comedian

The magnificent tomb of the theatre manager John Rich in the graveyard of St John the Baptist in Hillingdon reflects his successful career.

The ashes of the famous comedian, Tony Hancock, are interred in the graveyard of St Dunstan's Cranford.

Anthony (Tony) Hancock (1924–68), who is still remembered for his classic radio and television series, *Hancock's Half Hour*. His private life was far from being funny, with two divorces and a descent into alcoholism. He committed suicide in Australia while trying to revive his career. His ashes were brought back to England by the comedian Willie Rushton, and they were interred here with his mother's.

LONDON BOROUGH OF EALING

The famous Restoration actress **Elizabeth Barry** (1656?–1713) is buried in the vault of St Mary's, Acton, and she has a memorial high up on the west wall of the nave. Barry was no great beauty, but she had stage presence, a fine voice and a wide emotional range. She was an excellent comic actress, but also a great tragedian, who moved audiences to tears, and many dramatists created roles especially for her. She never married, but had several lovers, including the infamous Earl of Rochester, by whom she had a daughter. In 1710, after a long and successful career, she retired to Acton, where she died.

Hanwell Cemetery, on the south side of Uxbridge Road W7, was originally called the City of Westminster Cemetery, and is today run by the City of Westminster. It opened in 1854, and at only 23 acres is relatively small. After passing through the splendid wrought-iron gates, go straight ahead and turn left when you are level with the chapel. To the left of the War Memorial, in plot 24, is the simple grave, in the form of a book, of the comedian **Freddie Frinton** (1909–68). He is best known today for the popular television

In Hanwell Cemetery is the grave of the actor and comedian Freddie Frinton, best known in Britain for the television sitcom *Meet the Wife*.

sitcom, *Meet the Wife*, in which he starred with Thora Hird. Curiously, he is now better known in Germany and Scandinavia, where an 18-minute sketch, *Dinner for One*, in which he plays a drunken butler, is shown on television every Christmas and new year. Walk left and turn right and, about two-thirds of the way down this section, on the left in the fourth row, is the simple plaque to **Ian Nairn** (1930–83), the idiosyncratic architectural historian. He attacked the worst of new architecture and town planning, worked with Nikolaus Pevsner on his *The Buildings of England* series, and made a number of films for the BBC. His greatest legacy is the book *Nairn's London*,

66

which has recently been re-issued. He got his final wish, which was to be buried under the flight path to Heathrow Airport.

On the north side of Uxbridge Road, about 100 yards to the east, is the Royal Borough of Kensington and Chelsea Cemetery, which opened in 1855 as the Kensington Cemetery. At 10 acres, it is even smaller than Hanwell Cemetery, and when it began to fill up, a new cemetery was opened in Gunnersbury. Go up the long entrance drive and turn left, turning right up the next main path. Further up this path, on the left under a tree, is the unusual, semi-circular memorial to the songwriter **Paul Alfred Rubens** (1875–1917), with carvings of classically clad maidens dancing across it. Although little known today, Rubens was hugely successful in his lifetime, writing songs for many shows, including *Floradora*, which was a massive hit in the West End and on Broadway and included the famous sextet *Tell me Pretty Maiden*. Continue up this path and turn right and right again. On the right, by the path, is a large stone cross with a simple inscription and the words IN DEO SPES (In God Hope) on the cross. This is the grave of the sculptor **John Bell** (1811–95). Bell's most popular sculpture was *The Eagle-Slayer*, which was produced in various versions and was displayed at the Great Exhibition. He produced the *America* sculptural group on the Albert Memorial, the Wellington memorial in the Guildhall and the Guards Memorial in Waterloo Place. Continue down this path and turn left after the chapel. Behind the chapel is a Celtic cross commemorating the explorer **Sir Francis McClintock** (1819–1907), who is best known for his expeditions to

In the Royal Borough of Kensington and Chelsea Cemetery in Hanwell is the simple cross to John Bell, the sculptor of the Guards Memorial in Waterloo Place.

discover the fate of Sir John Franklin, who had died attempting to find the North-West Passage. His first search was in 1848, and he finally found evidence in 1859, with the help of the Inuit, including artefacts and skeletons.

At the eastern end of Church Road, Hanwell, is St Mary's church. Buried in the crypt is **Jonas Hanway** (1712–86), a successful merchant who traded for the Russia Company, and who financially supported many good causes. He is best known as the first man to carry an umbrella on the streets of London. He has no monument in the church, but has a memorial in Westminster Abbey. Also buried in the crypt is **William Thomas Wells** (1887–1967), the boxer known as Bombardier Billy Wells. Wells became the British heavyweight champion in 1911, winning the first heavyweight Lonsdale belt, defending the title 14 times and holding it for eight years. He is better known as the man who hits the gong at the beginning of J. Arthur Rank films. He is commemorated in the church by a plaque.

LONDON BOROUGH OF HARROW

St John the Evangelist church in Church Road, Great Stanmore, has an extensive churchyard, as well as the shell of an earlier church. Near the south-west corner of the new church is the white marble grave, with a winged angel, of **Sir William Schwenck Gilbert** (1836–1911), the playwright and wit who is best known for the Savoy operas, created with the composer Sir Arthur Sullivan. He was the first dramatist to be knighted. He died of a heart attack at his home, Grim's Dyke in Harrow Weald, while trying to rescue a girl from drowning in the lake.

In the churchyard of Christ Church in Roxeth Hill, South Harrow, is the grave of the celebrated chemist **Sir William Henry Perkin** (1838–1907). The Gothic headstone is in the overgrown eastern part of the graveyard. At the age of 18, Perkin

In the churchyard of St John the Evangelist in Great Stanmore is the grave of W. S. Gilbert, who co-wrote the Savoy operas with Arthur Sullivan.

carried out an experiment which went wrong, but which led to the discovery of the first aniline dye, known as mauveine or mauve. He built a chemical factory in Greenford Green to manufacture synthetic dyes, which soon replaced the natural dyes of the past. At his funeral, some wreaths were made up of mauve flowers.

James Brydges, 1st Duke of Chandos (1674–1744), made his fortune as paymaster-general to the Duke of Marlborough and, after his wife died, bought up her family estate at Cannons. He built a new house on the site, and also rebuilt the parish church, St Lawrence, Stanmore, in the baroque style. He employed George Frideric Handel as composer-in-residence, who composed a number of works for him, including 11 Chandos Anthems. The duke is buried in the grand, highly decorated, mausoleum off the north transept. It was designed by James Gibbs, and the colossal marble monument was designed by Grinling Gibbons. The duke stands in the centre, in Roman dress and wearing a long wig, and his two wives kneel on either side. In the churchyard, to the north of the church, is the modest headstone of the Baldry family, where the ashes of the blues singer **John William Baldry** (1941–2005) are interred. Known as Long John Baldry because of his height, he grew up in Edgware and he sang in the choir of St Lawrence. He discovered American blues music and from the early 60s performed with several groups, and with musicians such as Mick Jagger, Elton John and Rod Stewart. His biggest hit was the chart-topping *Let the Heartaches Begin.* He spent nearly 30 years in Canada, where he died.

In Pinner New Cemetery, in Pinner Road, is the grave of **David Edward Sutch** (1940–99), better known as Screaming Lord Sutch. The black marble grave, with a small angel on top, is over to the right, in front of a fence. Sutch was a minor rock 'n' roll star, whose act was ghoulish and Gothic, with props such as a coffin, skulls and live worms. He is now best remembered as an eccentric political candidate for the Monster Raving Loony

The grave of Sir William Henry Perkin, who created the first aniline dye (mauve), is in the overgrown graveyard of Christ Church in South Harrow.

The lavishly decorated mausoleum in St Lawrence Stanmore contains the monument to the Duke of Chandos, designed by Grinling Gibbons.

Party, contesting 41 by-elections, dressed in a top hat and a leopard-print jacket, and never winning one.

LONDON BOROUGH OF BRENT

In Beaconsfield Road, Willesden, is the United Synagogue Willesden Cemetery, which opened in 1873. It is an open cemetery, though you have to ring a bell to request admission.

In Section SP, to the left of the car park, is the grave of **Sir Charles Clore** (1904–79), a businessman who made his money by buying up businesses, such as Mappin & Webb and the bookmakers William Hill. He was also an art collector and philanthropist, and after his death the Tate Gallery opened the Clore Wing to house the paintings of J. M. W. Turner. Nearby is the grave of **Sir John Edward (Jack) Cohen** (1898–1979), the grocer who started his working life on a street stall in Hackney and went on to create the chain of Tesco stores. His grave is unusual in shape, and is said to resemble an early cash register. Over to the left in Section PLM is the simple grave of **Simeon Solomon** (1840–1905), the Pre-Raphaelite artist who painted biblical scenes as well as more mystical paintings containing androgynous figures. He was homosexual, and his career was seriously affected when he was arrested for importuning in a public toilet. He did begin to work again, with limited success, and lived in poverty for the rest of his life. He collapsed in the street and died in St Giles workhouse. Burne-Jones called him 'the greatest artist of all', but it wasn't until the late twentieth century that his work was fully appreciated.

At the left hand end of section N, beyond the chapel, is the modest grave of **Rosalind Elsie Franklin** (1920–58), the celebrated scientist whose research into the molecular structure of DNA laid the foundation for the work of Watson, Crick and Wilkins. Had she not died so young, she would surely have been included in the award of the Nobel Prize in 1962, but sadly it could not be awarded posthumously.

Further up the central path, and a little way to the right, is the first of the Rothschild family enclosures. On the left is **Lionel Nathan de Rothschild** (1808–79) who, in 1847, was the first Jew to be elected to Parliament, though he couldn't take his seat until 1858, when a bill was passed allowing him to take the oath of allegiance on the Old Testament. Next is the grave of his second son, **Alfred Charles de Rothschild** (1842–1918), who was the first Jewish governor of the Bank of England. On the right is the more elaborate grave of Lionel's first son, **Nathaniel (Nathan) Mayer, Lord Rothschild** (1840–1915), who was the head of the family bank and the first Jewish member of the House of Lords. Carry on up the main path; to the right of the roundabout is another enclosure with the graves of two sons of Nathaniel Mayer. Although both brothers did their duty as partners of the family business, they were more interested in natural history. **Nathaniel Charles Rothschild** (1877–1923) became an eminent entomologist, and his flea collection is now in the Natural History Museum. He also created Britain's first nature reserve at Wicken Fen in Cambridgeshire. **Lionel Walter Rothschild** (1868–1937) collected vast numbers of specimens for a zoological museum built on his father's estate in Tring, now part of the Natural History Museum. He also had a menagerie of exotic animals, and would ride around his estate in a zebra-drawn cart. On one famous occasion he visited Princess Alexandra at Buckingham Palace in a carriage drawn by zebras to demonstrate that the animal could be tamed.

At the far end of the cemetery, over to the right in Section QX, close to the wall, is the grave of the artist **Mark Gertler** (1891–1939). He studied at the Slade School of Fine Art, where he was a star pupil. He became a successful member of the London Group, but in his thirties began to have health problems; he later suffered from depression and committed suicide. His best-known work is *The Merry Go-Round*, painted during the First World War, which is now in the Tate. Take the western path back towards the exit and in the narrow section between the two paths is the grave of **Michael Winner** (1935–2013), the film director, best known for *Death Wish* and *Hannibal Brooks*.

Adjacent to the United Synagogue Cemetery, in Pound Lane NW10, is the Liberal Jewish Cemetery, which opened in 1914. Straight ahead is the Prayer Hall, which contains a columbarium, where the ashes of the writer **Israel Zangwill** (1864–1926) are to be found. Zangwill was a journalist and novelist who wrote about Jewish causes, including his most important novel *Children of the Ghetto*. In the middle of the section behind the Prayer Hall is the unusual grave of the Spanish opera singer **Conchita Supervía Rubenstein** (1895–1936). She was particularly associated with the revival of the operas of Rossini, though her most famous role was Carmen. Shortly after making her London debut in 1930, she married a Jewish businessman. She died tragically young in childbirth. Her tomb, designed by Edwin Lutyens, consists of a granite block resting on the backs of four tortoises.

Cross to the Holocaust memorial and take the path on the right. About one hundred yards on the left, by the path, is the grave of **Bernard Delfont** (1909–94), the theatre impresario. Born Boris Winogradsky in Ukraine, and brought up in the East End, he started out as an entertainer before moving into theatre management, putting on shows at the Palladium as well as dinner entertainment at the Talk of the Town. At the opposite end of this section, four rows back is the grave of his older brother **Lew Grade** (1906–98), the television and film producer, who was famous for his trademark cigars. He founded ATV, which started broadcasting in 1955, offering popular family entertainment, and later moved into film production. Seven rows back is the grave of the third brother **Leslie Grade** (1916–79), who was a highly respected theatrical agent. Further up in section 6, in the middle of a row, is the grave of **Arnold Goodman, Baron Goodman** (1913–95), a highly successful lawyer who came to prominence when Harold Wilson gave him a job, taking him into the heart of politics. He was chairman of the Arts Council for many years.

Paddington Cemetery, in Willesden Lane, NW2, also known as Paddington Old Cemetery, opened in 1855. Taking the second path on the right, to the left side of the path is the large tomb slab marking the grave of **Edward Middleton Barry**

The name of the architect E. M. Barry is picked out with moss on his tombstone in Paddington Old Cemetery.

(1830–80), the son of Sir Charles Barry and also an architect. At the start of his career he worked with his father and helped to build the new Houses of Parliament, completing it after his father's death. His other main buildings are the Royal Opera House in Covent Garden, the Charing Cross Hotel and the replica of the Eleanor Cross that stands in its forecourt. Take the next path on the left to find the grave of **Cuthbert Ottaway** (1850–78), a leading sportsman who has been almost forgotten, probably because he died so young. He represented Oxford University in five sports and was the first captain of an England football team, leading them in international matches against Scotland in 1872 and 1874. Over the years his monument was allowed to deteriorate, and in 1972 it was demolished by Westminster Council, but in 2013 a new gravestone was installed to mark the grave of this fine sportsman.

Just inside the gate of the graveyard of St Mary, Willesden, Neasden Lane NW10, at the north east corner of the church, is the tomb of the novelist and dramatist **Charles Reade** (1814–84). Though little read today, Reade was one of the most

The modern gravestone of Cuthbert Ottaway, the first captain of an English football team, in Paddington Old Cemetery.

The unusual grave of the author Charles Reade in the graveyard of St Mary's Willesden.

prolific and popular writers of his day, best known for his historical novel *The Cloister and the Hearth*. In 1853 he fell in love with a married woman, Laura Seymour, and they lived together until her death in 1879. Somewhat unconventionally for the time, he is buried in the same grave as Laura and her husband.

LONDON BOROUGH OF HAMMERSMITH AND FULHAM

At the north end of Putney Bridge is All Saints, Fulham. By the south-east corner of the church is the splendid tomb of **Sir Francis Child** (1641–1713), covered in carvings of heraldry and civic emblems. He ran one of London's most successful banks, based in Fleet Street, where it still operates, though now it is part of the Royal Bank of Scotland. Child, who lived in Fulham, was lord mayor in 1698–9. At the north-east corner of the church, opposite the door to the vestry, is the grave of the architect **Henry Holland** (1745–1806), which he designed for his parents in a plain classical style. He is best known for

his country houses, including Althorp and Woburn Abbey, and in London he built Brooks's Club in St James's and the Prince of Wales's short-lived Carlton House. In the north-west corner of the churchyard is the tomb of **Granville Sharp** (1735 1813), a leading activist in the fight for the abolition of slavery, and one of the founders, along with Thomas Clarkson and William Wilberforce, of the Society for the Abolition of the Slave Trade in 1787. His tomb had become overgrown and forgotten, but was re-discovered early this century, and money was raised for it to be restored and the inscription re-cut in time

The splendidly carved tomb of banker Sir Francis Child in the churchyard of All Saints Fulham.

The recently restored tomb of the anti-slavery campaigner, Granville Sharp, in Fulham churchyard.

The fine marble cross of the Polish-born British spy known as Christine Granville, in St Mary's Roman Catholic Cemetery in Kensal Green.

he is best remembered as a panellist on the television game show *What's My Line?* He was often brusque and rude, but the public loved him all the same, and Westminster Cathedral was packed for his requiem mass. Return to the top path and turn left. Take the second path on the left to find the large family plot, with a cross, of **George Joseph Edwardes** (1855–1915), the hugely successful producer of musical theatre. He began his London career working with Richard D'Oyly Carte on Gilbert and Sullivan's operettas before taking over the running of the Gaiety Theatre, which he ran for 30 years. He produced popular burlesques and musical comedies, making stars of his performers, and the theatre became the most important venue in the world for musical theatre. Return to the main path and turn left. Just after a brown stone mausoleum on the left is the white marble grave of **Countess Krystyna Gizycka** (1915–52), also known as **Christine Granville**. The Polish-born Krystyna was recruited as a British spy in the Second World War, taking the name Christine Granville, and she later worked for the Special Operations Executive. She was extremely brave, and after rescuing three French fighters from prison in Digne, she was awarded the George Medal by the British and the Croix de Guerre by the French. Sadly, she was murdered by a stalker in a hotel in South Kensington. A few yards further along the main path is a monument looking rather like a war memorial, a tall cross of granite and copper. It is the last resting place of **Thomas Power O'Connor** (1848–1929), the Irish politician and journalist who was a fervent supporter of home rule.

for the 200th anniversary of the 1807 Slave Trade Act, which abolished the slave trade in the British Empire.

St Mary's Roman Catholic Cemetery in the Harrow Road is adjacent to the more famous Kensal Green Cemetery, but is quite separate. It opened in 1858, on 29 acres of land between the railway and the Grand Union Canal. Take the first left after the chapel, where behind the white Gothic mausoleum is a simple cruciform ledger, the grave of **Gilbert Charles Harding** (1907–60), the popular radio and television celebrity. He was quizmaster of *Round Britain Quiz*, and was on the panel of *The Brains Trust* and *Twenty Questions*, but

The grave of the great conductor, Sir John Barbirolli, in St Mary's RC Cemetery.

The black marble gravestone of Sax Rohmer, author of the Fu Manchu novels, in St Mary's RC Cemetery.

Further along this path, past the junction, and over to the left, in the centre of the next section, is the low white marble grave of the Barbirolli family. Here, with his parents, are buried the ashes of **Sir John Barbirolli** (1899–1970), the great conductor, who worked with most of the world's great orchestras, but is best known for his long association with Manchester's Hallé Orchestra. Return along the same path, taking the second turning on the right, and on the left side of the central avenue is the last resting place of **Clarkson Stanfield** (1793–1867), an artist who went from painting stage scenery at Drury Lane to become a prolific painter of maritime landscapes. Unfortunately, the substantial tomb, with a large Celtic cross, became unstable, and has been dismantled for safety reasons. At

the time of writing, it is no more than a pile of earth, but hopefully it will soon be restored. Continue down this path, and after the trees finish, four rows to the right is the grave of **Philip William (Phil) May** (1864–1903), a headstone with rounded corners between two crosses. The inscription is very worn, but his name is just decipherable. May was a popular illustrator whose work was inspired by London's low life, including the music hall, gin palaces and fairgrounds. Take the next grass path on the right, then left and before you reach the end, on the right is a black marble tombstone in a sea of grey, the grave of **Arthur Henry Ward** (1883–1959), buried here with his parents. He is better known as **Sax Rohmer**, author of the popular Fu Manchu novels, mostly set among the opium dens of Limehouse,

The best-kept grave in St Mary's RC Cemetery is that of Mary Seacole, which is always covered in flowers.

The modest headstone to Carlo Pellegrini, the artist known as 'Ape', in St Mary's RC Cemetery.

and featuring what he called 'the yellow peril incarnate'.

At the end of the path turn left and then take the first right. After the Saint Rita burial ground, take the left fork up an incline. On the right, under a tree, is the grave of **Daniel Patrick Carroll** (1927–2009), better known as **Danny La Rue**, the famous female impersonator. He regularly appeared in the West End and in pantomime, as well as on television, and owned a nightclub in Mayfair. He is buried with his partner, Jack Hanson, who was also his manager. Return up the path where, after the next junction, over to the left, is the grave of **Mary Seacole** (1805–81), with

a striking white headstone decorated with palm trees. She was a Jamaican nurse whose work in Kingston, Panama and, especially, on the battlefields of the Crimea, has made her a black icon. She received little official recognition for her work, but the soldiers referred to her as the 'black Nightingale'. Her grave here was lost and forgotten for many years, but in 1973 it was restored, and it is now one of the best maintained in the cemetery, always covered in flowers.

Continue up this path, turn right, and ahead of you, in front of a small mausoleum, is the grave of **Sir Anthony Panizzi** (1797–1879), who became the principal librarian of the British Museum and built its famous round reading room. Behind is the grave of **Carlo Pellegrini** (1839–89), an artist whose caricatures of society notables, including Panizzi, produced under the pseudonym 'Ape' for *Vanity Fair*, were highly popular in his day and are still very collectable. His gravestone was paid for by the sale of a proof of his caricature of Whistler. Take the path heading north towards the chapel, and in the shadow of a mausoleum is a simple headstone of the grave of **Louis Wain** (1860–1939), the artist famous for his drawings of humanised cats. He was diagnosed as schizophrenic and spent many years in mental institutions, where he continued to paint cats. He was buried in his father's grave, but his name is not inscribed on the headstone. Over to the right, opposite the Belgian War Memorial, is the grave of Henry John Doyle, in which is also buried **Richard Doyle** (1824–83), the illustrator who worked for seven years for *Punch*, producing political cartoons and designing its famous cover. He also provided book illustrations for Dickens and Thackeray, and produced a book of fairy pictures called *Fairyland*, which is considered to be one of the best-produced illustrated books of the period. His work is little known these days, and he is best remembered as the uncle of Arthur Conan Doyle.

ROYAL BOROUGH OF KENSINGTON AND CHELSEA

In the south-east corner of the churchyard of All Saints Chelsea (Chelsea Old Church) in Cheyne Row is the splendid monument to **Sir Hans Sloane** (1660–1753), the physician and naturalist, whose vast natural history collections and library were

bequeathed to the nation and formed the core of the British Museum. He bought the manor of Chelsea and in 1722 leased four acres to the Society of Apothecaries for their physic garden, which survives to this day. Also buried here, but with no memorial, are the blind magistrate **Sir John Fielding** (1721–80), who succeeded his brother, Henry Fielding, the novelist, as magistrate in Bow Street,

The tomb of Sir Hans Sloane, Lord of the Manor, doctor and naturalist, in the graveyard of Chelsea Old Church.

The grave of the composer Charles Burney in the Royal Hospital burial ground.

the playwright **Thomas Shadwell** (*c.* 1640–92), who became poet laureate, and the sculptor **John Tweed** (1869–1933), whose London statues include Lord Clive in King Charles Street and Lord Kitchener on Horseguards Parade.

In Kings' Road, at the junction with Dovehouse Street, is a garden now known as Dovehouse Green. It was originally a burial ground, but it closed in 1824. The most celebrated person to be buried here was the Italian artist **Giovanni Battista Cipriani** (1727–85), but his grave can no longer be seen. He painted several neo-classical interiors for Robert Adam and Sir William Chambers, including rooms for the Royal Academy in Somerset House (now the Courtauld Gallery), but he is best known for his decoration of the Royal State Coach, which was made for George III in 1768 and is still used for every coronation.

On Royal Hospital Road, adjacent to the hospital, is its burial ground. Just inside the entrance, against an east-facing wall on the right, is the grave of **Charles Burney** (1726–1814), the composer and writer on musical history, and organist at the Chelsea Hospital. He is best known as the father of the novelist Fanny Burney. At the far end of the burial ground is the last resting place of **Margaret Thatcher, Lady Thatcher** (1925–2013), who was Britain's first female prime minister from 1979 to 1990. Nicknamed the Iron Lady because of her robust style, she was a powerful but divisive figure. Even her death was controversial, as she was granted an expensive ceremonial funeral with full military honours. Her ashes were interred in the burial ground in front of the hospital infirmary named after her, next to her husband Denis, who died in 2003.

At St Mary's Roman Catholic church in Cadogan Gardens is a memorial to **Anna Maria Tussaud** (1761–1850), better known as **Madame Tussaud**, founder of the world's most famous waxwork museum. She worked in Paris with Dr Curtius, making wax portraits of the royal family and, after the revolution of 1789, of many of those who were guillotined. In 1802 she brought her exhibition to England, touring the country before settling in Baker Street in London. She was originally buried in the Roman Catholic St Mary's chapel in Pavilion Road, but when the present church was built her remains were re-interred in the crypt. A memorial plaque can be seen in the north chapel.

The present St Mary Abbots church in Kensington is by Sir George Gilbert Scott, and many of the monuments from the earlier church have been preserved all round the walls. In the north transept is a memorial to Francis Colman, the father of **George Colman** (1732–94), a highly successful playwright and theatre manager who is buried in the family vault. George Colman was. He made a great success of running the Covent Garden theatre, putting on his own plays and offering the first performance of Goldsmith's *She Stoops to Conquer*. His most important play, co-written with Garrick, was *The Clandestine Marriage*, which is still performed today.

The ashes of Margaret Thatcher, Britain's first female prime minister, are interred in the burial ground of the Royal Hospital Chelsea.

BROMPTON CEMETERY

BROMPTON CEMETERY IS the most central of the Magnificent Seven cemeteries, and opened in 1840. It was built on land bought from Lord Kensington, which had previously been occupied by market gardens. The company soon ran into financial difficulties, and the cemetery was bought by the government; it is now maintained by the Royal Parks. The cemetery soon became popular, and it contains many tombs of the great and the good, including musicians, actors, writers and engineers. The Friends of Brompton Cemetery work with the Royal Parks to maintain the cemetery and its buildings, publish a guide, offer regular Sunday tours and hold an annual Open Day. For details check their website: www.brompton-cemetery.org.uk.

Starting from the northern entrance in Old Brompton Road, walk straight ahead down Central Avenue. About 40 yards down, on the left, is the grave of **Emmeline Pankhurst** (1858–1928), the great suffragette leader. In 1903 she formed the Women's Social and Political Union, which fought for many years, often violently, for the right of women to vote. She didn't live to see women over the age of 21 gain the right to vote, as she died two weeks before the law was passed. Her memorial is an unusual sandstone cross with a relief of Christ with his hand raised in blessing, with angels above, holding a chalice, and the hand of God appearing from a cloud. About 10 yards further down on the left is the tomb of the celebrated Austrian tenor **Richard Tauber** (1891–1948). Although an accomplished opera singer, his fame came from singing in operettas, including those of Franz Lehár, especially the song 'You are my heart's delight' from *The Land of Smiles*. His tomb is a large grey granite slab with, at its foot, a stanza from a verse by A. P. Herbert, in which he is called, 'A golden singer with a sunny heart'. When he died, Tauber left no money to pay for his grave, and Marlene Dietrich, a life-long friend, helped collect the money to pay for it.

Continue down Central Avenue, turn left, then right, and on the right is the grave of **Edward Alexander Wadsworth** (1889–1949), an artist who was a member of the Vorticists

Opposite: The cross on the grave of Emmeline Pankhurst, the celebrated suffragette leader, has a figure of Christ on the shaft and the hand of God at the top.

The Gothic grave of Squire Bancroft and his wife is all that is left of their mausoleum.

before turning to abstraction. The rather traditional headstone does not reflect the style of his work. Return along the path and continue to the far end. Just before the junction, on the left, is the pink granite headstone of the music hall star **Charles Coborn** (1852–1945). Born Colin Whitton McCallum, Coborn was famous for two songs, *Two Lovely Black Eyes* and *The Man who Broke the Bank at Monte Carlo*, the latter based on a true story, which was made into a film in which he appeared. He never retired and continued to sing the two songs throughout his long career. Continue to the end of the path and immediately to your left is the grave of **Sir Squire Bancroft** (1841–1926) and his wife **Lady Bancroft** (1839–1921), hugely successful actor-managers who were pioneers of natural acting and introduced drawing room comedy to the theatre. Their unusual Gothic tomb is actually the façade of their mausoleum, and it is not known why this is all that is left of it. Walk eastwards and a little further on the right is the tomb of **John Snow** (1813–58), the doctor who proved that the deadly disease cholera was water-borne, following his investigation

of an outbreak in Soho. He also worked in the development of anaesthetics, and gave chloroform to Queen Victoria at the births of two of her children. The white marble tombstone, surmounted by a draped urn, was erected by his friends and colleagues, and it was restored in 1895 and again in 1938. It was destroyed by a bomb in 1941, and was replaced by this replica in 1951.

Further along this path, on the left, is the coffin-shaped tomb, surrounded by railings, of the architect **Thomas Cundy the Younger** (1790–1867). The Gothic script makes the inscription rather difficult to read. Cundy was surveyor to the Grosvenor estate, working with Thomas Cubitt on the development of

The grave of John Snow, the doctor who first proved that infected water was the cause of cholera.

Belgravia and Pimlico. He also designed a number of London churches, including St Paul's Knightsbridge and St Barnabas Pimlico. Turn right down the eastern path where, about halfway down the block, on the right, beside the path, is the coped gravestone, with a cross, of **Thomas Joseph Pettigrew** (1791–1865). Pettigrew was a distinguished doctor who became surgeon to the dukes of York and Sussex. He was also an antiquarian, with a particular interest in Egyptology, especially mummies, and he was often referred to as 'Mummy' Pettigrew. He entertained guests to his parties by anatomising mummies, and the Duke of Hamilton was so impressed he arranged for Pettigrew to mummify him after his death. A few yards further on, also on the right and in the third row, is the pink granite gravestone of the artist and novelist **Charles Allston Collins** (1828–73), the brother of Wilkie Collins. Collins was never officially a member of the Pre-Raphaelite Brotherhood, but produced work in the same style, including his best known painting *Convent Thoughts*. He married Kate, the youngest daughter of Charles Dickens, and illustrated Dickens's unfinished novel, *The Mystery of Edwin Drood*.

A little further on, take the grass path on the left up to the upper terrace along the east wall. Look out for the stone distance markers in the brick wall, and just past the 450 stone is the white marble family grave of **William Terriss** (1847–97), the hugely popular actor and the greatest matinée idol of his day. He was stabbed at the stage door of the Adelphi Theatre by an out-of-work actor who bore him a grudge, and his ghost is said to haunt Covent Garden station to this day. His real

Buried here is William Terriss, one of the most popular actors of his day, who was murdered by another actor.

name, William Charles James Lewin, is on the gravestone along with his stage name. As he was a theatrical celebrity, his funeral attracted massive crowds, including many of London's theatrical élite, among them his mistress, the actress Jessie Millward, and Sir Henry Irving. Continue along this path, and just after the steps you can look down on the rather inconspicuous grave of the great designer and administrator **Sir Henry Cole** (1808–82). It is often lost in the undergrowth, as it has no headstone, and it was indeed lost for many years until re-discovered in 2001. Cole was a highly talented organiser who helped to plan the Great Exhibition of 1851, working closely

This humble grave is that of the important administrator and designer, Sir Henry Cole. For much of the year it cannot be seen, as it is often covered by long grass.

The grave of the writer George Borrow is visited every July by members of the George Borrow Society, who leave flowers.

with Prince Albert, and he also helped establish what would become the Victoria and Albert Museum.

Take the steps down and turn left. About 40 yards on the right is the tall, rather weathered, headstone to **William Railton** (1800–77), the architect who is best known as the designer of Nelson's Column in Trafalgar Square. Directly behind it is the damaged headstone of the grave of **Richard Redgrave** (1804–88), an artist who specialised in painting narrative scenes highlighting the conditions of poor working women, such as teachers and seamstresses. He also designed the impressive funeral carriage for Wellington's funeral. He later turned to arts administration, working with Henry Cole in setting up the Victoria and Albert Museum, and was surveyor of the queen's pictures for more than 20 years.

Return along the path and turn left onto the side path and right at the next one. Halfway along on the right is the pink gabled ledger of **Samuel Smiles** (1812–1904), the writer best known as the author of *Self Help*, a best-selling book which showed how ordinary people could improve their lives. Almost directly behind, in the centre of this block, is the white marble tomb of **George Henry Borrow** (1803–81), an author who wrote novels and travel books based on his own personal experiences. His best-known books are *The Bible in Spain* and the novel *Lavengro*. His tomb was restored in 2011 by the George Borrow Society, and members visit the cemetery on the anniversary of his death every July to leave flowers. Retrace your steps and just past the next junction, on the left, is the grave of **John Wisden** (1826–84), the Sussex and England cricketer who founded the famous Almanack, the cricketers' bible, which still bears his name. The present black marble headstone was installed in 1984, the centenary of his death. A few yards further on, in the third row on the right, is the simple headstone to **William Banting** (1797–1878), one of a distinguished family of undertakers based in St James's Street, who organised many royal funerals, including those of George III, George IV and Prince Albert, as well as the state funeral of the Duke of Wellington. Banting had a serious weight problem, and in 1863 he issued a popular pamphlet detailing a low-carbohydrate diet he was following. Even today, dieting is sometimes referred to as 'banting'. Take the next path on the right, by the Egyptian-style mausoleum, and 20 yards on the right is the grave of **Joseph Bonomi** (1796–1878), the artist and pioneer Egyptologist who produced many drawings to illustrate books on Egypt. He advised on the design of the Egyptian entrance to Abney Park Cemetery, and was involved in the design of the mausoleum you have just passed. He was later appointed curator of the Sir John Soane Museum. His

gravestone has Christian symbols at the top, and the Egyptian god Anubis, the protector of the dead, at the bottom. Go back to the mausoleum and turn right. At the end of this path, almost straight ahead, is the grave of **George Alfred Henty** (1832–1902), the war correspondent and author best known for his adventure stories for boys. The grave has, sadly, lost its cross.

Return to the eastern path for the massive tomb of **John Jackson** (1769–1845), surmounted by a wonderfully lugubrious lion. 'Gentleman Jackson', as he was called, because of his good manners, was a prize-fighter who became

The headstone of Joseph Bonomi's grave has Egyptian and Christian symbolism on it, and was created by Bonomi himself for his family.

A lion aptly features on the tomb of the famous prize-fighter John 'Gentleman' Jackson.

the champion of England, but retired after only three fights to train others, including Lord Byron. His splendid tomb was paid for by public subscription. It has a cameo relief of Jackson on one side, and a rather eroded inscription on the other. Originally large urns stood on plinths front and back. About 20 yards to the left of the Jackson monument, at the back, is the simple round-headed headstone to **Renton Nicholson** (1809–61), its inscription only just legible. Nicholson was an entrepreneur and gambler who was often in financial difficulties and spent much time in debtors' prisons. His claim to fame is that he set up the Judge and Jury Society, which put on satirical mock trials in taverns, with him presiding as 'Lord Chief Baron'. This was so successful that politicians, actors and other celebrities flocked to the performances, and it also toured the provinces. He later added saucy *poses plastiques* to the shows, consisting of semi-naked women imitating famous statues or paintings.

John Peake Knight's introduction of traffic lights to London was only a partial success.

Behind Jackson's tomb, to the left of the path, is the pedestal tomb, with a rather elegant urn, to **John Peake Knight** (1828–86), the railway manager who is now remembered as the man who introduced traffic lights to the streets of London. The first signals were set up outside the new Houses of Parliament in 1868, though a gas leak caused an explosion, injuring a policeman, and bringing the experiment to a temporary halt. It would be 50 years before traffic lights became a permanent sight on London's streets. Take the steps up to the raised path and turn right. A few yards down the path is the grave of shipping magnate **Sir Samuel Cunard** (1787–1865), a massive pink granite slab upon a block of grey granite, with his surname picked out in gold paint. A Canadian, Cunard started his shipping business with a small fleet of ships, trading in the West Indies and Latin America. He later created his own steam ship company in Britain, which was granted the contract to carry mail across the Atlantic. He soon offered the first regular passenger service from Liverpool to America, which was the beginning of what came to be called the Cunard Line. Three graves further on is the elegant family grave of **Philip Nowell** (1781–1853), in the form of a Gothic shrine. Nowell was the builder contracted to build most of the buildings and boundary walls of Brompton Cemetery. About

20 yards south of Nowell is the chest tomb of father and son **James Veitch** (1815–69) and **John Gould Veitch** (1839–70), the horticulturalists who were responsible for the planting of Brompton Cemetery. They were members of a gardening family that operated a famous nursery in the King's Road, Chelsea. The nursery was the first to sponsor plant hunters to travel the globe in search of new plants to offer for sale.

Continue along the upper track and after the next set of steps, take the unofficial path down to find the modest grave, marked only by a draped urn, of **Marquesa Luisa de Casati** (1881- 1957), an Italian heiress who was one of the most flamboyant figures of the early twentieth century. (If the path is inaccessible, go down the steps and reach the grave from the main path.) Though not a great beauty, she had flaming red hair and striking green eyes, which she emphasised using kohl, and her extravagant dress sense still influences today's fashion designers. She collected exotic pets, including cheetahs, which she would take for walks while wearing nothing but a fur coat. She also collected art, mixed with the cultural élite and, when entertaining, employed naked waiters covered in gold leaf. Sadly, the dream could not last and, bankrupt, she arrived in London in the 1930s, where she attracted a new circle of admirers. Buried with her is one of her stuffed Pekinese dogs, and the inscription, as well as mis-spelling her middle name, quotes appositely from Shakespeare's lines about Cleopatra, 'Age cannot wither her, nor custom stale her infinite variety'. Return to the upper path and continue right until, after about 30 yards, on the right, under a tree, is the grave to **Francis Fowke** (1823–65), a

Portland stone cross with kerbstones, but with no visible inscription. Fowke was an eminent engineer, who worked with Henry Cole on the construction of the Victoria and Albert Museum, but is best known as the designer of the Royal Albert Hall. Continue along the path and near the end on the left is the Gothic gravestone of **Sir John Fowler** (1817–98). Fowler was one of the greatest railway engineers, whose major achievement was the construction of the Forth railway bridge. In London, he built the first Grosvenor railway bridge over the

This simple grave marker is for the Marquesa Luisa de Casati, a flamboyant Italian socialite, whose fashion sense is still highly influential.

The Gothic headstone on the grave of Sir John Fowler, the engineer who designed the Forth railway bridge.

Sadly, the splendid tomb of champion oarsman Robert Coombes has been badly vandalised.

Thames, as well as the first Victoria Station, but he is best known in London for his work in building the early underground railway lines as engineer for the Metropolitan District Line.

At the end of the path, turn right. On the right is the large tomb of **Robert Coombes** (1808–60), the champion oarsman who won many races on the Thames and the Tyne, and later coached both the Oxford and Cambridge boat crews. He died in poverty, and the magnificent tomb of Portland stone was paid for by his friends and admirers. On top is an upturned boat, with his coat draped across it. In niches at the four corners are sculptures of watermen, all now, sadly, vandalised. Next to it is the grave of **Samuel Leigh Sotheby** (1805–61), the antiquary who helped to convert the family auctioneering business into the major company it is today. On the front of the granite memorial is a white marble relief of an angel guiding two figures, possibly Adam and Eve being expelled from the Garden of Eden. Directly opposite is the memorial to **Sir Francis Pettit Smith** (1808–74), the inventor of the screw propeller, which proved to be far superior to the paddle wheel. He worked with Isambard Kingdom

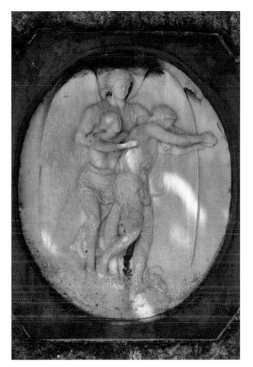

The marble relief on the monument to Samuel Sotheby, probably depicting the expulsion from Eden.

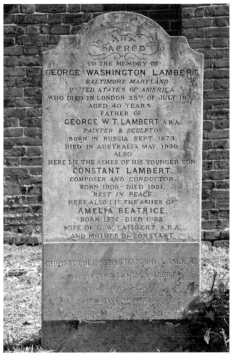

The grave of the composer Constant Lambert also contains the remains of his son, Christopher (Kit) Lambert, who managed The Who.

Brunel to replace his paddle steamers with screw propulsion. His grave is on the other side of the path, in amongst the trees, and is inaccessible. A few yards to the right, in the fifth row under some trees, is the grave, with a simple cross, of **William John Thoms** (1803–85), the antiquary who founded the scholarly periodical *Notes and Queries*, which offered a means for antiquaries and historians to exchange information. Charles Dickens was a regular reader, and the publication originally used Captain Cuttle's motto, 'When found, make a note of', from *Dombey and Son*. It is today published by Oxford University Press. Thoms was also interested in ancient customs and traditions, giving the word 'folklore' to the English language.

Retrace your steps and turn right along the southern perimeter path. Just after the next junction, on the left, is the grave of **Constant Lambert** (1905–51), the composer and conductor. He wrote music for Diaghilev's Ballets Russes and for the Sadler's Wells Ballet, as well as a good deal of purely orchestral music. Much of his music was influenced by jazz, such as *The Rio Grande*, his most popular composition. He was also a music critic, and wrote the influential book *Music Ho!* Several members of his family

The grave of the racing driver, Percy Lambert, who died young, includes a broken column, symbolising a life cut short.

The portrait sculpture on the grave of the opera singer Blanche Roosevelt Macchetta.

are buried in the grave, including his son **Christopher Sebastian (Kit) Lambert** (1935–81), who managed the rock band The Who, and produced many of their recordings. He had a flair for publicity, and it was his idea for the band to destroy their instruments at the end of their gigs. Take the path towards the chapel, take the first left and at the next corner, to the left of the path, is the broken column commemorating **Percy Lambert** (1880–1913), the racing driver who was the first person to drive one hundred miles in an hour, at Brooklands. Having lost his record, he was attempting to reclaim it when a tyre burst and he was badly injured, dying on the way to hospital.

He is not related to Constant or Kit.

Continue past the chapel and walk down towards Central Avenue. In the right-hand corner of the Grand Circle is an obelisk commemorating the composer **John Lionel Alexander Monckton** (1861–1924), who provided tuneful songs for musical comedies, including the international hit *The Geisha*, and other shows such as *The Arcadians* and *The Country Girl*. He was one of the most successful song writers of the Victorian and Edwardian theatre. On the other side of the main path is the marble portrait sculpture of **Blanche Roosevelt Macchetta** (1853–98), the American singer who had a highly successful operatic

The white marble cross to artist John William Godward stands out among the stone crosses.

even when modernist art was becoming the fashion. He committed suicide by gassing himself, and his death hardly got a mention in the press, but attitudes to Victorian art have changed in recent years, and his paintings now change hands for large sums of money.

Turn left at the end of the Great Circle and a few rows back is the large headstone of **John Hollingshead** (1827–1904), with carved quills on either side. Hollingshead made his name as a journalist and theatre critic, before turning his talents to theatre management. He ran the Alhambra in Leicester Square, then the Gaiety in the Strand, where he introduced electric lighting on stage. He produced the first Gilbert and Sullivan collaboration, *Thespis*, and was the first British manager to put on a play by Ibsen. Close by, on the other side of the path, marked by a memorial with a female figure standing by a pedestal, lies **Sir Augustus Henry Glossop Harris** (1852–96). Harris was an actor and theatre manager who, at Drury Lane, was famous for his spectacular shows with lavish special effects, including pantomimes and operas. He was so popular that many thousands attended his funeral. The monument, the work of Sir Thomas Brock, originally carried a bronze bust of Harris, but this was stolen in the early years of this century. Among the sculptural details are a violin and the masks of comedy and tragedy.

Now go north along the colonnade and, just after the steps down to the catacombs on the right, in the second row under a yew tree, is the simple ledger marking the grave of **Dame Emma Albani** (1847–1930), the renowned Canadian opera singer. Born Marie Louise Cécile Emma Lajeunesse,

career in Europe, and performed leading roles in the Gilbert and Sullivan operettas with the D'Oyly Carte Opera Company. Behind her memorial is the polished grey pedestal tomb of **(Walter) Brandon Thomas** (1848–1914), the actor and playwright who is best known for his brilliant farce *Charley's Aunt*, which was a huge success, breaking records in the West End. In the central area of the Great Circle, on the left, is the white marble cross marking the grave of **John William Godward** (1861–1922), an artist who specialised in painting female figures in flimsy classical drapery in the style of Alma-Tadema. He never changed his style or subject matter,

The theatrical monument to Augustus Harris has lost its bust. The photograph from 1967 (right) shows it as it once was.

she became the first Canadian opera singer to become a major international star. She starred at Covent Garden for 24 years, and also performed with great acclaim in America and Europe, specialising in coloratura roles. She was a favourite of Queen Victoria, who invited her to give a private performance at Windsor Castle. A little further on, on the right, is the tall, slim memorial to **Reginald Alexander John Warneford** (1891–1915), who was the first person to destroy a Zeppelin, in air combat over Ghent, and was awarded the Victoria Cross. Later the same month he died in an air accident, and it is estimated

that 50,000 people attended his funeral here. As well as his portrait, the memorial carries a relief of his aerial escapade.

Just off the Central Avenue to the right, in the second row, almost immediately after the end of the colonnade, are three graves of the Thesiger family. The first, low coped ledger is the grave of **Ernest Thesiger** (1879–1961), the celebrated stage actor. He also had a short but successful Hollywood career, and his most famous role was that of Dr Septimus in James Whale's *Bride of Frankenstein*. In the block behind, about six rows back, is the grave of **Sir William Howard Russell**

(1820–1907), the journalist who became famous as a war correspondent during the Crimean War. It was as a result of his reports that Florence Nightingale was sent there, and his criticism of the way the war was waged led to changes in the way it was run. Though he is not a well-known figure today, the new inscription, added in 2013, calls him 'the first and greatest war correspondent'. A few yards behind is the chest tomb of **Godfrey Sykes** (1824–66), a designer whose best known London work is to be found in the Victoria and Albert Museum, especially in the refreshment rooms. He also designed the tomb of William Mulready at Kensal Green.

Now take a short diversion along the path to the east of the colonnades. On the left is the Celtic cross marking the grave of the artist **Frederick George Stephens** (1827–1907). Stephens studied art at the Royal Academy and was a founder member of the Pre-Raphaelite Brotherhood. Because of his good looks he also worked as a model for his fellow artists. He soon realised he wasn't going to be a successful artist and destroyed most of his paintings, and he became a successful art critic, which allowed him to promote the works of his friends and to explain their radical ideas. Take the next left, then right, cross the next junction and about half way down on

Poppy wreaths were left at the grave of Reginald Warneford on the centenary of his death.

A new plaque on the grave of William Russell highlights his importance as the first war correspondent.

The white marble cross to the popular actress
Nellie Farren.

and his best-known work is the frieze of
sculptors and architects on the Albert
Memorial. Retrace your steps, turn left,
then right where, against the outer wall
of the colonnade is the white marble cross
of **Ellen (Nellie) Farren** (1848–1904),
the versatile burlesque actress. For many
years she worked for John Hollingshead
at the Gaiety Theatre, where she was
particularly noted for her 'principal boy'
roles. She was so popular that around 5,000
people attended her funeral.

Return to the Central Avenue and
head north. Immediately on the left is the
prominent chest tomb of the influential
Scottish geologist **Sir Roderick Impey
Murchison** (1792–1871). He explored
the geological structures of much of the
British Isles and Europe, and later promoted
exploration overseas. He received many
honours and was president of the Geological
Society and the Royal Geographical Society.
Many geographical features around the
world are named after him, including rivers,
islands and even a crater on the moon. A
little further on the left is the monument to
the sculptor **Matthew Noble** (1817–76),
a pedestal topped off by a draped urn.
Much of Noble's work is to be found in and
around Manchester, but he also produced
some fine statues for London, including
Sir John Franklin in Waterloo Place and
two prime ministers, Robert Peel and
the Earl of Derby, in Parliament Square.
Just after the next junction, on the left,
with a splendid anchor, is the tomb of the
famous magician **John Nevil Maskelyne**
(1839–1917). For 30 years he performed
at the Egyptian Hall in Piccadilly with a
celebrated levitation act, escapes from a box
and an array of clever automatons. Many

the right, next to the path, is the grave of
the eminent botanist **Robert Fortune**
(1812–80), with a new pink granite ledger.
Fortune travelled several times in the Far
East, collecting many new plants, which
were sent back to England, including
orchids, azaleas and chrysanthemums,
many of which bear his name. He is
probably best known for introducing tea
plants from China to India, thus creating
the tea-growing industry there. To enable
him to carry out this task, he adopted
Chinese dress, grew a pigtail, and learnt the
language. Somewhere in the overgrown area
behind him is the inaccessible grave of the
sculptor **John Birnie Philip** (1824–75).
Philip specialised in architectural sculpture,

The tomb of the magician John Nevil Maskelyne has a very prominent anchor, symbolising hope.

The fine tomb of the architect George Godwin, with a portrait flanked by the figures of Literature and Architecture.

of his illusions are still performed to this day. A few yards further on, on the right, is the splendid tomb of architect **George Godwin** (1813 88). Most of Godwin's work was in Kensington, where he lived, including The Boltons and its church, St Mary's. He edited *The Builder* for over 40 years, making it the most important journal of its kind, and wrote several books on architecture. The monument has a portrait medallion of Godwin, with the rather weathered figures of Literature and Architecture standing on either side. Below his portrait are carved an architect's tools, and on top of the memorial are three

books. Just after the next junction, on the right, is the pink granite cross marking the grave of **Henry Augustus (Gus) Mears** (1873–1912), co-founder, with his brother Joseph, of Chelsea Football Club, whose stadium overlooks the southern part of the cemetery.

Go back down the Central Avenue, take the second right and immediately turn right onto a parallel path. On the right is the tomb of **Valentine Cameron Prinsep** (1838–1904), a hugely successful artist associated with the Pre-Raphaelites. He also wrote plays and novels, and was the inspiration for Taffy in George Du Maurier's *Trilby*.

The grave of the artist Valentine Prinsep takes the form of a Gothic sarcophagus.

His unusual monument is in the form of a Gothic sarcophagus on eight columns. He married the daughter of **Frederick Richards Leyland** (1831–92), the ship-owning millionaire and art collector, whose grave is further up this path. He was patron to Dante Gabriel Rossetti, James McNeill Whistler and Edward Burne-Jones, and the latter designed his strikingly beautiful tomb, which is based on a Romanesque shrine. Surrounded by wrought iron railings, it consists of a chest tomb of white marble, with copper floral scrolls on all four sides and a copper roof. A short way further along this path, on the right, is the double width grave of **Sir William Crookes** (1832–1919), with its collapsed kerb and missing cross. Crookes was an influential chemist who helped in the discovery of X-rays and the electron, which led the way to nuclear physics, and he also worked on radioactivity. One of his more practical experiments was with anti-polarising glass for safety spectacles, now used in sunglasses. At the next junction is the tall memorial, with an armless female figure, to **Hiram Codd** (1838–87), the engineer who created the so-called Codd Globe Stopper bottle, which was filled with pressurised gas, forcing a marble into the neck to make a perfect seal. The bottles, especially the earlier ones, are now highly collectable.

Continue up this path and, after the next junction, in the middle of the block on the left, is the grave of **Tom Taylor** (1817–80), a successful playwright of comedies

Tom Taylor was a prolific and popular playwright and poet, but his work has not lasted well.

and burlesques, and writer of comic pieces for *Punch*, of which he was briefly editor. He was also an art critic with old-fashioned tastes, and testified against Whistler in the notorious libel case brought by John Ruskin. Abraham Lincoln was watching his play *Our American Cousin* when he was assassinated. His grave has a tall gabled headstone and a footstone. It is difficult to access when the grass is fully grown, but it can still be seen from the path. Retrace your steps and turn right to reach the grass bank by the railway line on the western side of the cemetery, which is the area where many recent burials have taken place. Almost directly opposite, close together, at the back by the wall, are the graves of **Brian Glover** (1934–97), the wrestler who had a successful second career as an actor, and **Bernard Levin** (1928–2004), the journalist and broadcaster best known for his combative interviews on the 1960s TV satire *That Was the Week That Was*. About 50 yards to the left, also at the back, is the grave of **Henrietta Moraes** (1931–99), an artists' model who inspired Francis Bacon and Lucian Freud, and was renowned for her love affairs. At the far left end of this section, by the path, is the grave of **Terence Feely** (1928–2000), the playwright who

Frederick Leyland's beautiful tomb was designed by Edward Burne-Jones.

wrote scripts for many famous television series, including *The Avengers*, *The Saint*, *Thunderbirds* and *The Prisoner*. The ledger has a long, loving, inscription and a round blue plaque at the top.

IN MEMORY OF

WILKIE COLLINS,
AUTHOR OF THE WOMAN IN WHITE
AND OTHER WORKS OF FICTION

KENSAL GREEN CEMETERY

KENSAL GREEN CEMETERY is the oldest of the Magnificent Seven cemeteries created in the first half of the nineteenth century. Founded by the General Cemetery Company, which still runs it today, it opened in 1833 in what was then a rural area outside the limits of London. It was a great success, and with the burial in 1843 of the Duke of Sussex became the most fashionable burial place in London. Within its 72 acres are interred many important people from all walks of life, including artists, writers, actors, engineers, doctors, politicians and royalty. It is still very much a working cemetery and is open daily. Check the website for opening hours: www.kensalgreencemetery.com. The Friends of Kensal Green Cemetery offer tours every Sunday from March to October, and on the first and third Sundays from November to February, starting at 2pm. They also hold an Open Day in July, when they offer a variety of tours and other events. Details can be found on their website: www. kensalgreen.co.uk.

The nearest rail and underground station is Kensal Green. Turn right along the Harrow Road to the western entrance, which is manned daily, and where you can buy a very useful concise guide and map to the cemetery and its principal burials.

Walking straight ahead, behind the mausolea on the left is the Rattigan family grave, a marble cross within a marble enclosure, where the playwright **Sir Terence Rattigan** (1911–77) is buried. He wrote many fine plays, a number of which were turned into successful films, such as *The Browning Version* and *The Deep Blue Sea*. For many years his work was considered to be rather old-fashioned, but the plays have recently been enjoying a successful revival. He died in Bermuda and his ashes were interred here, but there is no inscription to him. Continue down the main path, past an enormous new monument, and a little way further on, to the left, is a curious tomb in the form of a chair. This is the grave of **Henry Russell** (1812–1900), a popular singer and songwriter whose best-known song is *A Life on the Ocean Wave*. Another of his popular songs was *The Old Arm Chair*, which explains the unusual form of his grave.

Two rows behind, and three graves to the left, is buried the conductor **Sir Landon Ronald** (1873–1938), who was Russell's

Opposite: Novelist Wilkie Collins' grave is probably the best tended in the cemetery, with floral displays all year round (see page 104).

The ashes of playwright Sir Terence Rattigan are interred in the family tomb, but he has no inscription.

The unusual grave of Henry Russell, inscribed with lines from his popular song *The Old Arm Chair*.

son. He accompanied the singer Dame Nellie Melba in recitals before turning to conducting. He was a great champion of British music and an early supporter of the gramophone, recording with many great artists.

Take the next path to the right where, just before the next junction, four rows back on the left, is the grave of **Sir Leslie Ward** (1851–1922), an artist famous for the caricatures of prominent figures he drew for *Vanity Fair* for 40 years under the pseudonym of 'Spy'. Several of his subjects are buried in Kensal Green, including Sir John Tenniel, Anthony Trollope and George Grossmith. His great-grandfather, the artist

James Ward, is also buried here (see below). The cross is now missing, but the inscription is just about legible. Turn left down the next path and continue down through the gate marked 'The Rowan Garden'. At the end of the path, to the left, is the beautifully carved headstone marking the grave of novelist and playwright **Simon Gray** (1936–2008). He wrote many successful plays, including *Butley* and *Quartermaine's Terms*, as well as screenplays for television and the cinema. He also published eight volumes of diaries, where he spoke frankly of his addictions to drink and cigarettes. Go back the way you came and turn right at the gate. About 30 yards along, three rows back on the right, is the grave of the artist **John William Waterhouse** (1849–1917), who specialised in classical and literary subjects. His most famous painting is *The Lady of Shalott*, based on the famous poem by Tennyson, which is in the Tate collection. Soon after his death his work fell out of fashion, but in recent years there has been a revival of interest, culminating in an exhibition at the Royal Academy in 2009. The tall, slender headstone has a modern inscription. Continue along the lower path and about 20 yards past the next junction, on the left, is the grave of **George Grossmith** (1847–1912), with its simple cross. Grossmith is today celebrated for the novel *The Diary of a Nobody*, which he co-wrote with his brother, Weedon, starring Charles Pooter, one of literature's great comic creations. He was also a hugely popular entertainer, touring his sketches and comic songs all round the country. It was for Grossmith that Gilbert and Sullivan created many of the great comic characters in their Savoy operas, and he was the first performer to sing their famous 'patter' songs.

Take the grass path opposite and, at the top of the slope, over to the left, is the grave of **Dorothy Dene** (1859–99), marked by a tall cross. Dene was an actress, but is best known as Lord Leighton's favourite model, appearing in many of his most notable paintings, including *The Garden of the Hesperides*. It has been suggested that their relationship was the inspiration for George Bernard Shaw's *Pygmalion*. Return to the lower path and turn right where, on the right, is a Celtic cross marking the grave of **John Passmore Edwards** (1823–1911), the newspaper owner who was one

of London's greatest philanthropists. He paid for the construction of many libraries, museums, hospitals and convalescent homes, some in his home county of Cornwall, but mostly in London, especially in the East End. Sadly, many have since closed, though some have found new uses, and his name lives on, carved over their entrances. Take the next left and under a tree on the right is the grave of the influential fashion designer **Raymond 'Ossie' Clark** (1942–96). He was a massive star in the Swinging Sixties, making clothes for the rich and famous, as well as stage costumes for rock stars. He became a good friend of the artist David Hockney, who painted a portrait of him and his wife, Celia Birtwell, called *Mr and Mrs Clark and Percy*. Sadly his success did not last, bringing

The simple classical grave of artist John William Waterhouse, whose reputation has grown in recent years.

A Celtic cross marks the grave of philanthropist John Passmore Edwards.

Fashion designer Ossie Clarke's gravestone carries an Ankh symbol at the top and a Buddhist mantra carved along the bottom.

bankruptcy and drug addiction, and he was murdered in his council flat by his male lover. His grave is marked by a beautifully carved headstone, with, unusually, an Ankh, the Egyptian symbol of eternal life.

Return to the lower path, turn left, and take the next main path on the right. On the bend is the grave of **William Henry Smith** (1792–1865), a large chest tomb of pink and grey granite with an open bible on top. He was the newsagent who turned his small family business in London into a major national operation, now known as W. H. Smith. His great innovation was to send the London newspapers around the country, first by coach, then by rail. His son, also William Henry Smith, arranged a deal to set up bookstalls at railway stations, which made the company a household name.

Continue along the lower road and turn sharp left up the next grass path to find, to the left of a poplar tree, the grave of **James Henry Leigh Hunt** (1784–1859), a square marble block on a plinth. Leigh Hunt was a radical and influential journalist and literary critic, who promoted the work of

The chest tomb of William Henry Smith carries an open bible.

poets such as Keats, Shelley and Tennyson. He spent two years in gaol for insulting the Prince Regent. He was always positive and easy-going, and Dickens based his character of Harold Skimpole in *Bleak House* on him. The monument was erected in 1869, paid for by public subscription. It originally had a bust by Joseph Durham, which has, sadly, been stolen. Turn left after the poplar and follow the path. Just before it curves round to the right, on the left, behind the Paul headstone, but lost in the undergrowth, is the grave of engineer **Peter William Barlow** (1809–85), who is best known for designing the first Lambeth Bridge. He invented a new tunnelling shield, which he used to build the Tower subway under the Thames. The tunnel wasn't a success, but the shield was later adapted by his pupil, James Henry Greathead, to dig the tunnels for the Underground railway system.

About 60 yards further on, on the left, in the second row, is a cross marking the last resting place of **Richard Harris Barham** (1788–1845). Barham was a clergyman who, while working as a minor canon at St Paul's Cathedral, wrote the *Ingoldsby Legends*, which were published in *Bentley's Miscellany*. They purported to be tales recently discovered by Thomas Ingoldsby, but were actually re-workings of traditional legends and myths. The tales, with their mix of crime and the supernatural, were so successful that they were later issued as separate volumes, and they were illustrated by Tenniel, Cruikshank and Leech. When he died, he was buried in the church of St Mary Magdalene and St Gregory in the City of London, where he had been rector, but the church burnt down in 1886 and his remains were re-interred here. A little further on is

The pedestal tomb of Leigh Hunt once carried a bronze bust, but it was stolen some years ago (inset).

the pink granite cruciform raised ledger of the novelist **Anthony Trollope** (1815–82). For most of his life he worked for the Post Office, and introduced the pillar box to Britain. He was 33 before his first novel was published, and 46 more were to follow, plus many short stories and several travel books. The Barsetshire Chronicles and the Palliser novels are probably his best loved works. Trollope's reputation suffered somewhat after his death, but his work is now enjoying something of a revival.

Continue along this path to the West Centre Avenue where, on the right, is the splendid tomb of **Jean-François Gravelet** (1824–97), one of the most famous tightrope walkers of all time, performing

The grave of novelist Anthony Trollope, who worked for the Post Office for much of his life, and introduced pillar boxes to the country's streets.

under the name of **Charles Blondin**. He was celebrated for being the first person to cross the Niagara Falls, a feat he first carried out in 1859, and repeated several times with variations, including a crossing on stilts and another while blindfolded. He performed at the Crystal Palace in Sydenham, and after a successful provincial tour, took his show around Europe and the Americas. He died in Niagara House, his home in Ealing, and was buried here next to his first wife. The monument, of pink Peterhead granite and Carrara marble, carries relief portrait medallions of the two of them, and is topped off by the marble figure of Hope. Take the grass path almost opposite to the grave, with a stone cross, which marks the last resting place of the popular novelist **Wilkie Collins** (1824–89) (see page 98). It is a rather conventional grave for a writer who, in many ways, was very unconventional. He lived openly with a woman he never married, but who is buried with him, and had three children by another woman. He also took large doses of laudanum for 'rheumatic gout', which plagued him for much of his life. He is considered to be the originator of the 'sensation novel', including *The Woman in White* and *The Moonstone*, which are still his most popular books. Covered in colourful plants, his grave is one of the best maintained in the cemetery, tended by the Wilkie Collins Society.

Continue up this path, turn left and then left again onto the tarmac path. About 20 yards on the right is the grave of **William Harrison Ainsworth** (1805–82), with a slender urn on top. Ainsworth was a writer of historical novels, which were hugely successful during his lifetime, but are now rather out of fashion. Of some 40 novels, his best-known are *Rookwood,* for which he invented Dick Turpin's famous ride from York to London on Black Bess, and *Old Saint Paul's*. He lived for a number of years at Kensal Manor House, not far from the cemetery. A few rows behind is the grey granite sarcophagus of the architect **Decimus Burton** (1800–81). Among his many London buildings are the Athenaeum club in Waterloo Place, the Constitution Arch at Hyde Park Corner and the Palm House and Temperate House in Kew Gardens. He also designed several of the villas around the borders of Regent's

The impressive tomb of Charles Blondin, the famous tightrope walker.

The fine headstone of sculptor John Ternouth could well be his own work.

Park, and was responsible for laying out the grounds of London Zoo. Ten rows behind and two rows to the right is the distinctive gravestone of the sculptor **John Ternouth** (1796–1848), with a deep relief of a mourning female figure. His best-known work is *The Battle of Copenhagen* plaque on the pedestal of Nelson's Column in Trafalgar Square. His headstone may well be one of his own works. Return to the path, and behind the tree opposite is the short obelisk marking the grave of artist **Henry**

Nelson O'Neil (1817–80). At the Royal Academy Schools he formed a group of artists, including John Phillip and William Powell Frith (who are both buried in Kensal Green), whose plan was to paint modern historical subjects. His most successful pictures, because of their moving personal elements, were *Eastward Ho! August 1857* and *Home Again 1858*, depicting troops setting off to suppress the Indian Mutiny and returning after the conflict was over. Return to the path and turn left and left

The Egyptian-style mausoleum of the Duke of Cambridge, who was commander-in-chief of the British Army for many years.

again at the next junction, where on the left is the rather austere Egyptian mausoleum of **George William Frederick Charles, second Duke of Cambridge** (1819–1904), a grandson of George III who was commander-in-chief of the British army for nearly 40 years. Deposited with him is Louisa (or Sarah) Fairbrother, a dancer and actress he married, against the terms of the Royal Marriages Act, and who bore him three sons, who are also buried here.

At the Anglican Chapel, turn right and then right again onto the grass path at the corner. On the left is the gabled marble headstone to **Sir Charles Lock Eastlake** (1793–1865), a successful artist who later turned to arts administration. He was involved in organising the interior decoration of the new Houses of Parliament, was president of the Royal Academy for 15 years, and as director of the National Gallery bought many fine paintings for the collection. He died in Pisa, and was originally buried in the Protestant cemetery in Florence before being re-interred

here. On the other side of the path, in the third row, is the grave of portrait painter **William Salter** (1804–75), marked by a tapering column surmounted by an urn. Salter painted many notable people, including Wellington and Wilberforce, and his most important work is *The Waterloo Banquet at Apsley House*, containing portraits of 84 officers who fought with Wellington at Waterloo, which today hangs in Apsley House. A little over to the right, in the fourth row, is the marble cross on the grave of **Montagu William Lowry Corry, Baron Rowton** (1838–1903), who was Benjamin Disraeli's private secretary for many years. He became indispensable to Disraeli, and was often consulted by Queen Victoria, who became a personal friend. He later turned to philanthropy, in 1892 opening the first Rowton House, a poor man's hotel, in Vauxhall. Five more were built in the next few years, but only one still operates in London today. He was so popular that his obituary in *The Times* claimed that, 'Everyone loved him, from duchesses to dossers', and his funeral was attended by all social classes, including a few residents of Rowton House.

Return to the main path and turn right, and take the next on the right. A short way down, five rows back on the right, is the grave of the Arctic explorer **Sir John Ross** (1777–1856), appropriately decorated with an anchor. Ross had a distinguished career as a naval officer, being wounded 13 times and imprisoned several times by the French, but he is better known as a polar explorer, twice attempting, unsuccessfully, to find the North-West Passage, though he surveyed much new territory. At the age of 73, he led an expedition to locate Franklin's

The grave of Montagu Corry, Baron Rowton, who created the Rowton House 'hotels for the poor'.

ill-fated attempt to find the passage. On the other side of the path, to the right of an obelisk, is the pink granite slab marking the grave of the Scottish sculptor **William Calder Marshall** (1813–94). He produced statues for the Houses of Parliament and Westminster Abbey, but his best-known work is the *Agriculture* group on the Albert Memorial.

Return to the chapel and take the steps down to the right. On either side of Centre Avenue are impressive royal tombs. On the left is that of **Prince Augustus Frederick, Duke of Sussex** (1773–1843), the sixth son of George III. He became estranged from his father because of his radical views, but also because he twice married without royal assent. Members of the royal family were usually buried in

Windsor, and he was the first royal prince to be interred in a public cemetery, albeit with a full state funeral. His second wife, Cecilia Underwood, who was later created first Duchess of Inverness by Queen Victoria, was buried alongside him. The massive granite tomb is surrounded by bollards, which once held chains. On the south side of the path is the even more impressive tomb of his sister, **Princess Sophia** (1777–1848) who led a very sheltered life, due to her possessive father and a selfish mother. Only after her mother's death did she have any freedom, but by then it was too late. The elaborate monument consists of a Carrara marble sarcophagus and tomb chest on a granite base. It was designed by the German artist Ludwig Grüner, and carved by Italian masons.

Behind Sophia's tomb, and to the right, in front of the colonnade, is the large Egyptian-style headstone to **Sir Ernest Joseph Cassel** (1852–1921), the celebrated financier and philanthropist. Born into a Jewish family in Cologne, he arrived in England without a job, but

The rather severe tomb of the Duke of Sussex, whose burial in Kensal Green Cemetery made it the most fashionable place in London to be buried.

Princess Sophia's tomb is the grandest in the cemetery, designed by a German and created by Italian masons.

Return to Centre Avenue and take the grassy Inner Circle path to the left of Princess Sophia's tomb. About 30 yards on the right is the elaborately carved tomb of **William Holland** (1779–1856), an eminent furniture manufacturer, whose company supplied Buckingham Palace, Windsor Castle, the British Museum, government buildings and several prestigious London clubs. The company also worked as undertakers, and organised the funeral of Princess Sophia. The sarcophagus has angels at each corner, and rests on eight fish-tailed griffins. Four rows behind it is the grave of **George Frederick Carden** (1798–1874), the founder of Kensal Green Cemetery. He had been impressed by the Père Lachaise cemetery in Paris and wanted to create something similar in London, as an alternative to its dirty and overcrowded burial grounds. There was much opposition to the scheme, but in 1830 he got backing for the General Cemetery Company, which bought the land the cemetery now occupies. Carden later fell out with the directors and had no more to do with the business. The

quickly made his mark in banking. He was soon moving in high society, becoming a friend of Edward VII and an adviser to the government. Following the wishes of his wife, he converted to Roman Catholicism, and he was buried according to Catholic rites. Over to the left is the sober but impressive classical mausoleum of **John Forster** (1812–76), a writer who is best known as the biographer of Charles Dickens. He befriended many major authors, acting as both agent and advisor, but his most important association was with Dickens, who portrayed him in *Our Mutual Friend* as Podsnap. Forster wrote the first biography of Dickens, who had revealed to him facts about his life that he had kept secret, including his time working in the blacking factory at Hungerford Stairs.

The mausoleum of John Forster, Dickens' friend and biographer.

The highly decorative tomb to William Holland, furniture supplier to the royal family.

The simple grave of George Carden, founder of Kensal Green Cemetery.

simple headstone merely says 'Founder of this cemetery'.

Return to the path, and take the next path on the right. Five rows along on the left is the red granite ledger of **Philip Cipriani Hambley Potter** (1792–1871), one of the most important pianists and composers of the early nineteenth century. He wrote nine symphonies and much piano music, but it is not much performed today. He gave the first performances in England of three of the piano concertos of Beethoven, whom he met in Vienna. He also taught at the Royal Academy of Music, two of his pupils being William Sterndale Bennett and George McFarren. Return to the Inner

Circle path and a little further along are the graves of two railway engineers who often worked together. On the left is the pink granite tomb of **Joseph Locke** (1805–60), which is part of a large plot, which includes his wife's family. Locke worked on the Liverpool and Manchester Railway and the line from London to Southampton, as well as several railways in France and Spain. He also built the Richmond and Barnes railway bridges. On the other side of the path is the substantial granite chest tomb of **John Edward Errington** (1806–62), who worked with Locke on several major projects, and built a number of railway bridges, including that at Kingston.

Joseph Locke was an important civil engineer, specialising in railways and bridges.

When you reach Junction Avenue, turn right and right again along the first grass path to find the well-tended grave of **Walter Clopton Wingfield** (1833–1912), who is credited with being the inventor of lawn tennis. Others had played versions of the game before, but he patented it in 1874 as sphairistike, or lawn tennis, which was an outdoor fusion of real tennis and rackets. Many changes were made to the rules over the years, especially after the All England Croquet Club took the sport on board, so Wingfield's patent wasn't to prove very profitable for him. Return to Junction Avenue and turn right, and a little way down on the left is the grey granite raised ledger of **Charles Babbage** (1791–1871), an important mathematician who is considered to be the pioneer of the modern computer. He spent much of his life attempting to create two calculating machines, neither of which could be built with the technology available at the time. The first, the 'difference engine', was never completed, but what was built is now in the Science Museum. Continue to the end of Junction Avenue and turn left onto South Avenue. A few yards on the right is the

grave of **Howard Staunton** (1810–74), the chess player who organised the first international chess tournament, and was the first British world chess champion. He gave his name to the chess pieces still used in international competitions. He was also a Shakespearean scholar, and his grave carries a quotation from Henry VI Part 1. The present gravestone was erected in 1997 by the Staunton Society.

Return up Junction Avenue to the Inner Circle and turn right along it. To the left is the family vault of the de la Rue family, an inscribed marble block on a pink granite plinth. **Thomas de la Rue** (1793–1866) founded the famous printing company which today still bears his name. He came from a family of printers and stationers in

Walter Clopton Wingfield invented lawn tennis, though he didn't make much money from his patent.

110

Howard Staunton was a chess player and Shakespearean scholar, and his monument refers to both aspects of his life.

Thomas de la Rue founded the famous printing company that still prints postage stamps and banknotes for many countries.

Guernsey, but made his name in London, where he earned a reputation printing playing cards, later diversifying into the production of visiting cards, mourning stationery and railway tickets. They soon received contracts for printing postage stamps, both at home and for the colonies. The family lost control of the firm in 1923, but the company still carries the name and today prints banknotes for over 150 countries. About 10 yards further along, to the left, is the grave, with a Celtic cross, of **John Lawrence Toole** (1830–1906), the celebrated comic actor and theatre manager. He excelled as an actor in farces, but he was also a huge hit in the sentimental adaptation of Dickens' *The Cricket on the Hearth*. He was so popular that many hundreds came to the funeral and the gates had to be closed before the funeral cortège arrived. Further along, also on the left, is the pink granite pedestal marking the grave of **Thomas Hood** (1799–1845), a hugely popular poet in his day. His best-known works are *The Song of the Shirt*, about the poor conditions of seamstresses, and *The Bridge of Sighs*, inspired by a report of a girl's suicide. He died poor, and it wasn't until 1854 that the memorial was erected over his grave, paid for by public subscription. The work of Matthew Noble, it once bore a bronze bust of the poet, and bronze reliefs depicting

This pink granite monument to Thomas Hood once had a bust and reliefs depicting his poems, but these have been stolen. The engraving from the *Illustrated London News* (inset) shows what it once looked like.

marble headstone was erected by the Friends of Wallace in 2007. Behind is the pink granite obelisk marking the grave of **Michael William Balfe** (1808–70), a singer and composer of operas and operettas, which were internationally acclaimed in his day. His best-known work is the opera *The Bohemian Girl*, which was regularly performed until the 1930s, though rarely heard today, except for the aria *I Dreamt I Dwelled in Marble Halls*. He also wrote the well-known song *Come into the garden, Maud*.

two of his poems, *The Bridge of Sighs* and *The Dream of Eugene Aram*. Sadly these bronze elements were stolen some time ago.

On the other side of the path are the graves of two composers. **William Vincent Wallace** (1812–65) was an Irish composer of operas and instrumental music. He made his name as a performer in Australia and on a tour of the Americas. Once very popular, his reputation declined after his death, but new recordings of his work have recently become available. The

Three graves to the west is the stone chest tomb of **William Behnes** (1795–1864), a prolific and influential sculptor, especially of church monuments, including several in Westminster Abbey and St Paul's Cathedral. His outdoor statues in London include Sir Henry Havelock in Trafalgar Square and Sir Thomas Gresham on the clocktower of the Royal Exchange. Behnes' last years were sad, as he was made bankrupt and he also had a serious drink problem. He died in Middlesex Hospital after being found 'literally in the gutter, with threepence in his pocket'. An unsuccessful attempt was made to raise money for a bust to be erected on his grave, and the tomb has become quite badly damaged, with a corner broken off, and the inscription is almost illegible.

A little to the east of Wallace is the grave of **John Claudius Loudon** (1783–1843), a pedestal of Portland stone, with a rather chubby granite urn. Loudon was an important landscape gardener, who wrote many books on the subject, and he was also hugely influential on the design of cemeteries. He acted as consultant on the layout of Brompton Cemetery. Directly opposite, under a tree, is a pink granite

Celtic cross marking the grave of organist and composer **Sir John Goss** (1800–80), who wrote the music for the hymns *Praise my soul the King of Heaven* and *See Amid the Winter's Snow*. He was professor of harmony at the Royal Academy of Music for nearly 50 years, organist of St Paul's Cathedral and composer to the Chapel Royal. Further east, and about six rows to the left, is the cross marking the grave of **John Murray** (1778–1843), one of the most influential publishers of his time. Taking over his father's business in Fleet Street, he was soon able to move to Albemarle Street, where he entertained important literary and political figures. He published authors

The monuments to two Irish composers, William Vincent Wallace in the foreground, with the obelisk to Michael William Balfe behind.

The monument to John Claudius Loudon, who was very influential in the design of the new cemeteries.

John Murray was an important publisher, and his company still exists, though now as part of a larger company.

such as Jane Austen, Sir Walter Scott and Coleridge, and had a particularly close relationship with Lord Byron, who became a star overnight when Murray published the first two cantos of *Childe Harold's Pilgrimage*. However, Byron's posthumous memoirs proved so controversial that Murray burnt them, a great loss to posterity.

Continue to Centre Avenue, where on the left corner is the extraordinary mausoleum of **Andrew Ducrow** (1793–1842), the flamboyant equestrian artist and lessee of Astley's Amphitheatre on the south side of Westminster Bridge. There he gave displays of horsemanship, and put on spectacular pageants such as *The Battle of Waterloo*. His shows were so popular that even the royal family attended them. His mausoleum, which was originally built for his wife, is Egyptian in style, with lotus capitals and sphinxes, along with equestrian elements such as an urn decorated with horses' heads, and several depictions of the winged horse Pegasus. He clearly had a high opinion of himself, as the inscription says 'Erected by Genius for the reception of its own remains'. On the opposite side of Centre Avenue is another unusual monument, that of **John St John Long** (1798–1834), a quack doctor who claimed to have invented a cure for consumption. The lotion, which contained turpentine, acetic acid and egg yolk, could be inhaled or rubbed on parts of the body. He became the most fashionable quack doctor in London, with a strong female following. His practice wasn't unduly affected by three court cases against him for manslaughter, in two of which he was found guilty. He was clearly unable to heal himself, as he himself died of consumption. His tall monument, of Portland stone and Carrara marble, has classical medical symbols, including the staff of Aesculapius and a statue of Hygeia, the goddess of health. It is all presented with no sense of irony, with an inscription that asks us not to condemn him.

Continue along the Inner Circle, almost to Junction Avenue, and on the right is the marble chest tomb of **Sir Charles Locock** (1799–1875), the obstetrician who was physician accoucheur to Queen Victoria, and was present at the births of all of her children, using chloroform for the later births. A little further on, to the right, in the fifth row, is all that is left of the grave of

The splendidly idiosyncratic tomb of Andrew Ducrow, the equestrian showman who ran Astley's Amphitheatre.

This impressive monument is to the quack doctor, John St John Long.

the artist **James Ward** (1769–1859). The large headstone with a figure of the muse of painting by J. H. Foley lies flat and broken amid the ivy. Ward was a prolific artist, and is considered to be one of the greatest British painters of animals. He specialised in cows and horses, including portraits of Napoleon's *Marengo* and Wellington's *Copenhagen*. On the south side of the Inner Circle, two graves to the left of the tomb of Sir Robert Otway, is the marble cruciform ledger to **John Gould** (1804–81), whose name is on the lower left edge. He was a great ornithologist and publisher, famous for his beautifully illustrated books on birds from around the world. The books had lithographs, produced from his own sketches by his wife, who is buried with him, and other artists, including Edward Lear. Consulted by Darwin, he identified 12 birds from the Galápagos as being a family of related finches, a discovery that led Darwin to his theory of evolution. Many of Gould's specimens are now in the Natural History Museum, including his spectacular hummingbird cases.

Cross Junction Avenue and continue along the Inner Circle. To the right of the first path on the right, to the left of the Geisler chest tomb, is a large stone slab

The tomb of Sir Charles Locock, the obstetric physician who attended the births of all of Queen Victoria's children.

with no legible inscription. This is the grave of **Robert Coates** (1772–1848), probably one of the worst actors of his day, and possibly of all time. He inherited a fortune from his father, and set himself up in Bath as a man of fashion, dressing flamboyantly, wearing furs and diamonds, which earned him his first nickname 'Diamond Coates'. He considered himself to be an actor and played the part of Romeo in *Romeo and Juliet* with professional actors, but was usually laughed off stage by the end of the fourth act. When he did get to perform the death scene, he would dust the stage with a handkerchief to protect his clothes, and arrange himself in a suitable pose for death. Inevitably his new nickname was 'Romeo Coates'. He later performed in various major theatres in London, always unpaid and in aid of charity, despite the bad reviews and the jeers of the audience. Eventually theatre managers would not allow him to use their theatres and he ran up so many debts that he retired to Boulogne to escape his creditors. He returned to London a few years later, and, after attending a concert at Drury Lane, he was killed in a road accident, run over by a hansom cab. Continue along the Inner Circle until you reach Centre Avenue, then turn left. By the side of the path on the left is the large granite chest tomb, with a gabled top, of the civil engineer **James Meadows Rendel** (1799–1856). After training with Telford, he set up a business in Plymouth, designing bridges and chain ferries across the Tamar and Dart rivers, as well as Brixham harbour and the Millbay docks in Plymouth. He moved to London in 1838, where he was commissioned by the Admiralty to design docks and improve ports all over the country. One of his last

The cruciform ledger to John Gould, who published beautifully illustrated books on birds of the world.

116

jobs was to design a suspension bridge over the lake in St James's Park, but this was replaced in 1957.

At the crossroads, on the right hand side in the next section, is the pink granite raised ledger, with a floreate cross, to **Sir Augustus Wollaston Franks** (1826–97), a collector and antiquarian who worked for nearly 50 years for the British Museum, helping to build up its collections of British antiquities, and often buying objects with his own money. He left his own collection to the museum, including some of its greatest treasures. On the left side of Centre Avenue is the classical mausoleum of **George Birkbeck** (1776–1841), a successful doctor who, wishing to offer education to working people, gave free lectures on science, art and economics. This led to the foundation of the London Mechanics' Institution, which later became Birkbeck College, now part of the University of London. To its left is a monument to **George Cruikshank** (1792–1878), the famous cartoonist. Permission was granted for him to be buried in the crypt of St Paul's Cathedral, but he was buried here until space could be prepared for him. The pink granite pedestal once held a bronze bust by William Behnes, but this has been stolen. Just before the Long monument, in the second row, is the simple ledger stone to **Harold Pinter** (1930–2008), with an inscription finely cut by Emily Hoffnung. Pinter was one of the most celebrated British playwrights of the second half of the twentieth century. His plays have often puzzled the critics and audiences, with their unique use of language and famous dramatic pauses, but they are still good box office draws and are

regularly revived. Pinter was also successful as an actor, screenwriter and director, and in 2005 he was awarded the Nobel Prize for literature. Behind and to the left is the black marble headstone of the grave of **Maria Björnson** (1949–2002), the celebrated theatre designer. She designed sets and costumes for plays, operas, ballets and musicals, winning many awards. Her most famous work was the design for Andrew

Some of the British Museum's greatest treasures were given by Augustus Franks, who worked there for many years.

In the foreground is the simple gravestone of dramatist Harold Pinter, with a beautifully cut inscription by Emily Hoffnung. In the background is the black marble headstone of theatre designer Maria Björnson.

Lloyd Webber's *Phantom of the Opera*, with its famous falling chandelier. Just after the Long monument, on the left, is a memorial to the cult novelist **James Graham (J. G.) Ballard** (1930–2009), with a fine inscription carved by Richard Kindersley. He was cremated at Kensal Green, but he is not buried here.

Further along on the right is the large sarcophagus, raised on four square columns, of **John Cam Hobhouse, Baron Broughton** (1786–1869), the writer and politician. As a young man he travelled in Europe with Lord Byron, and was best man at his wedding. As an MP, he campaigned for prison reform and the regulation of factory labour, and he held several ministerial posts. He coined the phrase 'His Majesty's Opposition' in a debate in 1826. Take the path to the left of the Hobhouse grave to find the elaborate Gothic monument to the architect **John Gibson** (1817–92). Gibson worked with Sir Charles Barry on the new Houses of Parliament, but his major works in London are various branches of the National Provincial Bank, now Nat West, including its headquarters in the City. His monument, which he designed himself, is very Gothic, with bands of Portland stone and red Mansfield sandstone. To the south, on the other side of the path, is the cracked ledger of the grave of **Sir Julius Benedict** (1804–85), whose name is inscribed on the front edge. The German-born conductor and composer studied with Hummel and Weber before travelling to London, where he worked for the rest of his life. He conducted the first performances of operas by Balfe and Wallace, both of whom are buried nearby. He composed a symphony, two piano concertos and several operas, the most successful of which was *The Lily of Killarney*, but he is now almost forgotten.

Return to Centre Avenue and turn right. On the left is the splendid tomb of the Irish-born artist **William Mulready** (1786–1863), who specialised in genre scenes and landscapes. He was a pupil of John Varley, who is also buried in Kensal Green. He was renowned for his very fine technique, and his detailed realism inspired the Pre-Raphaelites. Designed by Godfrey Sykes, a terracotta effigy of the artist lies under a canopy supported by six Tuscan columns, wearing a gown of the Légion d'Honneur. Below the columns are carvings of palettes and brushes, and between them are reliefs of some of his best known paintings. Take the path to the right of the Mulready tomb, and tight behind it is the much more modest grey granite ledger of another artist, **John Phillip** (1817–67), who produced portraits and genre paintings. After several visits to Spain, its landscape and the art he saw there influenced his style, and he started painting scenes of Spanish rural life, which earned him the nicknames 'Spanish Phillip' and 'Phillip of Spain'. Queen Victoria bought three paintings from him as a gifts for Prince Albert.

Return to Centre Avenue and directly opposite is the tall pink granite obelisk to **Sir Richard Mayne** (1796–1868), a barrister who was appointed by Robert Peel as the first joint commissioner of his newly created Metropolitan Police Force in 1829, along with Sir Charles Rowan (who is buried in Catacomb B under the Anglican Chapel). Take the next grass path on the right, and about 15 yards on the

The architect John Gibson designed his own Gothic monument, using sandstone and Portland stone. It originally had stained glass windows.

William Mulready's grandiose monument includes scenes from his most popular paintings. The much simpler grave beside it is of artist John 'Spanish' Phillip.

left, in the fourth row, is the pink granite ledger to **Giovanni Battista Falcieri** (1798–1874), Lord Byron's faithful servant, usually known as Tita. A striking figure because of his black beard, Byron met him in Venice and took him with him on all his travels. He was with Byron when he died, and he helped bring his remains back to England, sleeping on the coffin on the ship to protect them. He later acted as travelling companion to Benjamin Disraeli, and worked as butler to Disraeli's father. Return to the path and a short way down on the left, beside the path, is the grave of **William Powell Frith** (1819–1909), a

prolific painter of scenes of contemporary life, most famously his trilogy of panoramic views *Life at the Seaside (Ramsgate Sands)*, *Derby Day* and *The Railway Station*. He had a very unorthodox private life, maintaining two large families within a short distance of each other, neither knowing about the other. The headstone is missing various lead letters, but enough of his name is visible to identify it. Almost opposite is the grave of **William Whiteley** (1831–1907), a marble pedestal topped off with a draped urn. Whiteley began his retail career by opening up a small drapery shop in Westbourne Grove, before the area became fashionable.

Far left: The grave of William Whiteley, the founder of London's first department store, who was murdered by a man claiming to be his son..

Left: Sir Charles Siemens' grave has a rather eroded portrait relief.

The business proved successful and he expanded into adjacent premises, creating London's first department store. Whiteley offered a wide range of merchandise, and he styled himself the Universal Provider. He was shot by a man claiming to be his son when he refused to offer him financial help. On the day of the funeral the store was closed and most of the employees attended the funeral. A short way further on to the left, in the second row, is the grave of **Sir Charles William Siemens** (1823–83), a pink granite Celtic cross with a bas relief portrait leaning against it. The German-born engineer is best known for his invention of the regenerative furnace, which was used worldwide for making steel and glass. He was also involved in cable-laying technology, designing the ship that laid the first cable across the Atlantic in 1874. Take the next path on the right to find the grave of the poet **Christopher Logue**

(1926–2011), a tall, narrow headstone with a palmette at the top. Logue was a rebel, claiming that poetry 'should play an active part in society', and was associated with protest, including taking part in the anti-nuclear Aldermarston march. He also wrote plays and several screenplays, including *Savage Messiah*, directed by Ken Russell. His most important works were his versions of Homer's *Iliad*, which won him the Whitbread Prize. He was better known to the general public for his Pseuds Corner column in the satirical magazine *Private Eye*.

Return along this path to South Branch Avenue and turn left. About 30 yards on the right, in the second row, is the grave (with an unusual cross) of **Sir John Tenniel** (1820–1914), a self-taught artist who for 50 years was a political cartoonist for the magazine *Punch*. He is today better known for his book illustrations, especially his iconic images for Lewis Carroll's *Alice's*

Far left: The distinctive cross of Sir John Tenniel, the artist who illustrated Lewis Carroll's two Alice books.

Left: Sir John Rennie was an engineer who worked with his more famous father, also John Rennie, especially in building bridges. He was knighted after building London Bridge to his father's design.

Adventures in Wonderland and *Through the Looking-Glass*. Further up South Branch Avenue, to the right of the path, is the grave of **Sir John Rennie** (1794–1874), the second son of the great engineer John Rennie. He worked with his father on the construction of Waterloo and Southwark bridges, and later built the new London Bridge after the death of his father, who designed it. On the other side of the path, and a little to the left, in front of the Leslie tomb, is a simple ledger stone with a very indistinct inscription, marking the grave of the actor **Charles Kemble** (1775–1854) and his daughter **Fanny Kemble** (1809–93). Charles was born into an acting family, which included Sarah Siddons and John Philip Kemble, so it was no surprise that he would also become an actor. Though never as famous as his siblings, he had a long and successful career, especially in Shakespeare's tragedies. His daughter became a popular

actress, especially for her portrayal of Juliet, joining her father on hugely successful tours of the United States. About 20 yards further on, to the right of the path, is the striking marble headstone of the grave of **Owen Jones** (1809–74), who was an architect and a hugely influential figure in Victorian design. He was a superintendent for the Crystal Palace, both in Hyde Park and at Sydenham, designing the displays and the controversial colour schemes. He produced interior decorative schemes for many important London buildings, including hotels, shops and private houses. Sadly, few of these buildings survive, and he has now gone out of fashion, but examples of his work can be seen in the Victorian and Albert Museum. He designed his own grave in the form of a Greek stele, with its decorative palmette finial.

At the top of South Branch Avenue at the junction with Centre Avenue is the

Gothic tomb of architect **Henry Edward Kendall** (1776–1875). Kendall worked in a variety of styles, and helped found the Institute of British Architects (now RIBA). His Gothic designs for the buildings at Kensal Green Cemetery won the competition, but did not meet with the committee's approval, and the present classical buildings are by John Griffith (who is also buried here). Kendall kept his prize money, and his grave, which he designed himself, has one of the most prominent positions in the cemetery. Behind Kendall's tomb is the grey granite obelisk marking the grave of the engineer **Thomas Russell Crampton** (1816–88). Crampton designed some of the earliest locomotives, but few of his designs were developed in Britain, and he had much more success in France. He was also involved in the laying of a submarine telegraph cable from Dover to Calais. There is a museum dedicated to him and his work in his native Broadstairs.

Henry Edward Kendall won the competition to build the cemetery's buildings, but, though he lost the job, his grave is on a very prominent site.

Continue along Centre Avenue and almost immediately on the left, just after the junction, is the chest tomb to **Henry Spencer Ashbee** (1834–1900), a hugely controversial character. A respected City merchant, he put together a huge collection of books of erotica, which he would show to fellow collectors. He also published three bibliographies of erotica under the nom de plume 'Pisanus Fraxi', a rude anagram of the Latin words for ash and bee. It is possible that he was the author of the infamous pornographic autobiography *Walter*. He bequeathed his entire collection, which included French and Spanish literature, to the British Museum, though it destroyed much of the erotica. About 30 yards before the end of Centre Avenue, on the left, just after a grass path, is a raised marble cruciform ledger, with a few of the original posts round it. This is the grave of the actor, playwright and theatre manager **Charles James Mathews** (1803–78) and his American-born actress wife **Elizabeth Mathews** (1806–99). He started out as an architect, working with Pugin and Nash, before turning to the theatre. His first wife was Madame Vestris, with whom he had a long and fruitful partnership; she is buried nearby, but her headstone has been destroyed, so it is hard to find. He met his second wife on an American tour, and they performed together with much success. Mathews was a hugely popular actor, playing over 200 parts in his career,

The grave of the popular actor Charles Mathews and his American wife.

and was most successful in comedy. Among the many mourners at his funeral, which was held in the Anglican Chapel, were Sir Henry Irving and Squire Bancroft.

Continue along Centre Avenue and turn right through the gate into South Avenue. About 50 yards on the right is the prominent Gothic spire marking the grave of **Feargus O'Connor** (1796–1855), an important radical politician and a charismatic orator. He was the leader of the Chartist movement, and was the main speaker at the demonstration on Kennington Common in 1848. During his last years he suffered mental problems and died penniless, but he was so popular that 50,000 people attended his funeral. Continue along South Avenue, and after about 30 yards on the left is the grave of the landscape artist **Richard Parkes Bonington** (1802–28). Bonington spent much of his short life in Paris, where he mixed with the most eminent artists and writers. His sensitive landscapes and seascapes of France, Italy and England were much admired, and many thought him the equal of Turner and Constable. He

died in London and was originally buried in St James's Chapel in Pentonville, but he was reburied in Kensal Green in 1837 in an unmarked grave. The pink granite slab was placed on his grave in 2003. Directly opposite is the grave of the novelist **William Makepeace Thackeray** (1811–63), a simple raised ledger surrounded by a low railing, which has traces of red paint. He began his writing career as a journalist, writing for *The Times* and *Punch*, using pseudonyms such as Fitzboodle and Yellowplush. His most important novels, including *Vanity Fair* and *Pendennis*, were serialised in monthly magazines. Despite his social realism and satire, his novels are now less well considered than those of Dickens and Trollope, but there have been a number of film and television adaptations. Two graves to the left is the plain marble slab, with no legible inscription, to **John Leech** (1817–64), the illustrator who gave the current meaning to the word 'cartoon'. For 20 years he produced humorous illustrations for the magazine *Punch*, and also worked for the *Illustrated London News*. He produced the illustrations for Dickens's *A Christmas Carol* and several novels by R. S. Surtees, with his depiction of the fox-hunting Jorrocks probably his most memorable character. Many artists and writers attended his funeral, and Sir John Tenniel was one of the pallbearers. A little further on, in the fourth row behind Maude Ada Dove's grave, is that of **Andrew Pears** (1766–1845), with a gabled ledger stone and headstone, and a badly worn inscription. Pears was a perfumier and soap-maker who developed the famous transparent soap, with its unique fragrance, which still carries his name.

The simple grave of the distinguished writer William Makepeace Thackeray.

Continue along South Avenue and about 50 yards on, on the raised section to the left, is the headstone to **John Varley** (1778–1842), the Hackney-born topographical watercolour artist who is considered to be the father of *plein-air* painting. He was also a successful teacher, whose pupils included John Linnell and William Mulready. The headstone, with its elegant inscription, was erected in 1996 by Dame Joan Varley. Retrace your steps and take the next grass path on the left where on the right is the modest grave of two of the finest nineteenth-century engineers, **Sir Marc Isambard Brunel** (1769–1849) and his son **Isambard Kingdom Brunel** (1806–59). The family grave, with its simple block of Carrara marble with lead lettering, was designed by Marc Brunel. He is best known for the construction of the first tunnel under the Thames, using a new tunnelling shield of his own invention. The project met with many difficulties, with the Thames often flooding the workings, and on one such occasion Isambard nearly drowned. The tunnel took over 20 years to build but was never a success, and it is now part of the Overground system. Isambard designed bridges, built the Great Western Railway, including Paddington Station, and constructed three great steamships. His most famous bridge, the Clifton suspension bridge over the Avon gorge, was completed after his death, using chains from his Hungerford Bridge in London, when it was converted into a railway bridge. Opposite, in the fifth row, next to the headstone of Cornelius Ward, is the tilted ledger to **Sir Charles Wheatstone** (1802–75), an important inventor whose research at King's College, London, where he was a professor, led to the general use of the electric telegraph. Among many other inventions are the rheostat and the bellows-blown concertina, which is still played today.

Now take the grass path to the right of the Brunel grave. On the left, directly in line with Thackeray's grave, is the badly broken chest tomb of the sculptor **John Thomas** (1813–62). Thomas mostly

The modest grave of two great nineteenth-century engineers, Marc Brunel and his son Isambard.

A modern headstone marks the grave of the influential artist John Varley.

worked as an architectural sculptor, and his most important work is the series of kings, queens and national heroes on the outside of the Houses of Parliament. His statue of Sir Hugh Myddleton stands on Islington Green. A little further along the path, on the right, opposite a Gothic shrine, is the double grave, with a single cross, of the architects **Philip Hardwick** (1792–1870) and his son **Philip Charles Hardwick** (1822–92). Both father and son worked in the City as well as for the railway companies, but much of their work has not survived. Hardwick Sr built the classical Goldsmiths' Hall and the Hall and Library at Lincoln's Inn, but his Euston Station and the Doric Arch that stood in front of it, were both, sadly, destroyed in the 1960s. His son also had a successful career, building Charterhouse School at Godalming and the Great Western Hotel in Paddington.

Continue along the path to Centre Avenue and turn right, continuing straight on into the Dissenters cemetery. By the side of the central path is the marble ledger of the publisher **John Cassell** (1817–65), who produced magazines and books aimed at educating the working classes. He was a radical, supporting universal suffrage and the abolition of slavery, and he published the first English edition of *Uncle Tom's Cabin*. Although his father was a publican, Cassell was a lifelong supporter of the temperance movement. His publishing company still exists as part of the Orion Publishing Group. A little further up the path, on the bend, is the gabled ledger

The double grave of two generations of architects, Philip Hardwick and his son Philip Charles Hardwick.

and large headstone to George Napoleon Epps and his daughter, **Laura Theresa Alma-Tadema** (1852–1909), the second wife of the artist Sir Lawrence Alma-Tadema. She met her husband at the house of Ford Madox Brown, and despite their age difference their marriage was a happy one. He gave her painting lessons, and she became a successful artist in her own right, painting sentimental scenes, many in the seventeenth-century Dutch style. Her husband was buried in St Paul's Cathedral. Continue along this path and at the next junction is the tomb, with an obelisk, to the Scottish-born explorer **John McDouall Stuart** (1815–66). Emigrating to Australia in his twenties, he carried out six expeditions to explore and survey its interior. He was the first person to cross the country from south to north, for which he was awarded £2,000. Several geographical features are named after him, as well as the Stuart Highway, which follows his route across the country. The obelisk was damaged by a bomb in the Second World War, and it was replaced in 2012.

Lady Alma-Tadema is buried with her family, instead of in St Paul's Cathedral with her more famous husband.

Leave the dissenters' section and turn right onto North Avenue. After about 60 yards, on the left by the path, is the narrow chest tomb of the celebrated journalist **Thomas Barnes** (1785–1841). He started his career as drama critic of *The Times*, and ended up as its editor from 1817 until his death, making him 'the most powerful man in the country' according to the Duke of Wellington. The newspaper became a voice for reform and it earned the nickname 'The Thunderer' under his editorship. He is buried here with his long-term companion, Dinah Mondet, whom he never married. The inscription on slate is a recent addition, as the original had eroded. To the right of the path, 20 yards further on, is the headstone marking the grave of **Mary Hogarth** (1819–37), the sister-in-law of Charles Dickens. Her sudden death at his home in Doughty Street left him distraught. He had been devoted to her and wore her ring for the rest of his life, even expressing a wish to be buried in her grave. He wrote the touching inscription on the tombstone, 'Young, beautiful and good, God in his mercy numbered her with his angels at the early age of seventeen'. The grave was restored by the Dickens Fellowship in 2015. About

This obelisk marks the grave of the explorer John McDouall Stuart, who was the first person to cross Australia from south to north.

Charles Dickens wrote the moving inscription on the grave of his beloved sister-in-law Mary Hogarth.

20 yards further on, in the third row on the left, is the leaning pedestal tomb of **Lewis Waller** (1860–1915), the stage name of the actor William Waller Lewis. Waller was a Victorian matinée idol, performing in Shakespeare and Ibsen as well as many new plays, including the premiere of Wilde's *An Ideal Husband*. The performance that made his name was as D'Artagnan in *The Three Musketeers*, and he excelled in such bravura roles. Four graves further on, in the second row, is the grey granite ledger of the artist **Daniel Maclise** (1806–70). Maclise made his name as a portrait painter, drawing many famous writers, and he was

soon moving in literary circles. Through John Forster he became a close friend of Charles Dickens, painting his portrait and illustrating some of his books. He excelled at painting historical scenes, the most important being the frescoes he painted for the Royal Gallery of the new Houses of Parliament.

About 30 yards further along North Avenue, in the fourth row, is the coped ledger of the sculptor **Thomas Milnes** (1810–88), behind a curiously shaped grave with a wheatsheaf on top to other members of the Milnes family. Milnes made his name as an animal sculptor, and

This plain pedestal tomb is of Lewis Waller, a celebrity actor famous for playing Shakespearean roles as well as romantic leads.

was asked to create the lions for the Nelson memorial in Trafalgar Square, but his designs were rejected and the commission was given to Landseer. Milnes' lions can now be seen in Saltaire. His only work in London is his statue of Wellington, made for the Tower of London where Wellington was constable, and which now stands in the Royal Arsenal in Woolwich. A little further along North Avenue, to the left of the path, is a Celtic cross marking the grave of **James Wyld** (1812–87), a cartographer who published many guides and maps, and was made geographer to the queen. His greatest success was the hugely popular 'Great Globe' in Leicester Square, housed in a massive sphere, which illustrated in great detail the surface of the earth. To the left of the next junction is the striking monument to the artist **Elizabeth Soyer** (1813–42), which also contains the body of her husband **Alexis Soyer** (1810–58), the famous French chef. Emma, as she was known, was a precocious artist, who exhibited at the Royal Academy at the age of ten. She mainly produced portraits and genre paintings, described as being in the style of the Spanish artist Murillo. She died in childbirth, and her husband designed this monument, which has a portrait relief of her on the front and the words TO HER. Her own easel used to be behind glass at the rear of the tomb. Topping off the tomb is a figure of Faith, which originally held a gilt-bronze cross. Alexis Soyer made his name as the chef of the Reform Club, where he produced magnificent banquets, but he also helped the poor, creating soup kitchens in Ireland and Spitalfields. He later went, unpaid, to the Crimea to improve the catering to the troops, designing a field stove that was to continue in use for over a hundred years.

Turn left at the junction down North Branch Avenue where, about ten yards on the right, by the path, is the grave of **Louis-Eustache Ude** (1767?–1846), a sloping ledger stone with a cross on top. His surname can just be read. Ude was a chef at the court of Louis XVI before arriving in London after the French Revolution. He soon became the most famous chef in London, especially during the ten years he worked at Crockford's, the famous gambling club. Take the next path on the right, and in the sixth row and five graves to the right of the path is the simple headstone to the celebrated doctor **James Barry** (*c.* 1799–1865). Barry qualified as a surgeon while still a teenager and went on to become an eminent army doctor, working in Canada, Malta, Corfu and the Crimea. Barry was short, dressed flamboyantly and had a squeaky voice, and questions were often asked about his sex or sexuality, but it was only after the doctor's death that he was discovered to be a woman, thus making her technically the first British woman to graduate as a physician, over 50 years before Elizabeth Garrett Anderson.

Return to North Avenue, turn left and then left again. To the left of the path, about 30 yards down, is a tall Corinthian column

This impressive monument marks the grave of the famous chef, Alexis Soyer, and was designed by him for his artist wife, Elizabeth.

marking the grave of inventor **Thomas Hancock** (1786–1865). Hancock created ways of working with rubber to make it more pliable, producing all sorts of articles at his Goswell Road factory, and allowing Mackintosh to improve his waterproof clothing. He also took out a patent for vulcanised rubber, which was much used in industry. Return to North Avenue, where straight ahead is the chest tomb of **William Debenham** (1794–1863), the founder of the famous department store. What is now a major multinational chain of stores began as a modest draper's in Wigmore Street. Continue along North Avenue and when you reach the colonnade above the catacombs, look for the large cross to the publisher **George Routledge** (1812–88). He made his name by publishing novels in cheap editions, especially of American authors, as there was no copyright law at the time. His Railway Library was particularly successful, as W. H. Smith placed a standing order to sell these books in their new station bookstalls. The company he founded is still in business as an academic publisher. Opposite the centre of the catacombs, in the fifth row, is the chest tomb, made of Portland stone, of **Sydney Smith** (1771–1845), the clergyman and famous wit. He was a radical thinker, which made him unpopular in certain quarters, so that for many years he failed to be given the senior position he deserved, but he was eventually made a canon at St Paul's Cathedral in his sixties. He is now best known for his many aphorisms and *bon mots*, including saying that 'I never read a book before reviewing it; it prejudices a man so'. Just past the catacombs, on the

This tall Corinthian column marks the grave of Thomas Hancock, the inventor who was a pioneer in the production and uses of rubber.

right under a tree, is the chest tomb of **Joseph Manton** (1766–1835), the finest gun maker of his age. There is a lengthy epitaph from Colonel Peter Hawker, a celebrated sportsman of the time. Manton was constantly making improvements to the design of his guns, which were expensive but much in demand. Despite this, he was imprisoned several times for debt, and was declared bankrupt in 1826. At the next junction is the large pedestal tomb of **John Griffith** (1796–1888), also known as 'John Griffith of Finsbury'. Although Henry Edward Kendall had won the competition to design Kensal Green's

buildings, the job went to Griffith, who was on the cemetery committee. He designed the two chapels and the main gate in Greek Revival style. Little else of his work is known.

Kensal Green has three catacombs, which cannot at present be visited. In Catacomb A, under the North Terrace Colonnade, lie **Sir William Beatty** (1773–1842), the naval surgeon who treated Nelson after he was shot at the battle of Trafalgar, and **Henry Mayhew** (1812–87), the journalist who wrote a series of articles for the *Morning Chronicle* about the street life of London, later published as *London Labour and the London Poor*.

In Catacomb B, under the Anglican Chapel, lie the following: **William Charles Macready** (1793–1873), the great Shakespearian tragedian and theatre manager who improved standards and restored much of Shakespeare's original text for his performances; **George Augustus Polgreen Bridgetower** (1780–1860), the famous Afro-European virtuoso violinist who performed for George III at Windsor Castle and gave the

Sydney Smith was a celebrated clergyman and wit, who once said that a friend's idea of heaven was 'eating pâté de foie gras to the sound of trumpets'.

first performance of Beethoven's 'Kreutzer' sonata, accompanied by the composer; **Sir Michael Costa** (1808–84), the composer and conductor, who founded the Royal Italian Opera, based at Covent Garden, and was the first conductor in England to use a baton; **Thomas Wakley** (1795–1862), the doctor who founded the influential medical journal, *The Lancet*, in which he campaigned for reform in the profession; **William Crockford** (1776–1844), who founded the famous gambling club, which still operates; **Sir Charles Rowan** (1782–1852), the army officer who became the first joint commissioner of the Metropolitan Police, along with Sir Richard Mayne.

Melvyn (Mel) Smith (1952–2013), the popular comedian, actor, writer and film director, best known for *Not the Nine O'Clock News* and *Alas Smith and Jones*, was cremated here and his ashes were scattered in the cemetery. Also cremated here was rock star Freddie Mercury, but his ashes were removed, although he is still thought by many to be buried here.

John Griffith was the little-known architect who designed the cemetery's buildings.

NORTH LONDON

LONDON BOROUGH OF BARNET

In the graveyard of St Andrew's Totteridge, in Totteridge Lane, are the graves of a major architect and two great golfing champions, both associated with the nearby South Herts Golf Club. They are all in the churchyard extension to the north east of the church. Go down the main path, and about 40 yards on the left is the unusual double headstone to architect **Thomas Edward Collcutt** (1840–1924). He made much use of terracotta in his work, which is very much in evidence in the façades of the Palace Theatre (originally the English Opera House) and the Wigmore Hall. He also built the Imperial Institute in Kensington, of which only the tower remains, and major extensions to the Savoy Hotel. Take the path on the right, where you will find the grave of **Henry William (Harry) Vardon** (1870–1937), who won 62 golf tournaments, including six Open Championships and one US Open. The overlapping grip he used is still referred to as the 'Vardon grip'. He also wrote books

Opposite: The impressive tomb of architect Banister Fletcher in Hampstead Cemetery was designed by his son (see page 154).

on golf and designed 14 golf courses. The South Herts Gold Club plays an annual Vardon Open tournament, when a wreath is laid on his grave. On the slope behind his grave are cremation burials, including that of **David James (Dai) Rees** (1913–83), who won many tournaments, but is probably best remembered for playing in the Ryder Cup team ten times, five times as captain, including the famous victory in 1957.

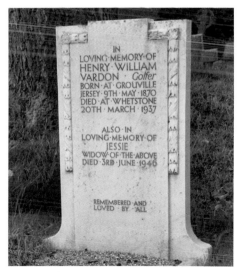

The grave of champion golfer Harry Vardon at St Andrew's Totteridge.

The plaque marking the grave of Sir Stamford Raffles, the founder of Singapore and the London Zoo, in St Mary's Hendon.

The grave of the sculptor Thomas Woolner, a founder member of the Pre-Raphaelite Brotherhood, in Hendon churchyard, has a stylised rosebush and a sculptor's tools carved on it.

St Mary's Hendon, in Church End NW4, contains the grave of **Sir Stamford Raffles** (1781–1826), the founder of Singapore and the London Zoo. He died young and in debt at his house in Hendon, and was buried in the churchyard. Raffles had campaigned against slavery, and as the vicar had investments in plantations in the West Indies, he refused him burial in the church vault and his grave was unmarked. In 1887 his family erected a brass plaque in his memory, which is now on a pillar in the north aisle of the church. When the church was extended in 1914 his grave was rediscovered, and it is now inside the church, in front of the chancel, with a new memorial stone. In the churchyard, under the east window, is the grave of **Herbert Chapman** (1878–1934), who is considered to be the first great football manager. He improved the fortunes of several teams, but it was at Arsenal that he really made his mark, leading them to four league titles. He was also an innovator, introducing floodlights and numbers on players' shirts, and he even managed to get the name of the nearest Underground station changed from Gillespie Road to Arsenal. On the north side of the church is the grave of the sculptor **Thomas Woolner** (1825–92), who was one of the founding members of the Pre-Raphaelite Brotherhood. He was particularly known for his portrait busts of the great and the good, but he also produced public statues, including that of John Stuart Mill on Victoria Embankment, and one of Raffles, which was erected in Singapore in 1887. His tombstone has carvings of a rose bush and sculptor's tools.

Hendon Cemetery in Holder's Hill Road NW4 opened in 1899 and was founded by the Abney Park Cemetery Company. Take

The Russian pianist and composer Nikolai Medtner lived in Golders Green for the last two decades of his life, and is buried in Hendon Cemetery.

Mill Hill Cemetery in Milespit Hill NW7 opened in 1936 as Paddington New Cemetery, but it was renamed when the City of Westminster took over its administration in the 1990s. In Plot B2 at the end of West Avenue is the grave of **Ronald Wycherley**, better known as **Billy Fury** (1940–83), the famous rock 'n' roll star from the 1950s and '60s. He wrote many of his own songs, but his most successful recordings were of American hits, including *Halfway to Paradise*. He was famous for his suggestive, hip-swivelling stage act, which was influenced by Elvis Presley. In Plot H1 is the simple plaque commemorating **Julian Maclaren-Ross** (1912–64), with the simple inscription giving his name and dates and the words 'Writer and Bohemian'. He wrote several novels and many short stories, and his work was admired by many leading authors; today he still has a cult following. He would spend much of the day drinking in the clubs and pubs of Soho, and liked to write late into the night, but he never missed a deadline.

Rock 'n' roll star Billy Fury's grave in Mill Hill Cemetery.

the second path on the left from the main drive and turn right and then left to find the grave of **Nicolai Medtner** (1880–1951), the Russian pianist and composer. Medtner left Russia after the Revolution to live and work abroad, finally settling in London, where from 1930 until his death he lived in Golders Green. He was a virtuoso pianist, second only to his friend Rachmaninov, and all his compositions include the piano either as accompanist or soloist. His works make only rare appearances in concert programmes, but there are many fine recordings, especially of his concertos and sonatas.

The grave of agony aunt Marje Proops in Hoop Lane Cemetery has a book with the words 'Dear Marje I have a problem...'.

In Hoop Lane NW11, directly opposite Golders Green Crematorium, is the Hoop Lane Jewish Cemetery, which opened in 1897. To the right are the horizontal graves of the Spanish and Portuguese congregation, while the more varied graves of the West London Synagogue are to the left. All the graves mentioned here are to be found in the latter section. The row numbers quoted are painted on the paths, though some have faded.

Passing through the arch, in row 2, on the left, is the grave of **Jack Rosenthal** (1931–2004), the celebrated television dramatist. He wrote some of the early episodes of *Coronation Street*, and went on to write many television dramas, including *Bar Mitzvah Boy*, which became a successful West End musical. He also wrote the script for the Barbara Streisand film *Yentl*. He was married to the actress, Maureen Lipman, who appeared in several of his plays. In row 3, just in front, is the white marble grave of **Erich Segal** (1937–2010), the author and screenwriter who is best known for his novel *Love Story*, which was turned into the hugely successful film of the same name. He also co-wrote the script for the Beatles'

film *Yellow Submarine*. A little further down the central path, in row 42, is the grave of **Marjorie (Marje) Proops** (1911–96), who was probably the best known of all the 'agony aunts'. Her career in journalism began as fashion editor for the *Daily Herald*, but on the death of the paper's advice columnist she took on the job herself, and she continued to write successfully at the *Daily Mirror* until her death.

Turn left at the little roundabout, go to the end of the path and turn left again. On the left, by the path, is the pink granite tomb of **Leslie Hore-Belisha, Baron Hore-Belisha** (1893–1957), the politician who, as Minister of Transport in the 1930s, made motorists take a driving test and introduced pedestrian crossings with black and white poles topped off with an amber globe, which were referred to as 'Belisha beacons'. Further up the path, on the right, is the grave of **Jacqueline du Pré** (1945–87), the great cellist whose career was tragically cut short when she contracted multiple sclerosis. She began playing the cello at the age of four and performed on television when she was only 13. Her professional career lasted a mere ten years, but during that time she performed to great acclaim in England and the USA, including both concertos and chamber music. She made many recordings, including Elgar's Cello Concerto, the work she is most associated with, with Sir John Barbirolli. In 1967 she married the pianist and conductor, Daniel Barenboim, after converting to Judaism.

East Finchley Cemetery opened in 1854 as the St Marylebone Cemetery, when the parish needed more space. Its name changed in 1965, when the City of Westminster took over its management. Turning right after

The grave of Jacqueline du Pré, the virtuoso cellist who died tragically young, in Hoop Lane Jewish Cemetery.

the chapel, a few rows back on the right is the grave of **Keith Blakelock** (1945–85), the police constable who was murdered during the riots at the Broadwater Farm estate in Tottenham. He was posthumously awarded the Queen's Gallantry medal. Turn right into Cypress Avenue, and to the left of the path by the next turning is the grave of **James Henry Holloway** (1897–1975), better known as **Jimmy Nervo**, the anarchic comedian who was for many years a member of the Crazy Gang. A little further along Cypress Avenue, behind a yew tree on the right, is an angel marking the grave of **William Henry Crump** (1865–1942), the music hall star who performed under the name of **Harry Champion**. He was best known for songs such as *Any Old Iron*, *The End of my Old Cigar* and *I'm Henery the*

Eighth I am. Continue along Cypress Avenue and turn right up the narrow path after Yew Avenue, opposite the Crematorium. About 30 yards on the right, in the third row, is the grave of **William Heath Robinson** (1872–1944), the book illustrator who became famous for his highly detailed drawings of complicated and impractical machines, designed to carry out absurdly simple tasks. They became known as 'Heath Robinson contraptions'. The white marble grave is easy to find, as it has recently been restored and given a new inscription.

Retrace your steps and turn right at the Nervo grave. About 30 yards down the path, on the left in the second row, is the grave of **Sidney Paget** (1860–1908), the artist best known for his illustrations to the Sherlock Holmes stories in *The Strand* magazine.

The grave of music hall star Harry Champion in East Finchley Cemetery is marked by an angel.

137

The grave of the popular artist Heath Robinson at East Finchley Cemetery.

Although he didn't always follow Conan Doyle's descriptions, his representation of the great detective is now iconic, including the famous deerstalker hat, which was never mentioned in the stories. His grave is easy to spot because of the carved capital P at the centre of the cross. At the bottom of the path turn left, and straight ahead is an oak tree. To the right of the tree is buried the sculptor **Edward Onslow Ford** (1852–1901), under a plain stone slab, with a bronze laurel wreath. He is best known for his memorial to Shelley at University College, Oxford, but his only London statue is that of Sir Rowland Hill in King Edward Street. Turn right and just round the curve, in the second row on the left, is the grave of naturalist and explorer **Henry Walter Bates** (1825–92). He spent 11 years in Amazonia studying its wildlife, especially insects, sending nearly 15,000 different species back to England, more than half of them new to science. His greatest discovery was what is now referred to as 'Batesian mimicry', where a harmless species looks like a poisonous variety, a clever survival tactic. This offered support to Darwin's theory of natural selection, and the two

A cross with a capital P marks the last resting place of Sidney Paget, the artist who illustrated the Sherlock Holmes stories, at East Finchley Cemetery.

became firm friends. His monument is a tall pedestal surmounted by a globe, with South America featuring prominently.

Continue to the roundabout and cross over it to see, on the left, the grave of **Sir George Hayter** (1792–1871), the portrait and history painter who became Queen Victoria's portrait painter, depicting the royal couple's marriage and producing state portraits. He designed his headstone for his third wife, Martha, whose name is more prominent than his. It has a fine carving of a male angel with an urn and an inverted torch. Return to the roundabout, where on the left is the monument to the composer **Sir Henry Rowley Bishop** (1786–1855), with a splendid bronze

The grave of naturalist Henry Walter Bates at East Finchley Cemetery, with a globe featuring South America, where he discovered thousands of new species.

The gravestone of the artist Sir George Hayter in East Finchley Cemetery, with a fine carving of an angel holding an inverted torch, representing a life extinguished.

portrait on the front of the plinth. In his time he was highly revered for his operas, ballets and oratorios, but today he is all but forgotten. His main claim to fame is as the composer of the ever-popular song *Home, Sweet Home*.

Turn left down Central Avenue and, behind some bushes on the left, is the grave of **Alfred Charles William Harmsworth, Viscount Northcliffe** (1865–1922), a simple stone slab with an inscription and an incised cross. Harmsworth began his career as a journalist before forming his own company, the Amalgamated Press Company,

and went on to create a new, more popular form of journalism. He founded the *Daily Mail* and later bought *The Times*, becoming the most powerful newspaper magnate in Britain, and during the First World War he was appointed director of propaganda. Further down Central Avenue, on the left after the second yew tree, is the grave of **Harry Relph** (1867–1928), better known as the music hall star **Little Tich**. He was only 4'6" tall, but his nickname originally referred to the fraudulent claimant to the Tichborne millions, and the current usage of the word 'tich' is due to his fame. He was

The tomb of composer Sir Henry Bishop at East Finchley Cemetery carries a fine bronze relief portrait.

a master of acrobatic dancing and mime, and was particularly famous for his big boot dance, in which he wore 28-inch long boots, often standing on their points. He was enormously popular in France, and his grave carries an epitaph in French, 'Le plus petit et le plus grand comique du monde'.

A little further down Central Avenue, on the right under an oak tree, is the simple grave of the biologist **Thomas Henry Huxley** (1825–95), with his monogram on top of the headstone. He was the most important scientific supporter of Darwin's revolutionary theories, and made the discovery that birds were descended from dinosaurs. He was the original 'agnostic', a

term he created for himself. The gravestone carries lines from his wife's poem *Browning's Funeral*, which contains agnostic sentiments. Further down Central Avenue, on the right just before it crosses South Avenue, is the last resting place of **Sir Austen Chamberlain** (1863–1937), a politician who is less well known than his half-brother, Neville. He was twice chancellor of the Exchequer and was in Lloyd George's War Cabinet. As foreign secretary he brought his French and German colleagues together in 1925 to sign the Locarno Pact, for which he was awarded the Nobel Peace Prize. Turn left into South Avenue and left into East Avenue. Just before the junction on the right is the headstone marking the grave of the famous conductor **Leopold Stokowski** (1882–1977). British-born, despite his fake middle European accent, Stokowski began his career as an organist and found fame in America, where he conducted several orchestras, most importantly the Philadelphia. He also appeared in a number of Hollywood films, most famously in Walt Disney's *Fantasia*, where he got to shake hands with Mickey Mouse. He spent his last years in England, where he died. He was often a controversial figure, who loved to

The grave of the great music hall star Little Tich at East Finchley Cemetery.

The scientist Thomas Huxley's gravestone in East Finchley Cemetery, bearing his monogram.

The famous conductor Leopold Stokowski is buried in East Finchley Cemetery.

'improve' scores by the masters, but his performances were never boring, and many of his recordings have stood the test of time.

Adjacent to the cemetery, but not connected to it, is the St Marylebone Crematorium. It was designed by **Sir Edwin Cooper** (1874–1942), an architect who designed many grand public buildings, including Marylebone Town Hall and the former Port of London Authority headquarters in Trinity Square. He usually worked in a classical style sometimes referred to as Edwardian Baroque, but the crematorium building is much more restrained. He was cremated here, and his ashes are in a niche in the cloisters,

with a small plaque. The ashes of two very different actors were scattered in the cloister. They are the versatile stage and film actor **Robert Donat** (1905–58), who won an Oscar for the role of Mr Chips in *Goodbye Mr Chips*, and **Kenneth Williams** (1926–88), who is best known for his many appearances in the *Carry On* films and in radio programmes such as *Round the Horne* and *Just a Minute*.

St Pancras and Islington Cemetery, in High Road N2, is the largest in London. The first section, consisting of 88 acres, opened in 1854 and another 94 acres were bought in 1877. It is now managed jointly by the boroughs of Camden and Islington.

The grave, in St Pancras and Islington Cemetery, of Henry Croft, the first Pearly King, once featured a statue of him, but it was vandalised and can now be seen in the crypt of St Martin-in-the-Fields.

Go straight ahead on Viaduct Road, which curves round to the left, and turn left into Tram Path. A short distance along it, to the left of the Harriett obelisk and in amongst the trees, is the headstone to the Irish artist **John O'Connor** (1830–89). He had a long career as a scenery painter in theatres in Dublin and London, but later painted many fine topographical views of London, several of which are in the collection of the Museum of London. He was never made a member of the Royal Academy, though the stonemason clearly thought so and had to correct his mistake on the headstone, changing an A for an H, as he was actually a member of the Royal Hibernian Academy in Dublin. Return to Viaduct Avenue and at the next junction is what is left of the grave of **Henry Croft** (1861–1930), a road sweeper who is considered to be the first Pearly King. His funeral was attended by many Pearly Kings and Queens and money was raised for a statue of him, dressed in his Pearly costume, to be placed on his grave. Sadly the statue was vandalised and it was removed in 2002 to be restored; it

can now be seen in the crypt of St Martin-in-the-Fields church, where the Pearlies used to hold their Harvest Festival service. A photograph on the headstone shows what the grave once looked like. Turn left into Cross Road and right up Chapel Hill, and on the slope on the right is the splendid mausoleum of the Mond family, in the form of an Ionic Greek temple. **Ludwig Mond** (1839–1909) was a leading figure in the British chemical industry, beginning with his improved process for making soda. He also collected art works, including early Italian paintings, most of which were left to the National Gallery. He was buried in the cemetery following Jewish rites, and his family later built the mausoleum to contain his remains and other family members, including his son **Alfred Moritz Mond, Baron Melchett** (1868–1930), who was responsible for the creation of ICI (Imperial Chemical Industries). Take the curving path to the left of the mausoleum to find the grave of the artist **Ford Madox Brown** (1821–93). Although never a member of the Pre-Raphaelite Brotherhood, he was closely associated with them and, like them, often painted outdoors. His best-known works are *The Last of England* and *Work*, which shows workmen building a water main in Hampstead. He was never as successful in his lifetime as his associates, but his work has been re-assessed in recent years and he is now considered to be an important and original artist.

Return to Chapel Hill and go right along Joint Road, which leads to Roman Road. Halfway along Roman Road there is an open space on the right where there was once a chapel. Go down the path at the far right and at the end is the simple

The classical mausoleum of the Mond family in St Pancras and Islington Cemetery.

headstone to (**Sally Myfanwy Amis**), the daughter of the author **Sir Kingsley Amis** (1922–95), whose ashes are also buried here. He made his name with *Lucky Jim*, which was considered to be the best comic novel of its time, but he wrote many more, including *Take a Girl Like You* and the award-winning *The Old Devils*. To the left of the Wieland mausoleum, at the back of the open space, take the path between the trees to find the grave of **Cora Crippen** (*c*. 1873–1910), a music hall singer working under the name of *Belle Elmore* who was murdered by her husband, Dr Crippen. The few human remains discovered in the cellar of their house were identified in court by Bernard Spilsbury, the eminent pathologist, as hers, though in recent years doubt has been cast on his findings. The burial was arranged by the Music Hall Ladies' Guild,

The artist Ford Madox Brown's grave in St Pancras and Islington Cemetery.

The remains of Cora Crippen, who was murdered by her husband, were interred in St Pancras and Islington Cemetery in Finchley.

LONDON BOROUGH OF ISLINGTON

In the churchyard of St Luke's Old Street (now redundant and used by the London Symphony Orchestra) is the impressive chest tomb of **William Caslon** (1692–1766), the type-founder who was famous for creating elegant types still used today in printing. His foundry was very close to the church. Also buried in the graveyard, but without a monument, is **George Dance the Elder** (c. 1694–1768), the architect who designed the Mansion House and a number of London churches, including nearby St Leonard, Shoreditch.

Although St James's Street Chapel in Pentonville Road, at the junction with Rodney Street, is now deconsecrated, the churchyard has been converted into the Joseph Grimaldi Park, where the grave of **Joseph Grimaldi** (1778–1837), who lived most of his life in the area, can be found. Grimaldi was a great clown, who first appeared on the stage of the Sadler's Wells theatre at the age of three, and continued to perform there for the next 42 years. He became the most celebrated pantomime clown of his age, adored by the likes of Byron and Hazlitt, and Dickens edited his memoirs. His nickname Joey is now often used to mean a clown.

Wesley's Chapel, in City Road EC1, is the home of Methodism, and the movement's founder, **John Wesley** (1703–91), lived in the house next door. He died in the house and is buried in the small graveyard behind the chapel. To find it, go through the central doors and then through the door on the right.

On the opposite side of City Road is Bunhill Fields, an important Dissenters'

of which Cora was a member. Continue up Roman Road and go up St Peter's Avenue. At the top on the left is the understated grave, with a cross, of conductor and composer **Sir Eugene Goossens** (1893–1962). His own compositions are rarely played today, and he is best remembered as a fine conductor, who gave the first British performance of Stravinsky's *Rite of Spring* and the premiere of Coleridge-Taylor's *Hiawatha*. During a long and successful career, he was also the principal conductor of the Carl Rosa Opera, the Cincinnati Orchestra in the USA and the Sydney Symphony Orchestra in Australia.

The last resting place of the great clown Joseph Grimaldi in the disused graveyard of St James's Street Chapel.

The fine monument to John Wesley behind Wesley's Chapel in City Road.

burial ground. It has been a burial place since Saxon times, and the name is said to be a corruption of 'Bone Hill'. From the seventeenth century it began to be used as a burial ground by non-conformists, and a number of prominent Puritans and Baptists are buried here. The last burial was in 1854, by which time many Dissenters were already using Abney Park Cemetery in Stoke Newington. Bunhill Fields is now maintained as a community garden, and in 2011 it was listed as a Grade I park, while several of the individual monuments were also listed. Although geographically in the borough of Islington, it is maintained by the City of London. Most of the graves are fenced off, but on weekday afternoons from 1–3 an attendant is available to allow you to see some of the more remote ones.

Entering from City Road, over to the right is the simple chest tomb of the preacher **Isaac Watts** (1674–1748), who is best known for his many hymns, including *O God, Our Help in Ages Past*. Watts spent much of his life as chaplain to the Hartopp family in Stoke Newington, where he died, and the original tomb was replaced by the Hartopps in 1808. In the central area are the

The chest tomb of hymn-writer Isaac Watts in Bunhill Fields.

three most important graves. On the south side is the tomb of **John Bunyan** (1628–88), the author of *The Pilgrim's Progress*. Bunyan was an outspoken and controversial preacher, and he was imprisoned in Bedford gaol for 11 years. There he wrote several books, including the first part of *The Pilgrim's Progress*, which is one of the most popular books ever published, and has been translated into more than two hundred languages. The tomb was originally a plain chest tomb, but in 1862 it was restored by Edgar George Papworth, who added the recumbent effigy of Bunyan and the carvings on the sides representing scenes from the book. Nearby is a marble obelisk commemorating the author **Daniel Defoe** (1660?–1731). As a non-conformist, Defoe wrote many political pamphlets supporting religious freedom, and he was once made to stand in the pillory for three days. He is best remembered as the author of *Robinson Crusoe* and *Moll Flanders*, two influential early novels. His grave originally had a simple headstone, but in 1870 the obelisk was erected, paid for by money raised by readers of a children's magazine, *Christian World*. Alongside is the simple headstone commemorating **William Blake** (1757–1827). Blake was both poet and artist, and produced the engravings for many of his own books of poetry. His visionary style

The tomb of John Bunyan in Bunhill Fields, with a fine effigy and carvings based on his book *The Pilgrim's Progress*.

The obelisk marking the grave of Daniel Defoe in Bunhill Fields.

People often leave coins and poems on this simple headstone, which marks the approximate location of William Blake's grave in Bunhill Fields.

is unique and instantly recognisable, and his work can be seen in many galleries. Although he lived mostly in poverty and obscurity, his reputation has grown hugely in recent decades, and people regularly leave flowers and coins on his gravestone. His grave was unmarked until 1927, the centenary of his death, when the memorial stone was erected on the spot, which is about 20 yards away in the grassy area of the gardens. When Bunhill Fields was rearranged in 1965 it was moved to its present, more prominent, location.

On the southern side of the cemetery, by the boundary wall, is the tomb of **Charles Fleetwood** (c. 1618–92), the parliamentary soldier who fought at the battle of Naseby and was later made commander-in-chief in Ireland. He was married to Oliver Cromwell's daughter. Further west is the grave of **Susanna Wesley** (1669–1742), the mother of John and Charles Wesley. Also buried here, but with no marked grave, is **Eleanor Coade** (1733–1821), the owner of the factory producing Coade stone, an artificial material which is resistant to weather, and was much used in architectural decoration and for tombs and memorials in graveyards, including several in Bunhill Fields.

Thomas Newcomen (1664–1729), the inventor of the atmospheric steam engine, is also buried here, but the location of his grave is unknown.

Across Banner Street, off Chequer Street, is Quaker Gardens, which was once the Quaker Burying Ground, now converted into a garden. It was opened in 1661 and operated until 1855. There were never any gravestones, but there is now a plaque in memory of those buried here. Among them is **George Fox** (1624–91), the founder of the Religious Society of Friends, or Quakers. He disagreed with many of the orthodox church's tenets, and his beliefs were considered more extreme than the Puritans, so that he was regularly imprisoned, but by the time of his death Quakers had been allowed the freedom to meet and practise their beliefs. Thousands accompanied his body to be buried at Bunhill. Although the exact location of his grave is unknown, a small gravestone with his name was placed in 1881 near the present meeting house.

The present St James Clerkenwell, in Clerkenwell Close, opened in 1792, replacing the nunnery church, which had been used as the parish church. The graveyard has been turned into a garden, with a few headstones around the wall, and the crypt was emptied in the early twentieth century. A few memorials remain from the earlier church, but none to the following notable people, who were buried in the old church. **John Robert Cozens** (1752–97) was an outstanding watercolour artist, painting romantic scenes, of Italy and Switzerland in particular. Constable called him 'the greatest genius that ever touched landscape'. Three important playwrights were also buried here: **Thomas Dekker** (c. 1572–1632), the prolific author, best known for *The Shoemaker's Holiday*; **Thomas Heywood** (c. 1573–1641), who wrote the tragedy, *A Woman Killed with Kindness*; and **William Rowley** (1585–1626), who collaborated with the other two, as well as co-authoring *The Changeling* with Thomas Middleton. The most notorious character to be buried here was **John (Jack) Ketch** (d. 1686), the hangman of London, who was infamous for his botched executions of Lord Russell and the Duke of Monmouth. Many successive hangmen were referred to as Jack Ketch, and his name was given to the hangman in Punch and Judy shows.

LONDON BOROUGH OF CAMDEN

Until the eighteenth century, Hampstead was just a small village, but it soon attracted many writers and artists, which is why the graveyard of the parish church, St John at Hampstead, in Church Row, NW3, has so many important permanent residents. Turn left inside the main gate and go down the path to find the large chest tomb, complete with its iron railings, of **Joanna Baillie** (1761–1851), a playwright and poet who lived most of her life in Hampstead. Though almost forgotten today, in her lifetime she was considered to be a major writer, and was admired by Sir Walter Scott and William Wordsworth, who visited her regularly. Five rows down is the plain chest tomb of **Robert Milligan** (1746–1809), the Scottish merchant and ship-owner who led a group of businessmen in building the West India Docks, the first of the enclosed docks, at a time when theft was rife at the riverside

The great artist John Constable is buried in Hampstead churchyard, close to where he lived.

wharves. The docks opened in 1802 and handled imports from the West Indies, such as sugar, rum and coffee. Against the south wall of the churchyard is the tomb of **John Constable** (1776–1837), the great Suffolk-born landscape painter. From the early 1820s he made many sketches on Hampstead Heath, particularly studies of clouds, and in 1827 moved with his family to Well Walk. The chest tomb was built for his wife, Maria, who died in 1828, and he was buried with her.

Take the next right and on the next bend is the grave of **William Westall** (1781–1850), the artist who accompanied Matthew Flinders on his 1801 expedition to Australia. Before returning he also spent time in China and India. He later produced some fine topographical views of the Lake District and London. The headstone has recently been restored and the inscription re-cut. A little further on, under a tree to the right, is the large chest tomb of **Richard Norman Shaw** (1831–1912),

the influential architect, Norman Shaw, as he is usually called, is best known for his Queen Anne-style houses in London, including artists' studios in Kensington and his own home in Ellerdale Road in Hampstead. Other key buildings in London are the Piccadilly Hotel and his only public building, New Scotland Yard, built as the headquarters of the Metropolitan Police on Victoria Embankment. By the south

The elegant Georgian-style chest tomb of architect Norman Shaw in the graveyard of St John at Hampstead.

The tomb, in the graveyard of St John at Hampstead, of John Harrison, who designed the first chronometer, which allowed sailors to calculate longitude and saved many lives.

transept of the church is the chest tomb of **John Harrison** (1693–1776), the watchmaker who designed a chronometer that allowed mariners to calculate longitude at sea. This was such a problem that a reward was offered, though he had to fight hard and long for the recognition he deserved, a story made famous by Dava Sobel's 1999 book *Longitude*. The chest tomb bears a long inscription relating his struggles. Another inscription states that the tomb was 'reconstructed at the expense of the Worshipful Company of Clockmakers' in 1879.

The old churchyard became overcrowded by the nineteenth century, and an extension was built across the road, though this is now also closed for burials. To the right, overlooking Church Row, is a group of important burials. The first is that of **Sir Herbert Beerbohm Tree** (1852–1917), whose ashes lie under a life-size statue of a mourning female figure. A very successful actor-manager, he built Her Majesty's Theatre in the Haymarket, where he put on accessible performances

of Shakespeare's plays as well as many important new plays. He also founded the Royal Academy of Dramatic Art. Next is the grave of an actor of the modern era, **Kay Kendall** (1927–59), who is best known for her roles in films such as *Genevieve* and alongside her husband, Rex Harrison, in *The Reluctant Debutante*. The gravestone is of green slate, with a well-cut inscription. Next is a more sober memorial to **Hugh Todd Naylor Gaitskell** (1906–63), a large urn on a plinth, all of Portland stone. He was chancellor of the Exchequer from 1950 to 1951 and Labour leader from 1955. Alongside it is the unusual wooden deadboard, with Celtic crosses at each end, which marks the grave of **George Busson du Maurier** (1834–96), the cartoonist and novelist. He worked as cartoonist for *Punch* for over 30 years, but also produced illustrations for the novels of Elizabeth Gaskell, Wilkie Collins and Thomas Hardy. His most important novel was *Trilby*, based on his experiences as a student in Paris. It gave two new terms to the language, the trilby hat and Svengali. The copper inscription on the right hand cross commemorates his son **Sir Gerald Hubert Edward Busson du Maurier** (1873–1934), who is also buried here. As a boy, Sir Gerald loved to dress up, and he later became a popular actor and theatre manager. He starred as both Mr Darling and Captain Hook in Barrie's *Peter Pan*, and was hugely successful as the gentleman thief in *Raffles*. By the far wall is the grave of **Anton Walbrook** (1896–1967), the Austrian actor who was the handsome leading man in many films. Jewish and born Anton Adolf Wilhelm Wohlbrück, he moved to America in 1936, when he

A view of the extension to the graveyard at St John at Hampstead, showing the graves, in the foreground, of Hugh Gaitskell and George du Maurier, and behind, Sir Herbert Beerbohm Tree and Kay Kendall.

The grave of the Austrian-born actor Anton Walbrook in the extension of Hampstead graveyard.

changed his name. He moved to London, where he appeared in *The Red Shoes* and *The Life and Death of Colonel Blimp*. He was also a successful stage actor, appearing regularly in the West End. He died of a heart attack during a performance in Munich, and his body was brought back to be buried in Hampstead, close to his home in Frognal.

Walk up the paved path to just before the cross-path where on the left is the large Gothic headstone, with an eroded inscription, of **Eliza Acton** (1799–1859), who is considered to be the first of the modern cookery writers. Her best-known book, *Modern Cookery for Private Families*, was published in 1845, and was a standard text for many years. Walk up to the upper part of the extension, turn right at the cross-path and take the second path on the left. About halfway up, on the left, is the grave of the architect **Basil Champneys** (1842–1935), in the form of a gabled granite cross, with a bronze figure of Christ. Champneys worked in a variety of styles, and designed buildings in Oxford, Cambridge and London. In the

capital he built St Luke's in Kentish Town, the chapel at Mill Hill School, and his own house in Frognal Lane. Continue to the top, take the second path on the left and about 30 yards down, on the right, is the grave of the architect **Temple Moore** (1856–1920), with a crucifixion scene and an inscription in an elegant Gothic font. Moore studied with George Gilbert Scott junior (see below) and in his turn taught his master's son, Giles Gilbert Scott. Moore became an important architect of the Gothic revival, designing many churches, including several in London.

The gravestone of architect Basil Champneys in the Hampstead graveyard extension.

The grave of architect Temple Moore in Hampstead churchyard, with a fine carved crucifixion.

Return to the top path, turn left and take the second path on the left, where a little way down on the left is the sharply cut headstone marking the grave of the writer **Eleanor Farjeon** (1881–1965). She is best known as the author of beautifully crafted children's poetry and stories. She also wrote the words for the hymn *Morning Has Broken*. She spent the last 45 years of her life in Perins Walk, Hampstead. Continue along the top of the cemetery and turn down the fourth path on the left. Just after the path turns left, on the right is the hipped cruciform ledger marking the grave of **George Gilbert Scott Junior** (1839–97), the eldest son of Sir George Gilbert Scott, and like his father an architect. He had a brief successful career, though most of

his London churches no longer exist, and he suffered mental problems in his later years. He built his own house in Frognal Way. Go down the paved path on the left and shortly before the cross-path, on the right, is the grave of the author **Sir Walter Besant** (1836–1901). Besant was a prolific fiction writer, though his novels are little read today, but his most important work are his histories of London. He was also involved in the campaign for author's rights, helping to found the Society of Authors. Continue down the path and halfway down the lower section, on the right, is the distinctive yellow sandstone headstone, with a Celtic cross cut in relief, to **Eva Gore-Booth** (1870–1926), the Irish poet and suffragist. In Italy she met and fell in love with

The simple grave of architect George Gilbert Scott Junior in Hampstead graveyard.

The London historian Sir Walter Besant's gravestone in Hampstead graveyard.

Esther Roper, who worked in the suffrage movement in Manchester, and they worked for the cause for the rest of their lives. They were particularly successful in attracting working class women to join the suffrage movement. They also ran a radical journal called *Urania*, which reflected their ideas about gender and sexuality. Eva and Esther are buried together in the grave. A more recent resident of Hampstead is **Peter Cook** (1937–95), the great comedian and satirist. He became famous as one of the original performers in *Beyond the Fringe*, and later with Dudley Moore in the television show *Not Only But Also*. He was cremated at Golders Green and it is said his ashes are buried here in the extension, close to where he lived.

By the mid-nineteenth century Hampstead graveyard was reaching its capacity, so Hampstead Cemetery was created about a mile away in Fortune Green Road, opening in 1876. The great and good of Hampstead are buried here, with a particular emphasis on architects, writers and actors.

From the entrance go straight ahead and a short way down, on the left, is the grave

The distinctive gravestone of suffragette Eva Gore-Booth in the extension of Hampstead graveyard.

The family grave, in Hampstead Cemetery, of John Richard Clayton, whose stained glass can be found in many churches throughout Britain.

The grey granite ledger of the famous surgeon, Sir Joseph Lister, in Hampstead Cemetery.

of **John Richard Clayton** (1827–1913), a large double-fronted headstone with classical columns. Clayton was an artist and sculptor who joined up with Alfred Bell to create Clayton and Bell, one of the most famous nineteenth-century producers of stained glass, which can be seen in churches throughout the country, including many in London. Ten graves after the next path, on the left, is the large cross marking the grave of **Edwin Longsden Long** (1829–91), a hugely successful artist who began his career painting portraits before specialising in detailed portrayals of the ancient world. His commercial success allowed him to commission two large studio houses in Hampstead from Norman Shaw.

Cross the public footpath and turn left at the chapel. At the next junction is the splendid classical monument to the architect **Banister Fletcher** (1833–99) (see page 132). He had an extensive practice, designing shops, factories and houses, including a number in Hampstead. He also wrote books on architecture and was a professor at King's College, London. The family tomb was designed by his eldest

son, Sir Banister Flight Fletcher, and the central pedestal once held a bronze bust of the architect. Walk west along the main path where, about 50 yards on the left, is the grey granite raised ledger of **Joseph Lister, Baron Lister** (1827–1912), the surgeon who initiated antiseptic surgery, using carbolic acid to kill germs, which greatly increased the survival rate of patients after an operation. Listerine mouthwash is named after him. He received many honours and was offered burial in Westminster Abbey, but he wished to be buried at Hampstead with his wife. **Catherine (Kate) Greenaway** (1846–1901) is buried in her family grave nearby, but it is very difficult to locate, as it is in amongst the undergrowth to the left. It can occasionally be glimpsed through the bushes. Kate was one of the most popular and important book illustrators of the nineteenth century, mostly of children's books, and her work is instantly recognisable. The Kate Greenaway medal was set up in 1955 to recognise today's best illustrators of children's books. About 50 yards further on, to the right, is the modest headstone

The family grave of Kate Greenaway, the famous book illustrator, in Hampstead Cemetery.

The grave of Sir Francis Dicksee, president of the Royal Academy, in Hampstead Cemetery.

to the composer **Sir George Alexander Macfarren** (1813–87), which lists none of his many achievements. He studied at the Royal Academy of Music, and was later its principal. He wrote operas and symphonies and was music director at Covent Garden. His music is mostly forgotten today, as it was old fashioned even when it was written, but in his day he was highly respected.

Continue on this path until you reach the roundabout with a large cedar in the middle. Behind the trees on the left is the grave of the artist **Sir Francis Dicksee** (1853–1928). Dicksee was influenced by the Pre-Raphaelites, painting in a romantic style, and he specialised in rather sentimental and often erotic subjects. He was also a fashionable portrait painter. He

became president of the Royal Academy in 1924. Head back along the central path towards the chapel, and about 100 yards on the left is the granite cross marking the grave of electrical engineer **Sebastian Ziani de Ferranti** (1864–1930). Ferranti was a pioneer in the generation and distribution of electricity, and later became involved in the production of radios and household electrical goods. The firm that carried his name continued to produce electrical equipment for over a hundred years, but went bankrupt in 1993. He had

The family grave of the Italian electrical pioneer Sebastian de Ferranti in Hampstead Cemetery.

The grave of sculptor Sir William Goscombe John in Hampstead Cemetery, with the shadow of the sculpture he created for his wife. Pictured right is a photograph of the memorial before the statue was stolen.

lived in Hampstead for much of his life, and he was buried in the family grave along with his parents. A little further on, on the left behind the large Waterhouse tomb, is the headstone marking the last resting place of **John Hargrave** (1894–1982), the writer and artist who is best known as 'White Fox', and who founded the rather unorthodox Kibbo Kift movement in 1920 as an alternative to the Boy Scouts, with whom he had fallen out. They wore a uniform of green shirts and were attacked by extremists of both left and right, but attracted such eminent writers as H. G. Wells and Havelock Ellis. When the gravestone was unveiled in 1984 there was a gathering of ex-members of the group.

To the left of the chapel is the grave of the Welsh sculptor **Sir William Goscombe John** (1860–1952). He produced memorials for St Paul's Cathedral and Westminster Abbey, and also created the memorial to Sir Arthur Sullivan in Victoria Embankment Gardens. He made this memorial for his wife, and it originally featured a life-size bronze of a female figure, but sadly this was stolen in 2001, though its outline is still clearly visible. The statue was returned after it turned up at an auction, but was stolen again before it could be re-installed. Take the road on the left and just before the row of trees, over on the left, on the edge of some bushes, is the tall pedestal tomb of **Sir William Randal Cremer** (1828–1908),

The grave of Sir William Cremer, Nobel Prize winner, in Hampstead Cemetery.

The family grave of Frederick Gaisberg, who made some of the earliest gramophone recordings, in Hampstead Cemetery.

a radical politician and a tireless campaigner for international arbitration. In 1903 he was awarded the Nobel Peace Prize as well as the cross of the Légion d'Honneur. Return to the chapel, turn left and just before the public footpath, on the left, is the grave of **Frederick William Gaisberg** (1873–1951), a leading figure in the early years of the gramophone. American-born, he came to London to set up the new studio of the Gramophone Company (later renamed HMV), where he recorded music-hall stars and famous singers such as Nellie Melba, Chaliapin and Caruso. In the tenth row of the left hand block on the other side of the public footpath, and rather difficult to find,

is the simple stone grave with a carved cross of **Francis James Barraud** (1856–1924), who worked with Gaisberg, as he was the artist whose painting of the dog 'Nipper' listening to an old gramophone became the trademark of the His Master's Voice record label.

Turn left and at the next crossroads, on the right, is the impressive tomb of **Henry Brodribb Irving** (1870–1919), the son of the famous actor, Henry Irving. Although his father didn't want him to follow in his footsteps, he became a successful actor in his own right, his most famous part being the lead in J. M. Barrie's *The Admirable Crichton*. He only appeared on the same

The large tomb of actor Henry Brodribb Irving, son of the great Sir Henry Irving.

The grave of the famous film actress, Gladys Cooper, in Hampstead Cemetery.

stage as his father on one occasion. Turn left and walk back towards the public footpath and just before the fence, on the right, are two more graves of actors. The first is **Fred Terry** (1863–1933), the actor son of Ellen Terry, who was a fine Shakespearean actor but spent much of his career in more romantic parts, his most famous role being that of Sir Percy Blakeney in *The Scarlet Pimpernel*. A little further along is the simple headstone marking the grave of **Dame Gladys Constance Cooper** (1888–1971), the celebrated stage and screen actress. She began her career as a Gaiety Girl but soon became a professional actress, and also managed the Playhouse theatre on the Embankment. She left London for America in the 1930s and became a successful Hollywood actress, appearing in such films as *Rebecca* and *Now Voyager*.

Return to the crossroads, turn left and then right where, on the left, is the grey marble grave of **Charles Forte, Baron Forte** (1908–2007), the Italian-born caterer and hotelier who began his career working in an ice cream parlour in Weston-super-Mare. He went on to create an empire that included hotels, restaurants,

motorway cafeterias and bingo halls. On the same path, a little before the War Memorial, is the prominent tomb of the actor-manager **Sir Charles Wyndham** (1837–1919). Born Charles Culverwell, he worked for some years as a doctor, but had always been attracted to the stage and after successful amateur performances turned professional, using Charles Wyndham as his stage name. He had great stage presence and played dashing young heroes in popular farces well into middle age. He built Wyndham's Theatre and the New Theatre, now renamed the Noel Coward. Continue past the War Memorial and about 20 yards further on, to the right of the path, is the Celtic cross marking the grave of **Marie Lloyd** (1870–1922), the popular music hall star. Born Matilda Alice Victoria Wood, she first performed aged 14, and soon became a big star, famous for her bawdy asides as much as her renditions of songs such as *My Old Man Says Follow the Van* and *A Little of What You Fancy Does You Good*. Many thousands of people lined the streets to watch her funeral and at least a dozen cars were needed just to carry the flowers.

Behind Marie Lloyd's grave, about halfway between this path and the main avenue, is the easily overlooked grave of the great Russian ballerina **Tamara Platonovna Karsavina** (1885–1978). The headstone bears the name of her English husband, Henry James Bruce, and her name is inscribed on the grave slab. A leading ballerina at the Maryinsky theatre in St Petersburg, she fled from Russia during the Revolution, never to return. She performed in Europe with Diaghilev's Ballets Russes, dancing with Nijinsky, and created major roles in several of Fokine's productions. She also played a major part in the development of British ballet, coaching dancers such as Margot Fonteyn in her own most important roles. Return to Marie Lloyd's grave, turn right and left at the end of the path. On the right, in the third row, close to the boundary wall, is the simple headstone commemorating the virtuoso horn-player **Dennis Brain** (1921–1957). A child prodigy, Brain went on to become the principal horn of the Philharmonia Orchestra and many composers wrote music especially for his unique skills. Many of his recordings are still played today, in particular his classic performances of Mozart's four horn concertos. He had a great sense of humour and once performed on a hosepipe at a Hoffnung concert. He also had a taste for fast cars, and sadly he died when he crashed his sports car on the

The family grave of actor-manager Sir Charles Wyndham in Hampstead Cemetery.

The grave of the much loved music hall star, Marie Lloyd, in Hampstead Cemetery.

The modest grave of the famous Russian ballerina Karsavina in Hampstead Cemetery. She is buried in her husband's grave, and her name is inscribed on the gravestone.

The simple grave of Dennis Brain, the great horn-player, in Hampstead Cemetery.

Barnet by-pass. Further along this path, to the right of the flamboyant Bianchi tomb, is the grave of **Alan Coren** (1938–2007), the humorous writer and broadcaster. He wrote for various magazines and newspapers, and was editor of *Punch* in the 1970s and '80s, hence the representation of Mr Punch on his headstone. He was one of the wittiest men in England and appeared on both radio and television, including the long-running quiz show *Call My Bluff*. He lived for many years in Cricklewood and he was often referred to as the 'Sage of Cricklewood'.

St Michael's in South Grove, Highgate, is the last resting place of the great Romantic poet **Samuel Taylor Coleridge** (1772– 1834). He is best known for *The Rime of the Ancient Mariner* and *Kubla Khan*, which he claimed to have written under the influence of laudanum. He took laudanum for medical reasons, but soon became addicted. In 1816 he went to live with Dr James Gillman in Highgate in the hope that he could be cured of the addiction, and he spent the rest of his life there. He was buried in the local churchyard, but in 1866 a new chapel for Highgate School was built over the vault, and the grave became neglected. In 1961 he was reburied in the crypt of St Michael's church. There is a modern stone slab in the nave aisle, which includes the original inscription, written by the poet, 'Beneath this sod A poet lies or that which once seem'd he. O lift one thought in prayer for S.T.C.'.

The church of St Giles-in-the-Fields in St Giles High Street behind Tottenham Court Road is the third on the site,

Opposite: The grave of poet Samuel Taylor Coleridge in St Michael's Highgate.

NEAR UNTO THIS PLACE LYETH THE BODY OF ANDREW MARVELL ESQUIRE, A MAN SO ENDOWED BY NATURE, SO IMPROVED BY EDUCATION, STUDY & TRAVELL, SO CONSUMMATED BY PRACTICE & EXPERIENCE; THAT JOINING THE MOST PECULIAR GRACES OF WIT & LEARNING WITH A SINGULAR PENETRATION, & STRENGTH OF JUDGMENT, & EXERCISING ALL THESE IN THE WHOLE COURSE OF HIS LIFE, WITH AN UNALTERABLE STEADINESS IN THE WAYS OF VIRTUE, HE BECAME THE ORNAMENT & EXAMPLE OF HIS AGE; BELOVED BY GOOD MEN, FEAR'D BY BAD, ADMIR'D BY ALL, THO IMITATED ALASS! BY FEW, & SCARCE FULLY PARALLELLED BY ANY, BUT A TOMB STONE CAN NEITHER CONTAIN HIS CHARACTER, NOR IS MARBLE NECESSARY TO TRANSMIT IT TO POSTERITY, IT WILL BE ALWAYS LEGIBLE IN HIS INIMITABLE WRITINGS, HE SERVED THE TOWN OF KINGSTON UPON HULL, ABOVE 20 YEARS SUCCESSIVELY IN PARLIAMENT, & THAT, WITH SUCH WISDOM, DEXTERITY, INTEGRITY & COURAGE AS BECOMES A TRUE PATRIOT, HE DYED THE 16. AUGUST 1678 IN THE 58TH YEAR OF HIS AGE.
SACRED
TO THE MEMORY OF ANDREW MARVELL ESQR AS A STRENUOUS ASSERTER OF THE CONSTITUTION; LAWS & LIBERTIES OF ENGLAND, AND OUT OF FAMILY AFFECTION & ADMIRATION OF THE UNCORRUPT PROBITY OF HIS LIFE & MANNERS. ROBERT NETTLETON OF LONDON MERCHANT, HIS GRAND NEPHEW HATH CAUSED THIS SMALL MEMORIAL OF HIM, TO BE ERECTED IN THE YEAR 1764.

The memorial to the poet Andrew Marvell in St Giles-in-the-Fields church extols his many virtues without mentioning his literary output.

built in the 1730s. Halfway down the north aisle is the memorial to the poet **Andrew Marvell** (1621–78), who lived nearby. Marvell was also a politician with republican sympathies and wrote many political satires as well as odes in honour of Oliver Cromwell. He also wrote love poems, including his most famous lyric *To his Coy Mistress.* The inscription extols his many virtues, but makes no mention of his literary talents. At the east end of the north aisle is the monument to the playwright **George Chapman** (1559–1634). Today his plays are rarely performed, and he is better known as the first person to translate Homer's *Iliad* and *Odyssey* into English. The gravestone once marked his burial in the

churchyard, and was designed by Inigo Jones in the form of a Roman altar. On the second column of the south aisle is a memorial to **Luke Hansard** (1752–1828), the printer of the daily records of debates in the House of Commons; today's reports are still referred to as 'Hansard'. Also buried here, but with no monument, is the portrait painter **John Greenhill** (1644?–76). He was considered to be one of the best pupils of Sir Peter Lely and painted many fine portraits of important people of the time, including actors and playwrights. He led a rather dissolute life, dying young after collapsing drunk into the gutter in Long Acre after a drinking session at the Vine tavern. There is also no memorial to the

George Chapman's monument in St Giles-in-the-Fields church was designed by Inigo Jones and once stood in the churchyard.

The body, or 'auto-icon', of Jeremy Bentham now resides in a cabinet in University College.

playwright **James Shirley** (1596 1666), who was buried here. His plays are now all but forgotten, but his comedies and masques were highly praised at the time. His career was affected by the Civil War, as the theatres were closed by Cromwell, and he died a victim of the Great Fire of London in 1666.

University College London, in Gower Street WC1, is the rather unusual last resting place of philosopher and social reformer **Jeremy Bentham** (1748–1832). He left instructions that his body should be anatomised and that his skeleton be preserved as an 'auto-icon'. After the dissection, his skeleton was wired together,

but the preservation of the head was unsuccessful and a wax head was created. The skeleton was dressed in Bentham's clothes and placed in a chair, holding a walking stick. The hair you see today is his own. The auto-icon was donated to University College, and he now sits in a glass-fronted cabinet in the South Cloisters, accessible by the door to the right of the pediment. There is an urban myth that his body attends college meetings, and is recorded as being 'present, but not voting'.

To the north of St Pancras Station, on Pancras Road, is St Pancras Old Church. Its surrounding gardens are but a small part of its original graveyard, which

The architect Sir John Soane designed his tomb, which stands in what was the graveyard of St Giles-in-the Fields, now an extension of the graveyard of St Pancras Old Church.

included the separate burial ground of St Giles-in-the Fields, as much of it was lost to make way for the railway line into St Pancras Station in the 1860s and '70s. The most important tomb, in the centre of the gardens, is that of the architect **Sir John Soane** (1753–1837), which he designed for his wife in Carrara marble and Portland stone. The symbolism includes a pine cone, an ancient symbol of rebirth, as well as a snake biting its own tail, symbolising eternal life. The central part of the tomb was to inspire Giles Gilbert Scott in his design for the telephone box. Soane was an important architect, with his own unique neo-classical style. His major London buildings are the Dulwich Picture Gallery, the Bank of England (of which the external walls are all that remain), and his own house in Lincoln's Inn Fields, now Sir John Soane's Museum, which houses his extensive collection of antiquities, paintings and architectural drawings.

Close by is the simple monument to **Mary Wollstonecraft** (1759–97), the early feminist writer, and her husband, the philosopher **William Godwin** (1756–1836). They were originally buried here, but in 1851 their remains were moved to St Peter's in Bournemouth, where they were re-interred alongside their daughter,

The sculptor John Flaxman is buried in the graveyard of St Pancras Old Church.

Mary Shelley, the author of *Frankenstein*. A few yards further west are two sloping tomb slabs to the Flaxman family, the left one being the last resting place of **John Flaxman** (1755–1826), the sculptor best known for his funerary monuments, including the Earl of Mansfield in Westminster Abbey and Lord Nelson in St Paul's Cathedral. The inscription on his gravestone is now almost illegible.

Several other notable people were buried in the graveyard, but their graves have been lost. There is, however, alongside the Burdett-Coutts sundial, a memorial plaque to the composer **Johann Christian Bach** (1735–82), the youngest son of J. S. Bach. He is often referred to as 'the London Bach', as he spent the last 20 years of his life in London, where he became an influential and successful composer and performer. Another musician buried here, but with no memorial, is **Karl Friedrich Abel** (1723–87), the German composer and viola da gamba virtuoso, who had a successful career in London, working in collaboration with J. C. Bach. The satirist **Edward (Ned) Ward** (1667–1731) also has no memorial. He is best known as the author of the hugely popular *The London Spy*, a book that exposed the seedy side of life in London. The most eccentric character to be buried here was the **Chevalier D'Éon** (1728–1810), who was a French soldier, diplomat, spy and transvestite. He was a fine swordsman and gave fencing exhibitions dressed as a woman. During his last years he lived as a woman in a boarding house in Bloomsbury, and his landlady was shocked to discover on his death that he was a

The baroque cartouche to the great miniaturist, Samuel Cooper, in St Pancras Old Church.

man. The infamous thief-taker **Jonathan Wild** (1683–1725) was briefly buried here after his execution at Tyburn, but was later dug up, and what is said to be his skeleton is now displayed in the Hunterian Museum in Lincoln's Inn Fields. **Samuel Cooper** (1607–72), the miniature painter, is buried in the church, and he has a monument on the east wall. Cooper was hugely successful, producing 'warts and all' portraits of Oliver Cromwell and, after the Restoration, of Charles II and several of his mistresses.

St James Gardens, down an alley on the east side of Hampstead Road, was bought in 1788 as an additional burial ground for St James, Piccadilly, and a chapel was built in 1793, but this was later demolished. At one time there were

The curious cross marking the grave of auctioneer James Christie in St James Gardens.

about 50,000 burials here, but in 1887 it was turned into a public garden, and most of the gravestones were removed and laid around its perimeter. At the entrance is a curious cross, the memorial to the Christie family, including **James Christie** (1730–1803), who founded the famous auction house in 1766, which still operates in St James's. Christie was involved in many great sales, including the studio sale after Gainsborough's death, and he also valued the collection of Sir Robert Walpole, which

was sold to Catherine the Great. Other important people buried here, but with no memorial, are the celebrated portrait painter **John Hoppner** (1758–1810), **George Morland** (1763–1804), an artist who painted landscapes and genre scenes, and **John Charles Felix Rossi** (1762–1839), a sculptor who created several major memorials for St Paul's Cathedral. Also buried here were **Matthew Flinders** (1774–1814), the explorer who surveyed much of the coast of Australia, and **William Roy** (1726–90), the eminent surveyor who founded what was later called the Ordnance Survey.

LONDON BOROUGH OF ENFIELD

In the south-western part of the churchyard of All Saints, Edmonton, is the grave of writer **Charles Lamb** (1775–1834). Although he worked for 33 years as a clerk for the East India Company, he was a prolific author, writing poetry and essays, using the pseudonym Elia. With his sister, Mary, who is buried with him, he wrote *Tales of Shakespeare*, re-telling the stories for children. After Mary had killed her mother in a fit of madness, Charles cared for her, and they moved several times, lastly to Edmonton, where their cottage can still be seen in Church Street.

In the graveyard of the Winchmore Hill Friends Meeting House in Church Hill N21 is buried **Luke Howard** (1772–1864), the chemist and meteorologist who created the classification of clouds, a system that is still in use today. The location of his grave had been lost for many years, but it is now marked by a new headstone, which stands alone, just behind the meeting house.

The grave of the writer Charles Lamb and his sister in the graveyard of All Saints Edmonton.

Luke Howard, whose classification of clouds is still used, was buried at the Winchmore Hill Friends Meeting House.

LONDON BOROUGH OF HARINGEY

Tottenham Cemetery, in Prospect Place N17, which opened in 1856, is a large, sprawling space, situated to the north of the medieval All Hallows church. Its most famous inhabitant is **William Butterfield** (1814–1900), the architect of many High Victorian churches in the Gothic style. His most important London church is All Saints, Margaret Street, with its polychromatic brickwork and ornately decorated interior. He designed his own grave in the Gothic style, with a carved cross on top. The easiest way to find his grave is to take the path north from the graveyard of All Hallows (one of many churches he restored); it is just

The great Victorian architect, William Butterfield, is buried in Tottenham Cemetery in a grave of his own design.

inside a gate on the right. The grave was restored in 2014 with funds raised by the Ecclesiological Society, who had been ardent supporters of Butterfield.

HIGHGATE CEMETERY

Highgate Cemetery is London's most famous cemetery, due to the presence of the grave of Karl Marx, which draws many thousands of visitors every year. It was the third of the 'Magnificent Seven' cemeteries to open, created in 1839 by the London Cemetery Company. In 1860 an extension on the eastern side of Swain's Lane was opened, adding another 19 acres. For many years it was a highly profitable commercial enterprise, but by the 1970s it was no longer viable and the company closed it, leaving it open to vandalism and allowing nature to take its course. In 1975 the Friends of Highgate Cemetery were founded, and they now manage it, restoring its monuments and landscape. The Eastern Cemetery is open daily and there is a small admission charge. To visit the Western Cemetery you have to take a guided tour. There is one tour on weekdays, and at the weekend there are tours throughout the day. See the website for further details: www.highgatecemetery.org.

The Eastern Cemetery has one main path, which goes round in a loop. The route described follows this circuit, but with a number of diversions. Take the first path on the right to see the grave of **Leslie Hutchinson** (1900–69), the Caribbean entertainer known as Hutch, the most popular cabaret star of the 1920s and '30s. He made his name as a pianist and singer in Paris, and later had a successful career in London, appearing in cabaret and West End revues. After the Second World War he went out of fashion and, sadly, only 42 people attended his funeral. Back on the main path, to the right of the Dalziel mausoleum, by the path, is the grave of

Lesley Hutchinson, known as 'Hutch', was a popular cabaret artist of the 1920s and '30s.

The novelist George Eliot (see page 176) is buried next to her long-term partner, whom she could not marry.

The grave of Bruce Reynolds, who was a key player in the Great Train Robbery.

The gravestone of Shura Cherkassky, one of the greatest pianists of the twentieth century, carries his signature in Russian.

Herbert 'Bert' Jansch (1943–2011), the award-winning Scottish singer and composer, who was a key figure in the 1960s folk music revival. He died of cancer in a hospice in Hampstead. To the left of the mausoleum is the grave of playwright **Anthony Shaffer** (1926–2001), whose most famous play, *Sleuth*, was a massive hit in the West End and on Broadway, and was later made into a successful film. On the reverse of the headstone is carved the logo of the film of *Sleuth*.

Almost directly opposite is the grave of **Bruce Reynolds** (1931–2013), the criminal who is best known for his part in the Great Train Robbery of 1963. His ashes were buried at Highgate on the 50th anniversary of the robbery, and the headstone bears the inscription 'C'est la Vie', the words he uttered when he was arrested in 1968. The bronze death mask was created by his son, Nick. A little further down, on the right, is the grave of **William Alfred Westropp Foyle** (1885–1963), founder of the famous bookshop in Charing Cross Road. To the left of the path is the simple headstone of **Corin Redgrave** (1939–

2010), the well-known film and theatre actor. He was also a political activist and a member of the Workers' Revolutionary Party. On the opposite side of the path is the grave of the great Russian pianist **Shura Cherkassky** (1909–95). His family fled from the Russian Revolution and settled in America and in 1961 he moved to London, though he continued to perform around the world. Almost opposite is the memorial to **Douglas Adams** (1952–2001), the acclaimed author of the hugely successful *The Hitch-Hiker's Guide to the Galaxy*, which began as a radio comedy series before being adapted for television. So many fans stuck pens in the earth around the grave that a pot has now been placed there to keep it tidy.

Take the next path on the right for a short detour. A simple cross marks the grave of **Frank Matcham** (1854–1920), the architect who built many theatres the length and breadth of Britain, famed for their exuberant interiors. In London he built the London Coliseum, the Hackney Empire and the London Palladium. Continue up this path and then left to find, by the external fence, the white Gothic memorial

The grave of Frank Matcham, an architect who is famous for his many theatres up and down the country.

The grave of Douglas Adams, author of *The Hitch-Hiker's Guide to the Galaxy* is regularly visited by his many fans, who often leave pens.

to **William Friese-Greene** (1855–1921), the inventor and photographer who is credited with the invention of motion pictures, or Kinematography, as it is spelt on the monument. The inscription includes his patent number, 10,131. At the time of his burial, a two-minute silence was observed in many of the country's cinemas.

Return to the main path, take the right fork and on the left is the grave of the author **Alan Sillitoe** (1928–2010), best known for his novel *Saturday Night and Sunday Morning* and the short story *The Loneliness of the Long-Distance Runner*, both of which were made into successful films. Further down, on the left, is the grave of

The Gothic memorial to William Friese-Green, the father of the cinema.

The simple headstone of Alan Sillitoe, a novelist who wrote about the life of the working classes and is often considered one of the 'angry young men'.

Sir Colin St John Wilson's grave is in the form of the entrance to the British Library, his most important building.

Sir Colin St John Wilson (1922–2007), the architect of the British Library, which opened in 1997 and is now a Grade 1 listed building. His grave has been designed in the form of its main entrance. Further down on the right is the grave of the artist **Patrick Caulfield** (1936–2005), with its highly original headstone with the word DEAD cut out of the stone. His work is characterised by its use of bold colour and strong outlines, and he designed his own gravestone. Almost directly opposite is the rather more traditional ledger of the great actor **Sir Ralph Richardson** (1902–83) who, after many years of acting in the plays of Shakespeare, Shaw and Priestley, turned to modern plays by Orton and Pinter. Just after the next path, in the second row on the right, is the simple cross of the grave of **Sir Eyre Massey Shaw** (1828–1908), who helped to create the Metropolitan Fire Brigade, which he ran for nearly 30 years. He was a known womaniser, and he was in the audience on the first night of

Patrick Caulfield's unusual gravestone has the word DEAD as his only epitaph.

books, which explains his memorial. Just after the next path on the left is the grave of the actress **Sheila Gish** (1942–2005), with a star cut out of the stone. A versatile actress, she was particularly associated with the plays of Tennessee Williams. Further down, on the left, is the black marble headstone to **Malcolm Robert Andrew McLaren** (1946–2010), who was an influential figure in the punk movement. His gravestone has a bronze death mask by Nick Reynolds, son of Bruce Reynolds, the Great Train Robber.

Gilbert and Sullivan's *Iolanthe*, when the love-sick fairy queen first sang the line 'Oh Captain Shaw'.

A short way down, on the right, is the grave of the broadcaster **Jeremy Beadle** (1948–2008), with its shelf of books. He was best known as the presenter of television programmes such as *Game for a Laugh*, and he was once voted the most hated man in Britain because of the pranks featured in his shows. Privately, he was very well read, with a huge collection of

Continue all the way round the main path until you come to Highgate's most famous resident, **Karl Marx** (1818–83), the political philosopher and author of the revolutionary book *Das Kapital*. He spent much of his life in London, studying at the British Museum, always short of money and living off his friends. He and his family were originally buried in a modest plot about 100 yards south of the present memorial, which was erected in 1956 with a monumental bronze bust by Laurence Bradshaw. It has become a place

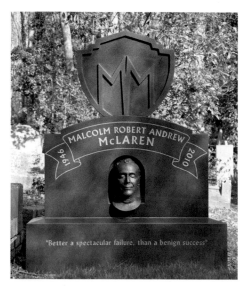

Malcolm McLaren, an important figure in the punk movement, gave himself an unusual epitaph, 'Better a spectacular failure than a benign success'..

Opposite Karl Marx is the grave of the philosopher Herbert Spencer.

of pilgrimage but, sadly, it has also been the target of vandals, and in 1970 there was an attempt to blow it up. As well as Marx and his wife, their youngest daughter **Eleanor Marx** (1855–98) is also buried here. She wrote her father's biography and wrote and campaigned tirelessly for workers'

and women's rights. She was cremated in Woking, where her ashes remained until they were interred with her parents when the new monument was installed.

A number of radical figures are now gathered around Marx. To the left is the grave of **Claudia Vera Jones** (1915–64), a Trinidadian journalist who became involved in the civil rights movement, first in America and later in England. In 1958 she took part in the protests against the race riots in Notting Hill, and a year later organised an annual event that developed into the Notting Hill Carnival. Immediately opposite Marx's tomb is the sarcophagus of **Herbert Spencer** (1820–1903), the philosopher who developed an evolutionary theory four years before Darwin published *The Origin of Species*, and coined the phrase 'survival of the fittest'. To the right is the simple headstone of **Paul Foot** (1937–2004), the left-wing investigative journalist, who was a member of the Socialist Workers' Party and wrote regularly for *Private Eye*. Over to the right, a few rows back, is the grave of **Eric Hobsbawm** (1917–2012), the eminent historian who, as a committed Marxist and a life-long member of the Communist Party, wrote many articles for *Marxism Today*.

To the north is the grave of the Polish-born artist **Feliks Topolski** (1907–89). He settled in London in 1935, where he built a reputation designing book covers and stage sets, and was an official war artist. He also produced murals, such as *Memoir of the Century*, which is displayed under the arches

Opposite: Karl Marx's monument has been a place of pilgrimage since it was erected in 1956.

The grave of the Polish artist Feliks Topolski.

Max Wall had a varied career, from the music hall to Samuel Beckett.

of Hungerford Bridge on the South Bank in what was his studio. Three rows behind is the simple grave of comedian and actor **Max Wall** (1908–90), whose real name was Maxwell George Lorimer. A major music hall star, he went on to work in radio and television, his best known role being Professor Wallofski, dressed in black tights, black wig and huge boots. With the decline of variety, he carved out a new career in the theatre, performing in the works of Samuel Beckett.

Return to the Marx memorial and turn right, then right again. The obelisk on the right marks the last resting place of the great novelist **George Eliot** (1819–80), the pen-name of Marian Evans (see page 168). She began her literary career writing for the *Westminster Review*, where she met George Henry Lewes, with whom she had a life-

long relationship, though they could never marry as he already had a wife. He is buried in the grave behind hers. With novels such as *Silas Marner* and *Middlemarch*, she became a celebrity and her work is still popular today. Because of her unconventional life, and because she was not a Christian, it was deemed inappropriate for her to be buried in Westminster Abbey. Return to the main path, turn right and take the next path on the right. A short way up on the right, in the third row, is the grave of the Australian artist **Sir Sidney Nolan** (1917–92), famous for his series of paintings of Ned Kelly, the notorious bushranger and folk hero. He spent many years working in London, where he designed sets for opera and ballet as well as book covers. Almost opposite, in the second row to the left of the path, is the grave of the architect

The grave of Sir Leslie Stephen, who founded the *Dictionary of National Biography*.Beckett.

Charles John Phipps (1835–97), marked by a stone cross. Less well known than his rival, Matcham, he is, nevertheless an important figure in the late-nineteenth-century flowering of theatre building. His most important buildings are the Savoy Theatre, the Lyceum and Her Majesty's Theatre. Continue up this path and turn right up a side path where, up against the boundary wall is the grave, with lilies carved on the headstone, of **Sir Leslie Stephen** (1832–1904), the writer whose most important legacy is the *Dictionary of National Biography*, which he edited for ten years. He was the father of the novelist Virginia Woolf and the artist Vanessa Bell.

Although the Western Cemetery has been tidied up since it reopened in the 1970s, it still has more of a wild and romantic feel than the Eastern Cemetery.

Tours last about an hour and do not take you round the whole site, so some of the graves mentioned here may not be seen on a tour.

A short way up the main central path, on the right, is the fine chest tomb of **Edward Blore** (1787–1879), the architect who completed the construction of Buckingham Palace for Queen Victoria. He also worked at Windsor Castle and Hampton Court, and built a large number of country houses. He was known as 'the cheap architect' because he always kept to his estimates. At the first junction, to the left, is the grave of **Alexander Litvinenko** (1962–2006), the Russian ex-secret service officer who was killed in London with the radioactive poison polonium-210. In Russia he had accused his superiors of corruption, and fled to Britain where he was granted asylum. He worked as a journalist and repeated his earlier allegations openly. The public enquiry in 2015 named the main suspects and claimed the murder was approved by senior figures in Russia, though they are unlikely to be brought to trial. At the next junction, an obelisk marks the grave of the Wyatt family, including the sculptor **Matthew Cotes Wyatt** (1777–1862). His most admired work is the equestrian statue of George III in Pall Mall, but he also produced a colossal equestrian statue of the Duke of Wellington for the Constitution Arch at Hyde Park Corner, which was widely ridiculed, and was eventually taken down.

By the side of the path opposite the Wyatt memorial is the dark granite chest tomb of the great artist **Lucian Freud** (1922–2011). The grandson of Sigmund Freud, he was considered to be the greatest

The dark granite chest tomb of the great artist Lucian Freud.

Alexander Litvinenko's grave is designed as a modern broken column, denoting a life cut tragically short.

figurative painter of his time, specialising in portraits and fleshy nudes. His funeral, which was a private family occasion, was conducted by Dr Rowan Williams, the then Archbishop of Canterbury. A little further on, on the right, is the simple ledger stone to **James Bunstone Bunning** (1802–63), the architect who was surveyor to the London Cemetery Company, working at both Highgate and Nunhead. The path going left from the Wyatt memorial takes you round a curve, and up a side path on the left is the grave of the Rossetti family. Here is the poet **Christina Georgina Rossetti** (1830–94), the younger sister of the artist, Dante Gabriel Rossetti, for whom she often sat as a model. Also buried here

is **Elizabeth Eleanor (Lizzie) Siddal** (1829–62), the model and later the wife of Dante Gabriel. She sat for other members of the Pre-Raphaelite Brotherhood, most notably as the drowned Ophelia for Millais. She died of an overdose of laudanum and Rossetti placed a book of his unpublished poems in her coffin. He later regretted this act, and obtained permission to exhume her body so the book could be retrieved and the poems could be published.

Return to the Wyatt memorial and continue up the central path. Over to the

Buried in the Rossetti family grave are the poet Christina Rossetti and Lizzie Siddal, Dante Gabriel Rossetti's wife.

The controversial novelist Radclyffe Hall is buried in this vault with her first partner.

The mausoleum of Carl Rosa, whose eponymous opera company performed opera in English.

right, and now inaccessible, is the simple headstone marking the grave of **Stephen Geary** (1794–1854), the architect who created Highgate Cemetery. A little further on to the right is the tomb of **Charles Alfred Cruft** (1852–1938), who founded the prestigious Cruft's Dog Show, which is still held annually. On the left is the astonishing Egyptian Avenue, the entrance to the Circle of Lebanon, which is surrounded by vaults. In one of the vaults is buried **Marguerite Antonia Radclyffe-Hall** (1880–1943), the author of the controversial novel *The Well of Loneliness*, which was banned in England because of its depiction of lesbianism; it wasn't published in Britain until 1949. Using the pseudonym

Radclyffe Hall, she wrote six other novels, as well as poetry. She is buried in the vault of her first partner, Mabel Batten, and a plaque to the left of the door was placed there by her later companion, Una Troubridge. Here, too, are a number of mausolea, including that of **Carl Rosa** (1842–89), founder of the eponymous opera company, which performed in London and the provinces, offering opera in English. Looming over the Circle of Lebanon is the huge family mausoleum built by **Julius Beer** (1836–80), the German-born financier who owned *The Observer* newspaper. The interior has a domed ceiling with Salviati mosaics and a sculpture of his daughter Ada, who died young.

IN MEMORY
OF
ANN WOMBWELL,
WIDOW,
DIED 1st SEPTEMBER 1876
AGED 88

TO THE MEMORY
OF
GEORGE WOMBWELL
(MENAGERIST)
BORN 24th DECr 1777
DIED 1st NOVr 1850

The sarcophagus of Mrs Henry Wood, the author of popular sentimental novels.

Up some steps to the west of the Circle of Lebanon is the impressive pink granite sarcophagus of **Mrs Henry Wood** (1814–87), the popular novelist. She was married to a shipping agent, whom she supported with her writing after he retired early. Her most successful novel was *East Lynne*, which was a blend of the sentimental and the sensational. She asked for a quiet funeral, but it attracted a large crowd. Close by is the grave of **George Wombwell** (1777–1850), the proprietor of a celebrated travelling menagerie, which included many exotic animals from around the world. It is marked by a statue of a sleeping lion, based on Nero, his most famous exhibit. Further south, but not accessible, are the graves of the family of Charles Dickens. Buried here are his parents, **Elizabeth** (1789–1863) and **John** (1785–1851), and his long-suffering wife **Catherine** (1815–79).

A short walk east of the Circle of Lebanon is the grave of **Frederick Warne** (1825–1901), the publisher of books by Edward Lear, Kate Greenaway and, most famously, Beatrix Potter. Nearby is the tomb of **Tom Sayers** (1826–65), one of the last of the bare-knuckle fighters, and the most celebrated of his day. More than 10,000 people attended his funeral, and his dog Lion had its own carriage in the cortège. On front of the chest tomb is a portrait medallion of Sayers, and it is guarded by a sculpture of Lion. Take the main path back past Egyptian Avenue and then the next path round to the left. A short distance along it, on the right, is the curious tomb of **Francis Montague Holl** (1845–88), with its grave marker standing on top of a large stone block. Holl was an artist who painted scenes from everyday life, including scenes of grief and tragedy, depicting the life of the poor. He later became a very successful portrait painter of the great and the good. Just round the next bend is the grave of novelist

Frederick Warne was the publisher of Beatrix Potter and Kate Greenaway.

Opposte: Nero the Lion guards the tomb of George Wombwell, the menagerist.

The grave of the pugilist Tom Sayers is watched over by his dog, Lion.

Dame Beryl Bainbridge (1932–2010). She won many awards for her writing, and was shortlisted five times for the Booker Prize, whose judges gave her a special posthumous award.

A short distance away, in an unconsecrated area by the outer wall of the cemetery, is the grave of the great scientist **Michael Faraday** (1791–1867), who is most famous for his work on electromagnetism. He was an elder of the Sandemanian church, a sect of primitive Christianity, and was buried according to their practice in silence and with no ceremony. Continue round the bend and at the bottom of the slope, on the left, is the simple headstone of **Philip Harben** (1906–70), the popular television chef. Self-taught, Harben's broadcasting career began, somewhat bizarrely, giving cooking demonstrations on the radio. Close by is the grave of the actor **Patrick Wymark** (1926–70), real name Patrick Carl Cheeseman, who worked in film, theatre and television. On the other side of the path is a plaque to **Jacob Bronowski** (1908–74), the mathematician who is best remembered for his ground-breaking television series *The Ascent of Man*, in which he explained to a lay audience the development of science.

A number of other important figures are buried in the Western Cemetery, but their graves are not seen on a tour. They include:

Edward Hodges Baily (1788–1867), the sculptor who is best known for his statue of Nelson in Trafalgar Square.

Henry Hugh Armstead (1828–1905), the sculptor who, with John Birnie Philip, worked on the frieze of the Albert Memorial.

Samuel Sanders Teulon (1812–73), an architect who designed many churches in his own idiosyncratic Gothic style.

Sir James Pennethorne (1801–71), a pupil of John Nash who spent much of his career working on metropolitan improvements, designing parks and new streets, but also built the former Public Record Office in Chancery Lane.

Henry Wallis (1830–1916), the artist best known for his *The Death of Chatterton*.

Sir William Charles Ross (1794–1860), the finest miniaturist of his age, who became 'Miniature Painter' to Queen Victoria.

Albert Joseph Moore (1841–93), a member of the aesthetic movement, specialising in painting women in classical dress.

Stella Gibbons (1902–89), the novelist who wrote the comic classic *Cold Comfort Farm*.

Henry Gray (1826/7–61), the surgeon who wrote the influential *Anatomy, Descriptive and Surgical*, usually shortened to *Gray's Anatomy*, which is still in print today.

Henry Willis (1821–1901), the famous organ builder, who created the organs at St Paul's Cathedral and the Royal Albert Hall.

Rowland Mason Ordish (1824–86), the engineer who designed the Albert Bridge and helped William Barlow in the design of the roof of St Pancras Station.

David Devant (1868–1941), the great magician, many of whose illusions are still performed today.

The grave of the popular novelist Beryl Bainbridge.

GOLDERS GREEN CREMATORIUM

THE FIRST CREMATORIUM in England opened in Woking in 1885, followed by five more in the north of the country. London had to wait until 1902, when the London Cremation Society opened Golders Green Crematorium in what was then a rural location within driving distance of central London. It has since become the best known and most respected of all Britain's crematoria, and over 300,000 cremations have taken place there since it opened. The dignified red-brick buildings in Lombardic style were designed by Sir Ernest George and Alfred Yeates, and the restful gardens were laid out by William Robinson.

If you visit on a weekday, you can collect a map and guide from Reception, where you can also ask to visit the columbaria, which are normally locked for security reasons. There are also maps posted around the grounds. Many famous people have been cremated there, some of whose ashes have been buried or dispersed elsewhere. The guide informs you of those whose ashes are either in one of the columbaria, scattered on the lawn or buried under a rosebush or

tree. There are many plaques on the walls commemorating people whose ashes have been dispersed or interred here, too many to be listed in these pages, and what follows is just a selection.

In the West Memorial Court there are plaques to entertainers and musicians whose ashes were scattered on the lawn, including the formidable harmonica player **Larry Adler** (1914–2001), jazz musicians **Tubby Hayes** (1935–73) and **Ronnie Scott** (1927–96), comedian **Bernie Winters** (1930–91), and rock legend **Keith Moon** (1946–78). Other plaques are to novelist and scriptwriter **Wolf Mankowitz** (1924–98), **Alexander Baron** (1917–99), the author of gritty novels set in the East End, and **Cyril Lord** (1911–84), the textile millionaire. On the north wall is a plaque to singer and comedian **Bud Flanagan** (1896–1968), famous as one of the 'Crazy Gang', who recorded the music for *Dad's Army*. His ashes are in a niche behind the plaque. A few plaques are to people whose ashes are interred here, who will get a separate mention. They are **John Stephen** (1934–2004), the 1960s fashion designer known as the 'king of Carnaby Street', rock star **Marc Bolan** (1947–77), and the impresario **Val Parnell** (1892–1972).

Opposite: The ashes of Sir Henry Thompson (see overleaf), the founder of the Cremation Society, are in the West Columbarium.

IN EVERLASTING MEMORY
OF
BUD FLANAGAN
(WINTHROP)
DIED 20th OCTOBER 1968
HIS DEVOTED WIFE
ANN (CURLY)
DIED 30th MAY 1975
AND THEIR SON
BUDDY
DIED 29th FEBRUARY 1956
TOGETHER AGAIN

IN MEMORY OF
BERNIE
WINTERS
DEARLY LOVED
HUSBAND AND FATHER
WHO DIED ON
4th MAY 1991.
*You are in our hearts
always.*

The plaques to Bud Flanagan and Bernie Winters in the West Memorial Court.

On the outside wall is a plaque to talent show host **Hughie Green** (1920–97), and on the wall of the West Columbarium to the east is a simple plaque to the versatile TV actor **Ian Hendry** (1931–84). In the West Columbarium itself is the casket containing the ashes of **Sir Henry Thompson** (1820–1904), the surgeon who founded the Cremation Society, of which he was the president, and who helped to create Golders Green Crematorium. He also has a bust in the West Chapel.

On the west wall of the first bay of the West Cloister are plaques to the sculptor **Sir William Reynolds-Stephens** (1862–1943) and the romantic novelist **Elinor Glyn** (1864–1943). In the fifth bay is a colourful ceramic plaque to

Havelock Ellis (1859–1939), author of the controversial but influential *Studies in the Psychology of Sex*. In the seventh bay is the circular ceramic plaque to the society portrait painter **John Collier** (1850–1934). Four bays further east is the simple stone plaque to **Sir Ernest George** (1839–1922), the architect who designed the buildings here. In the Anna Pavlova Rose Bed opposite is where the ashes of **Max Jaffa** (1911–91), the popular violinist and band leader, are interred. Six bays further on is a plaque to **Eric Coates** (1886–1957), the composer of light music, famous for the *Dambusters March*. The next bay is an elaborate memorial to **William Robinson** (1838–1935), the gardener who laid out the gardens of the crematorium. The Latin

The urn containing the ashes of Bram Stoker, the author of *Dracula*.

inscription states that 'Those who walk in a garden can hear the voice of God'.

Just past the West Cloister is the East Columbarium, where on the ground floor are the remains of **Abraham (Bram) Stoker** (1847–1912), who worked for many years as Henry Irving's business manager at the Lyceum, but is more famous as the author of the novel *Dracula*.

In Cloister Walk Rose Bed A are buried the ashes of the popular violinist and 1950s band leader **Cyril Stapleton** (1914–74). He also has a plaque on the east wall in Bay 30. In Bed B are the ashes of the famous ballet dancer **Dame Marie Rambert** (1888–1982), whose dance company continues to flourish. On the wall to the left of the entrance to the Ernest George

Columbarium are plaques to **Benjamin Frankel** (1906–73), the composer of film music, and the popular TV magician **Robert Harbin** (1908–78).

The most famous remains are housed in the Ernest George Columbarium. To the right is the urn containing the ashes of **Anna Pavlova** (1881–1931), one of the most famous ballerinas of all time. Figurines of the dancer and a swan flank the urn, though her ballet shoes were stolen some time ago. Pavlova performed many times in London and in 1914 made her home in Golders Green. In 1993 Russia asked for her ashes to be returned to Moscow, and arrangements were made for the transfer, but at the last moment the request was withdrawn, and

The ashes of the great ballerina, Anna Pavlova, are in the Ernest George Columbarium. Her ballet shoes were originally on display here, but were stolen some years ago.

Pavlova's ashes now remain at Golders Green in perpetuity.

To the left is the last resting place of **Sigmund Freud** (1856–1939), the Austrian founder of psychoanalysis. Freud escaped from Nazi-occupied Vienna in 1938 and spent the last 15 months of his life in Hampstead, where his home is now a museum. His ashes, along with those of his wife, are contained in an ancient Greek urn, which was part of his own collection. On New Year's Day 2014, an attempt was made to steal the urn, which was smashed and left scattered on the floor. It has now been painstakingly restored and replaced on its plinth. The ashes of other members of his family are also here, including his youngest daughter **Anna Freud** (1895–1982), who was also a psychoanalyst, specialising in the study of children.

There are several other important people in the Ernest George Columbarium, including the sculptor **Sir George Frampton** (1860–1928), best known for his statue of Peter Pan in Kensington Gardens, and **Dame Adeline Geneé** (1878–1970), the Danish-born ballet dancer who has a theatre named after her in East Grinstead. Sharing a niche are the ashes of **Simon Marks** (1888–1964) and **Israel Sieff** (1889–1972), who together worked to make the retailer Marks & Spencer the business it is today.

In the East Cloister, high up on one of the arches, is a bust of **Ivor Novello** (1893–1951), the popular composer, playwright and actor best known for his musicals and songs such as *Keep the Home Fires Burning* and *We'll Gather Lilacs*. His ashes are, appropriately, interred under a lilac tree in front of the Martin Smith Mausoleum, just a short distance away. From the East Cloister there is access to the Hall of Memory, which is another columbarium. Go down the steps to the right to find the urn containing the ashes of **Frank Pick** (1878–1941) in a niche straight ahead. Pick was the man responsible for developing the Underground's identity and visual style, commissioning artists to create original advertising posters and architects to design distinctive new stations. On the top floor are the remains of the artist **Percy Wyndham Lewis** (1882–1957), a founder member of the short-lived Vorticist movement. He was an official war artist in the First World War, producing two of his finest paintings.

Beyond the East Cloister is a wall of plaques curving round and up the eastern side of the gardens. In Bay 8, overlooking the Cloister Garden, are plaques to the bandleader **Ray Ellington** (1916–85) and the comedian **Peter Sellers** (1925–80), whose ashes are under a rose bush a few yards away. On the buttress between bays 20/21 is a stone plaque to **Emanuel (Manny) Shinwell** (1884–1986), the legendary left-wing politician who had a very long career, serving under Ramsay MacDonald, Attlee and Harold Wilson. In Bay 27 is a small plaque to the rock 'n' roll star **Johnny Kidd** (1935–66), leader of The Pirates, who was killed in a car accident.

Under a cypress tree in Eastern Bed B is **Val Parnell** (1892–1972), the theatre impresario who was famous for his variety shows, including the television show 'Sunday Night at the London Palladium'. In section K of the East Central Bed, alongside the main lawn, are the ashes of **Bernard Bresslaw** (1934–93), the actor best known for his roles in the 'Carry On' films. Further up, in the Keats bed overlooking the Cedar Lawn, is buried the popular dance bandleader **Victor Silvester** (1900–78). In the top left-hand corner is a summer house, which has simple memorials to the actor **David Kossoff** (1919–2005) and his son **Paul Kossoff** (1950–76), the legendary rock guitarist.

Sigmund Freud's ashes are contained in an antique Greek urn, which has been restored after an attempt was made to steal it.

John Stephen (1934–2004) is buried with his partner Bill Franks by the New Pond, where there is a plaque. On the Cedar Lawn West bed were scattered the ashes of the famous Irish playwright **Sean O'Casey** (1880–1964). Nearby, in West Statue Bed 5 under a rose bush, are buried the ashes of the legendary rock musician **Marc Bolan** (1947–77). A wooden T-Rex bench overlooks the spot.

Finally, here is a small selection of the many celebrities whose ashes have been scattered on the crocus lawn. Among the many actors are **Sir Cedric Hardwicke** (1893–1964), **Jack Hawkins** (1910–73), 'Carry On' star **Sidney (Sid) James** (1913–76), character actress **Irene Handl** (1901–87), and the inimitable **Joyce Grenfell** (1910–79). Musicians include the composer **Richard Addinsell** (1904–77), who wrote the 'Warsaw' concerto, and pianist **Dame Myra Hess** (1890–1965), famous for her recitals at the National Gallery during the Second World War. Among writers whose ashes have been scattered here are the novelist **Leslie Poles (L. P.) Hartley** (1895–1972), and the notorious playwright **Joe Orton** (1933–67), whose ashes were mingled with those of his lover **Kenneth Halliwell** (1926–67), who murdered him before committing suicide.

Artists include **Charles Ginner** (1878–1952), founder member of the Camden Town Group, and **Ben Nicholson** (1894–1982), the abstract artist who was married to Barbara Hepworth. Also here are the architects **Charles Francis Annesley Voysey** (1857–1941), famous for his interior designs, and **Ernö Goldfinger** (1902–87), whose modernist house in

Marc Bolan's ashes are buried under a rose bush.

Hampstead is now owned by the National Trust and open to the public.

Also scattered here were the ashes of **Sir Isaac Pitman** (1813–97), who devised the famous shorthand system, legendary footballer **Alex James** (1901–53), **Sir Neville Cardus** (1888–1975), the celebrated writer on music and cricket, and **Sir Bernard Spilsbury** (1877–1947), the eminent forensic pathologist whose evidence helped to convict Dr Crippen.

Opposite: Ivor Novello's ashes are buried, appropriately, under a lilac tree.

EAST LONDON

LONDON BOROUGH OF HACKNEY

ST LEONARD'S SHOREDITCH is very close to the site of the first purpose-built London playhouse, called The Theatre, which opened in 1576, so it is no surprise that a number of actors associated with the theatre are buried here. Their graves have long since disappeared, but in the church is a memorial to them at the top of the south staircase, erected in 1913 by the London Shakespeare League. Among them are **James Burbage** (*c*. 1531–97), who founded the theatre, his eldest son, **Cuthbert Burbage** (1564–1636), who arranged for the theatre to be dismantled and re-erected on Bankside as the Globe, and the younger son, **Richard Burbage** (1568–1619), one of the finest actors of the era, who played many of Shakespeare's greatest roles. Also buried here were **William Somer** (d. 1559), the court fool, **Richard Tarlton** (d. 1588), the celebrated clown, and **Gabriel Spencer** (*c*. 1572–98), the actor who was killed in a duel by Ben Jonson. From a much later

period, the surgeon **James Parkinson** (1755–1824) was buried here, and he has a memorial in the south aisle of the

The memorial in St Leonard's Shoreditch to the actors buried there, all of them associated with the Elizabethan theatres that operated in the neighbourhood.

Opposite: The grave of Herbert Campbell, (see overleaf) one of many music hall stars buried in Abney Park Cemetery.

George Leybourne and Albert Chevalier, two music hall stars united by marriage, are buried in the same grave in Abney Park. Chevalier's rather extravagant full name was Albert Onésime Britannicus Gwathveoyd Louis Chevalier.

church. He first described the disease 'shaking palsy', which is now known as Parkinson's disease.

Abney Park Cemetery in Stoke Newington was for many years the principal burial place for dissenters. It opened in 1840, by which time Bunhill Fields had become full. The 30-acre cemetery was created by the Abney Park Cemetery Company on the estate of Abney House, the home of the leading nonconformist, Sir Thomas Abney. In 1979 it was bought for £1 by the Borough of Hackney, which has slowly but surely restored it. Very few burials take place here, but it is now an important nature reserve, with many different species of shrubs and trees. Just inside the Egyptian-style entrance gates is an information centre, which has trail leaflets, maps and an excellent guide to the cemetery.

Take the central path ahead of you, called New Road, and on the right is an information panel on music hall stars buried in the cemetery. Visible from here is the pink granite obelisk that is a memorial to **Herbert Campbell** (1844–1904), a popular singer of comic songs and a great pantomime star at Drury Lane, often in partnership with Dan Leno. He is actually buried in the family grave, marked by a white marble headstone beside the obelisk, which was erected by his friends. About 40 yards further on there is a narrow path on the right which leads to the grave, in the third row, of the music-hall stars **George Leybourne** (1842–84) and **Albert Chevalier** (1861–1923). Leybourne performed under the name Champagne Charlie, the name of the song that made him famous. He had many other hit songs, including *The Daring Young Man on the Flying Trapeze*. His daughter Florence married Chevalier, a comedy actor whose most successful songs were *My Old Dutch* and *Knocked 'em in the Old Kent Road*. Nearby is the newly restored grave of **Nelly Power** (1854–87), the music hall performer who was the first to sing the popular song *The Boy I Love is Up in the Gallery*.

Continue along New Road, take the next left and go across the next junction. On the left by the path is the chest tomb of **James (Bronterre) O'Brien** (1804–64), one of the most prominent Chartists, along with Feargus O'Connor, with whom O'Brien had a falling out. He gave voice to his radical views as a journalist and editor of various newspapers, and was once imprisoned for sedition. Take the next right and turn right along Road A. Opposite the Church Street Gate are the graves of **William Booth** (1829–1912) and his wife **Catherine Booth** (1829–90), the founders of the Salvation Army, which began life as the Christian Mission in Whitechapel. General Booth's funeral attracted many thousands of people who lined the streets to watch the cortège's progress. The grave consists of a large Salvation Army shield made from blue sandstone. Buried opposite is their eldest son, **William Bramwell Booth** (1856–1929), who succeeded his father as general. Continue along this path and turn right into Branch B, where on the left is the white stone monument

The grave of William and Catherine Booth, founders of the Salvation Army, in Abney Park.

Below: The grave of the menagerist, Frank Bostock, in Abney Park, is marked with a sculpture of a sleeping lion.

to **James Braidwood** (1800–61), who for nearly 30 years was superintendent of the London Fire Engine Establishment. He died when a wall fell on him while fighting the Tooley Street fire. He was so popular that his funeral procession was a mile and a half long. Go up Dr Watts' Walk and turn left into Road F after the Watts statue. At the end of this path on the right is the finest memorial at Abney Park, a splendid sleeping lion marking the grave of menagerie-owner and showman **Frank Charles Bostock** (1866–1912), known as 'The Animal King'. As well as performing lions and tigers, his show featured a boxing kangaroo and a chimpanzee that behaved like a man, drinking, smoking and riding a bike. Turn right and then second right to the ruined chapel, then left and take the right fork to go up Little Elm Walk. About 25 yards before the boundary road, the granite obelisk to **George William Hunt** (1830–1904) can be seen on the right, a few rows back. Hunt wrote songs for the music hall, his most famous song being *Macdermott's War Song* written to support British naval action in the Russo-Turkish war of 1877. Its chorus of 'We don't want to fight, but by jingo if we do, we've got the ships, we've got the men, we've got the money too', gave the word 'jingoism' to the English language.

In the churchyard of St John-at-Hackney, at the northern end of Mare Street E8, is the large chest tomb of **Sir Francis Beaufort** (1774–1857), the naval officer who gave his name to the Beaufort Scale, which measures the strength of the wind. He devised his wind scale while serving on HMS *Woolwich* in 1805, based on the effect wind had on the ship's sails.

LONDON BOROUGH OF WALTHAM FOREST

In St Patrick's Roman Catholic Cemetery in Langthorne Road, Leytonstone E11, are buried two victims of major crimes. Turn left and immediately take the gravel path on the right, then take the path opposite and turn down the next gravel path on the left. About 50 yards on the right, by the path, is the grave of **Timothy John Evans** (1924–50), who was hanged for the murder of his daughter Geraldine. Three years later John Reginald Halliday Christie was found guilty of murdering six women, including Evans' wife, Beryl, and hanged. In 1966 Timothy Evans was given a posthumous pardon and his remains were removed from Pentonville Prison and re-interred here. Return to the chapel and walk round it to the left and up the path by the outer wall. About 50 yards on the right, halfway along a row of simple graves, is that of **Mary Jane Kelly** (1863–88), the last of Jack the Ripper's victims, who was murdered in her room in Miller's Court and brutally mutilated. The funeral was held at St Leonard's church in Shoreditch, and large crowds watched the funeral procession as it made its way to the cemetery. The small headstone bears her

The grave of Mary Kelly, the last of Jack the Ripper's victims, in St Patrick's Roman Catholic Cemetery.

The Kray twins and their family have their own corner of Chingford Mount Cemetery.

The grave of sculptor Joseph Wilton in the graveyard of St Mary the Virgin Wanstead is marked by a shelter that doubled as a lookout for body-snatchers.

given name, Marie Jeanette Kelly, and it is easily found because of the flowers that are regularly left there.

In a quiet corner of Chingford Mount Cemetery, in Old Church Road E4, are buried **Reginald Kray** (1933–2000) and **Ronald Kray** (1933–1995), the infamous and legendary East End criminals, who mingled with film stars and sporting celebrities and inspired many books as well as several films. The twins are buried in the same grave, and portraits are engraved on the black marble headstone. Alongside them are their brother **Charles James Kray** (1926–2000), who aided the twins and, like them, was imprisoned, and their parents, **Violet Kray** (1910–82) and **Charles David Kray** (1906–83). The twins were devoted to their mother, and were allowed

out of prison to attend her funeral. Both of the twins had old-fashioned East End funerals, with plumed black horses pulling a traditional black hearse, followed by a cavalcade of limousines, and they attracted huge crowds, which lined the streets from the church to the cemetery. Also here is the grave of **Frances Kray** (1943–67), Reggie's first wife, who left him after two months and later killed herself.

In 1895 all the coffins at Whitefield's Chapel in Tottenham Court Road were moved to Chingford Mount. Among them were the remains of **John Bacon** (1740–99), the most important sculptor of his time. Some of his finest works are in London, including the monument to Thomas Guy in Guy's Chapel and the statue of William III in St James's Square.

Dr Barnardo's grave
in the grounds of the
home he built for
girls in Barkingside
is marked by an
impressive memorial
by George Frampton.

CHILDREN TO COM
THE KINGDOM OF

IN AS
OF TH

I HOPE TO DIE AS I HAVE LIVED
IN THE HVMBLE BVT ASSVRED FAITH OF
JESVS CHRIST
AS
MY SAVIOVR MY MASTER AND MY KING

LONDON BOROUGH OF REDBRIDGE

In the large churchyard of St Mary the Virgin Wanstead, to the south of the church, is the grave of the sculptor **Joseph Wilton** (1722–1803). It takes the form of a large neo-classical sentry box and was erected in 1813 to commemorate him, but was also used to house a guard to deter body snatchers. Wilton was the most distinguished sculptor of his period, and became sculptor in ordinary to George III. He created the monument to General Wolfe in Westminster Abbey, produced the sculpture for William Chambers' Somerset House, and made the elaborate carving on the royal state coach, which is still used for coronations and other royal occasions.

Off Tanners Lane in Barkingside is Barnardo's Village, a small part of the Girls' Village Home founded by **Thomas John Barnardo** (1845–1905) to house destitute girls. He was a popular social reformer and the streets were lined with large crowds along the funeral route from Liverpool Street Station to Barkingside, where he is buried under the magnificent memorial by George Frampton.

LONDON BOROUGH OF TOWER HAMLETS

In the chapel of St Peter ad Vincula, in the Tower of London, are the bodies of a number of people who were executed at Tower Hill or on Tower Green. **Sir Thomas More** (1478–1535) and **John Fisher** (1469–1535), bishop of Rochester, were both executed on Tower Hill for refusing to accept Henry VIII as head of the English church, and both are now Catholic saints. Their heads were displayed on London Bridge. **Anne Boleyn** (1500–36), Henry VIII's second wife, was accused of adultery and treason and beheaded on Tower Green because she was unable to give the king an heir, and his fifth wife, **Katherine Howard** (1520–42), was executed only six years later. **Thomas Cromwell** (1485–1540) was Henry's principal adviser, but lost the king's favour and was executed on Tower Green. **Lady Jane Grey** (1537–54), whom Edward VI had made his heir, was queen for only nine days before Mary I claimed the throne, and she was executed on Tower Green. **James, Duke of Monmouth** (1649–85), Charles II's illegitimate son, rebelled against James II but was beaten at the battle of Sedgemore and beheaded on Tower Hill. The executioner needed five attempts to finish the job. After the battle of Culloden, several of the Jacobite rebel leaders were brought to London and executed on Tower Hill, including **Simon Fraser, Lord Lovat** (1667–1747), who was the last person to be publicly beheaded in Britain; several spectators were killed when some of the seating collapsed.

LONDON BOROUGH OF NEWHAM

The City of London Cemetery in Aldersbrook Road E12 opened in 1856 to replace the grossly inadequate churchyards of the City, which were now overcrowded and a hazard to public health. Two hundred acres of land near the southern end of Epping Forest were bought and the City Surveyor, William Haywood, designed the buildings in the Gothic style. It is the largest municipal cemetery in Britain, and is well maintained by the City of London.

The monument in the City of London Cemetery that covers the re-interred remains from St Helen's Bishopsgate, including those of Robert Hooke.

On weekdays, a map and history are available from the office. Tours are also on offer; check the website for details: www.cityoflondon.gov.uk/cemetery.

Go straight ahead down Chapel Avenue and on the left is the Gothic mausoleum which contains the ashes of the cemetery's architect, **William Haywood** (1821–94), and which was made to his design. As the City engineer and surveyor, a post he held for almost 50 years, he worked with Joseph Bazalgette on the new sewage system and carried out many street improvements. Inside the mausoleum are busts of Haywood and his wife.

Along both sides of Central Avenue are a number of large monuments which cover the re-interred bones from City churchyards, including, on the right, the church of St Helen's Bishopsgate, where the remains of the polymath **Robert Hooke** (1635–1703) are now buried. Turn left into St Dionis Road and, after the Traditional Crematorium, in the Memorial Garden on the right is a simple plaque under a magnolia to **Bobby Moore** (1941–93), the great football captain who led the England team to victory at the World Cup in 1966. He joined West Ham aged 17 and played over 500 matches for them before joining Fulham, and he captained England 90 times.

Continue up Limes Avenue and turn right into Gardens Way. About 50 yards ahead are the last resting places of two of the five known victims of Jack the Ripper. On the right is **Mary Ann (Polly) Nichols** (1845–88), the first casualty, and a little further on the left is **Catherine Eddowes** (1842–88), who was the fourth. Both were buried in unmarked graves, but plaques now mark their locations.

Return to the Traditional Crematorium and continue down St Dionis Road to the roundabout. Take the first path on the left and over to the right is the grave of the actress **Dame Anna Neagle** (1904–86) and her husband, the film director **Herbert Sydney Wilcox** (1890–1977). She was very much a local girl, born in Forest Gate, and she became a hugely popular film actress, most famous for her portrayal of Queen Victoria, directed by her husband. They are buried in her family grave, and her name, added at the bottom, is her married name, Florence Marjorie Wilcox.

The ashes of the great footballer Bobby Moore are interred under a magnolia tree in the City of London Cemetery.

The grave in the City of London Cemetery of the actress Anna Neagle and her husband, the director Herbert Wilcox.

To make it easier to find the grave, a new marble plaque was added and unveiled by the Princess Royal in 2014.

Another of Jack the Ripper's victims is buried in nearby Manor Park Cemetery. Go down Whittard Road to enter the cemetery, walk down Centre Drive and take the first grass path on the left. On the left is an area of common graves, where **Annie Chapman** (1841–88) was buried in an unmarked grave, and there is now a simple memorial to her.

In the East London Cemetery, in Grange Road E13, is the grave of **Terry Spinks** (1938–2012), the boxer who in 1956 was the youngest Briton to win a boxing medal at the Olympic Games. His professional career was cut short by ill health, but he was awarded the MBE in 2002. The grave is to the left of the main path shortly before the chapels. It is of black marble and carries the Olympic rings and photographs of the boxer. Turn left at the chapel and continue to the end of that path and left again. On the right, set back from the path, is the simple headstone marking the grave of **Elizabeth Stride** (1843–88), the third known victim of Jack the Ripper.

SOUTH-EAST LONDON

LONDON BOROUGH OF LAMBETH

ST MARY'S CHURCH, next to Lambeth Palace, was once the parish church of Lambeth, but has been redundant since 1972. It now houses the Garden Museum, which is highly appropriate as in the eastern churchyard is the extraordinary sarcophagus of **John Tradescant the Elder** (d. 1638) and his son **John Tradescant the Younger** (1608–62), the famous gardeners who introduced many new and exotic plants to Britain. They lived in Lambeth where, as well as a garden, they created a museum of curiosities known as Tradescant's Ark. They were both made keeper of the king's gardens. The tomb was erected in 1662, and is carved on all sides with reliefs of trees, animals, antique ruins and fantastic creatures. Also in the churchyard is the tomb of **William Bligh** (1754–1817), who led the ill-fated expedition of the *Bounty* to take breadfruit plants from the Pacific to the West Indies. Under the leadership of Fletcher Christian, the crew mutinied and set Bligh and 18 men adrift in

a launch; amazingly, they reached land after two months at sea with the loss of only one crew member. The tomb, of Coade stone, is topped by a flaming urn.

In the north-east corner of the churchyard of St Leonard's Streatham, against the wall and missing its cross, is the tomb of **William Dyce** (1806–64), an artist closely associated with the Pre-Raphaelite Brotherhood. His best-known painting is *Pegwell Bay – A Recollection of October 5, 1859*, which is in the Tate, but he also produced frescoes for the new Palace of Westminster, including the Arthurian frescoes in the Robing Room. He moved

Opposite: The magnificent memorial in Guy's Chapel to Thomas Guy, founder of the eponymous hospital (see page 208).

The finely carved tomb of the Tradescants (father and son), the celebrated gardeners, in the graveyard of St Mary's Lambeth, now home to the Garden Museum.

The tomb of Captain William Bligh, who will always be associated with the mutiny on the *Bounty*, in St Mary's churchyard, Lambeth.

LONDON BOROUGH OF CROYDON

The archbishops of Canterbury were lords of the manor of Croydon for centuries, and Croydon Palace (now a girls' school) was one of several on the way from Lambeth to Canterbury. Six archbishops were buried in the parish church, now called Croydon Minster, and two very fine tombs survived the fire that destroyed much of the church in 1867. In the south-east chapel of St Nicholas is the brightly painted alabaster tomb of **John Whitgift** (*c.* 1530–1604), who is shown recumbent and praying. He was archbishop during the reign of Elizabeth I and was in attendance at her deathbed. His main legacy can be seen in Croydon, where he founded the Whitgift School and almshouses, both of which still exist. A shopping centre is also named after him. In the south aisle is the marble tomb of **Gilbert Sheldon** (1598–1677), who had asked to be buried next to Whitgift. He is shown reclining on a mat, with skulls and hour-glasses all round the base of the tomb. Sheldon is now best remembered for Wren's Sheldonian Theatre in Oxford, which he financed.

Also buried here is the American painter **John Singleton Copley** (1738–1815) who, after making a name for himself painting sensational portraits in colonial America, came to London, where he painted stunningly realistic history paintings as well as portraits of London luminaries. His largest canvas, *The Siege of Gibraltar*, which hangs in the Guildhall Art Gallery, is so large that the new gallery had to be specially designed to display it. He died penniless and was buried in the grave of fellow Bostonian Thomas Hutchinson.

with his family to Streatham in 1856, and decorated the chancel of St Leonard's, where he was a churchwarden, but the frescoes were destroyed in a fire in 1975. In the Chapel of Unity, at the south-west corner of the church, is the colourful memorial to **Edmund Tilney** (1535–1610), who, as Master of the Revels under Elizabeth I, organised the court entertainment, licensed actors and censored plays.

The splendid tomb, in Croydon Minster, of Archbishop Whitgift.

There is a wall memorial in the north aisle with a relief portrait of the artist.

Mitcham Road Cemetery, in Mitcham Road, Croydon, is a vast and sprawling site, but the two graves mentioned here are easy to find. From the Mitcham Road entrance go up to the chapel and take the path on the right, which leads you to block R6. Here is the grave, marked by a broken column, of **William Martin Yeates Hurlstone** (1876 1906), a promising composer who died tragically young. He studied with Charles Stanford at the Royal College of Music and composed several very assured pieces including a piano concerto and some fine chamber music, which is occasionally performed today. He suffered from asthma from an early age, so a concert career was out of the question. He moved to Croydon, where he taught and conducted until his

The memorial in Croydon Minster to the celebrated American artist John Singleton Copley.

The grave in Mitcham Road Cemetery of Derek Bentley, the victim of an infamous miscarriage of justice.

The grave, in the graveyard of All Saints Upper Norwood, of Robert Fitzroy, naval captain and meteorologist, who took Darwin on the ground-breaking voyage to South America.

untimely death. Return to the main track, turn right and continue to the second roundabout. Just before it, on the right, is the grave of **Derek William Bentley** (1933–53), the victim of an infamous miscarriage of justice. Bentley, who had a low IQ, was found by police on the roof of a warehouse in Croydon along with Christopher Craig. Bentley had already been seized by police when Craig opened fire, killing a policeman. Both were found guilty, though the jury recommended mercy for Bentley. Craig was too young to hang, but Bentley was sentenced to death. It was not until 1998 that the conviction was considered to be unsafe and Bentley was given a posthumous pardon. Bentley's body had been buried at Wandsworth Prison, but in 1966 it was exhumed and re-interred here, originally with no marker. The present black marble headstone was installed in 1994, and it carries the inscriptions 'A victim of British justice' and 'The truth will out'.

In the western part of the graveyard of All Saints, Upper Norwood, on Beulah Hill, is the last resting place of **Robert Fitzroy** (1805–65). He was the naval officer who commanded the *Beagle* on a five-year voyage to South America, when he was accompanied by Charles Darwin, whose studies during the journey led to his ground-breaking theory of evolution. Fitzroy's greatest legacy was his work as head of the new Meteorological Service at the Board of Trade, where he instigated an early version of weather forecasting. In 1865 he moved to Upper Norwood, where his health deteriorated, and he committed suicide. The grave is surrounded by a fence and the headstone has a carving of a cross and an anchor. The grave was restored by the Meteorological Office in 1981.

LONDON BOROUGH OF SOUTHWARK

One of the oldest and most splendid memorials in Southwark Cathedral is the colourful canopied tomb of the poet **John Gower** (d. 1408) in the north aisle. Gower was a friend of Chaucer and worked at court, writing verse in three languages, English, French and Latin. He rests his head on three books, including his most important work, *Confessio Amantis*. The monument was restored and repainted in 1958.

Bankside was London's main entertainment district in the age of Shakespeare, and what is now Southwark Cathedral was then the parish church, so people associated with the theatre would have attended services here, and a few are buried in the church. On the floor of the choir are three grave slabs, though they do not mark the actual graves, and it is not known where exactly they are buried. One is to **Edmund Shakespeare** (1580–1607), an actor who was the youngest brother of William Shakespeare. Next is **John Fletcher** (1579–1625), a playwright who collaborated with several other writers, including Shakespeare and Philip Massinger. His work with Francis Beaumont includes his best-known work, *The Knight of the Burning Pestle*. **Philip Massinger** (1583–1640) was another playwright who often worked in collaboration with others, including Fletcher. His best-known play is the comedy *A New Way to Pay Old Debts*. He asked to be buried in the same vault as his friend and collaborator Fletcher.

The colourful tomb of the medieval poet John Gower in Southwark Cathedral.

Also buried in the chancel, but with no memorial, was **Philip Henslowe** (c. 1555–1616), who was one of the most important impresarios of the Elizabethan theatre. He built the Rose playhouse on Bankside and the Fortune to the north of London Wall, working in partnership with the actor, Edward Alleyn.

The reconstruction of the Globe Theatre on Bankside is one of London's most popular and successful theatres. It was the brainchild of the American actor, **Sam Wanamaker** (1919–93) who sadly did not live to see it finished. Appropriately, his ashes are interred beneath the stage.

Guy's Hospital, in St Thomas Street, was founded by **Thomas Guy** (1644/5–1724), (see page 202) a printer and publisher who had invested in South Sea stock and made his fortune by selling it before the bubble burst. He was originally buried in nearby St Thomas's church, but in 1780, after the west wing of the hospital was finished, he was re-buried in the crypt of Guy's Chapel, and a splendid monument by John Bacon was erected at the west end of the chapel that shows Guy helping a half-naked man in front of a relief of the hospital. Also buried in the crypt is **Sir Astley Paston Cooper** (1768–1841), the influential surgeon who studied and taught at St Thomas's Hospital, later becoming the principal surgeon at Guy's. He earned his baronetcy after operating on George IV, and later attended Queen Victoria. Like all surgeons of the period, Cooper was forced to use body snatchers for his supply of cadavers, which he needed for research and teaching purposes. However, he made certain that his own body would not be anatomised, as it is entombed in a double stone sarcophagus.

Camberwell New Cemetery, in Brenchley Gardens, opened in 1927, as the old cemetery was reaching its capacity. To the left of the chapel is the family grave of **George Cornell** (*c.* 1928–66), a member of the infamous South London Richardson gang, who was shot by Ronnie Kray in the *Blind Beggar* in Whitechapel, after calling Ronnie a 'fat poof'. In the parallel path behind is the Richardson family grave, where **Charles (Charlie) Richardson** (1934–2012), one of the leaders of the gang, was buried, though at the time of writing his name had not been added to the headstone. The Richardson

The grave of the popular boxer, Freddie Mills, in Camberwell New Cemetery, complete with a boxing glove and an engraved portrait.

gang rivalled that of the Krays, and carried out all kinds of criminal activities, including theft, fraud and protection rackets. At Richardson's trial in 1967, the jury heard horrific accounts of torture inflicted on those who crossed him, and he was sentenced to 25 years in prison. He received a traditional gangster's funeral, attended by several of his old associates. Towards the end of the path, on the left, is the grave of **Frederick (Freddie) Mills** (1919–65), the popular boxer who was the world light heavyweight champion from 1948–50. After losing his title, he retired and worked as a television entertainer. He opened a Chinese restaurant in Charing Cross Road, which was later turned into

The grave of singer Anne Shelton, the 'forces' favourite', in Camberwell New Cemetery.

The actor Edward Alleyn's grave in the nave of Christ's Chapel, Dulwich.

a nightclub, and he was found one night in his car behind the nightclub, shot in the head. The inquest decided he committed suicide, but there are many who doubt the verdict and think he was murdered. The black marble headstone shows Freddie in action, and there is a boxing glove on a plinth in the centre of the tombstone. Return to the main path and turn right, continuing round to the left to the grove of trees. Next to the path at the further end is the white marble grave of **Anne Shelton** (1923–94), the popular singer who became the 'forces' favourite', her songs, including *Lili Marlene*, being broadcast to the troops. Her fame soon spread and she sang with both Bing Crosby and Glenn Miller, but luckily she chose not to accompany Miller on his fatal plane trip to France.

Edward Alleyn (1566 1626) was one of the greatest actors of his time, famous for his performances in plays by Christopher Marlowe, who wrote parts specifically for him. In 1605 he bought the manor of Dulwich and founded the College of God's Gift, better known today as Dulwich College. Christ's Chapel, on the site of the original 'hospital', adjoining the Dulwich Picture Gallery, was consecrated in 1616, and as founder Alleyn was buried in its choir, where his tomb can still be seen, though the original gravestone was replaced in 1816. The chapel is open on Tuesday afternoons, and access is via the Picture Gallery.

Jenny Hill, the popular music hall artiste, is buried in Nunhead Cemetery.

The pedestal tomb of the pioneering omnibus operator, Thomas Tilling, in Nunhead Cemetery.

Nunhead Cemetery, in Linden Grove SE15, was opened in 1840 as All Saints Cemetery by the London Cemetery Company, the owners of Highgate Cemetery. It has had a chequered history, having suffered from fraud and vandalism, and in 1975 was bought by the Borough of Southwark for £1. Built on a hill, it is now as much a nature reserve as a cemetery, with a wealth of wildlife and a huge variety of trees. Take the first path on the right and fork left at the obelisk of the Scottish Martyrs Memorial. To the left of the path, set back among the trees but visible from the path, is the grave of **Jenny Hill** (1848–96), the popular music-hall artiste, with a fine angel carved on the headstone. She was a vivacious performer, which earned her the nickname 'The Vital Spark', and she performed in London and the northern counties as well as making a brief tour of America. Return to the entrance and turn right towards the chapel, then take the road up to the right. About halfway up it, on the left, is a path into the trees, where the large stone tomb of **Thomas Tilling** (1825–93) can be found. One of the first omnibus operators, Tilling ran a bus service called The Times to and from the Great Exhibition in 1851, and he soon became the biggest operator in south London. He supplied horses and carriages for Queen Victoria's 1887 jubilee, and was granted the royal warrant.

The curved ledger stone of Sir Charles Fox, the engineer who built the Crystal Palace, in Nunhead Cemetery.

The family grave, in Nunhead, of Bryan Donkin, inventor of an air-tight tin for canning food.

At the top of the slope, on the left, is the plain granite ledger of **Sir Charles Fox** (1810–74), the engineer who specialised in building bridges and railways. He was knighted for his work in the construction of the Crystal Palace for the Great Exhibition of 1851, and he later took it down and re-erected it in Sydenham. On the left, just before the next junction, a marble cross marks the grave of **Frederick Gorringe** (1831–1909), who in 1858 opened a small draper's shop in Buckingham Palace Road, Victoria, which became Gorringe's department store, one of the most fashionable shops in London until it closed in the 1960s. Almost directly opposite, a ledger stone on a brick vault marks the grave of **Bryan Donkin** (1768–1855), an engineer and inventor who created a paper printing machine, worked with Marc Brunel on his Thames Tunnel, and built Charles Babbage's difference engine. His main claim to fame is as the inventor of an air-tight metal tin for canning food, for which he built a canning factory in Bermondsey.

LONDON BOROUGH OF LEWISHAM

Ladywell and Brockley Cemetery opened in 1858 as two separate cemeteries, but were combined in 1948. The graves mentioned here are all in the Ladywell section, accessed from Ladywell Road. A few yards to the right of the main drive, in the third row, is the large but somewhat dilapidated tomb of the artist **Sir John Gilbert** (1817–97). Mainly self-taught, Gilbert worked in oils, watercolour and wood engraving. He produced many paintings on historical or literary subjects, but he was most famous for his book illustrations. He was the first

The grave of the 'decadent' poet Ernest Christopher Dowson in Ladywell Cemetery.

The family grave of the celebrated artist David Jones in Ladywell Cemetery.

artist to be granted the freedom of the City of London. Walk past the war memorial and the chapel, and just past the war graves, straight ahead, is the white marble grave of **Ernest Christopher Dowson** (1867–1900), the so-called 'decadent' poet. T. S. Eliot considered him to be the most gifted poet of the period. He knew Oscar Wilde and Aubrey Beardsley, and produced work for the *Yellow Book*. He led a self-indulgent life and died tragically young, but he is still remembered for such inspired phrases as 'The days of wine and roses' and 'Gone with the wind'. His grave, missing its cross, was restored in 2010. Go down the path to the left and take the first left to find the grave of **David Jones** (1895–1974) about 10 yards down the path in the second row. Jones was an artist who exhibited with Henry Moore and John Piper, as well as a poet of great intensity. He won many awards and was made CBE in 1955 and Companion of Honour in 1974. He is buried in the family grave, and he has an inscription on a circular plaque. Return to the main path, turn right and take the second left after the war graves. Continue to the outer wall and on the right side of the triangular patch is the stone cross to the musicologist **Sir George Grove** (1820–1900). He was secretary to the Crystal Palace when it moved to Sydenham, where he put on a series of popular concerts. He later helped found the Royal College of Music, of which he was the first director, but he is now most famous as the editor of the *Dictionary of Music and Musicians*, which is still referred to as 'Grove'.

At Deptford Green is the church of St Nicholas, famous for the stone skulls on either side of the entrance to the

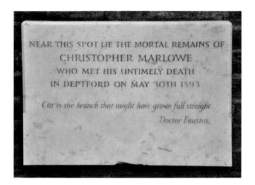

The playwright Christopher Marlowe is buried in an unmarked grave in the graveyard of St Nicholas Deptford.

graveyard. This is the last resting place of **Christopher Marlowe** (1564–93), the great Elizabethan poet, playwright and spy, famous for his heroic verse in such plays as *Doctor Faustus* and *Tamburlaine the Great*. He died in a house in Deptford, stabbed by Ingram Frizer, but the circumstances have never been satisfactorily explained. The exact location of his grave is unknown, but on the east wall of the graveyard is a modern memorial plaque, and there is another inside the church. Both have, as an appropriate epitaph, the line from *Doctor Faustus*, 'Cut is the bough that might have grown full straight'.

In the old churchyard of St Margaret's on Lee Terrace in Lee, across the road from the current church, is buried the Astronomer Royal **Edmond Halley** (1656–1742), who is famous for predicting the orbit of the comet which is named after him. There is a map showing the position of his tomb, which was restored in 1854 when a replica tombstone was installed; the original now adorns a wall of Flamsteed House at the Royal Observatory in Greenwich.

ROYAL BOROUGH OF GREENWICH

In St Alfege church in Greenwich is buried **James Wolfe** (1727–59), the military hero who in the campaign to drive the French from Canada led a successful battle to capture Quebec on the Plains of Abraham, but died at the moment of victory. There is a brass plaque at the back of the church and a modern commemorative stained glass window. Also buried here, under the chancel of the earlier church, is **Thomas Tallis** (*c*. 1505–85), the organist and composer of much church music, including the complex forty-part motet *Spem in alium*. As a gentleman of the Chapel Royal, he would have been living in Greenwich when he died. There is a plaque to him in the south-west corner of the church, and also a memorial stained glass panel.

The memorial in St Alfege Greenwich to the great military leader James Wolfe, who is buried there.

The window celebrating the composer Thomas Tallis in St Alfege church in Greenwich.

In the churchyard of St Mary Magdalene in Woolwich is the tomb of the great bare-knuckle boxer **Tom Cribb** (1781–1848). It takes the form of a splendid lion, with its paw resting on an urn that carries the words 'Respect the ashes of the dead'. Defeated only once in his career, he later ran several pubs, including the Union Arms in Panton Street, which is now the *Tom Cribb*.

At St Luke's church in Charlton is buried **Spencer Perceval** (1762–1812), the only British prime minister to have been assassinated, shot in the lobby of the Commons by John Bellingham, who had a grudge against the government. He was buried in the church near his birthplace and where his wife's family lived. At the back of the church, to the right of the

The great pugilist Tom Cribb is buried in the St Mary Magdalene churchyard in Woolwich, his grave marked by a splendid lion.

Spencer Perceval, Britain's only prime minister to be assassinated, is buried in St Luke's in Charlton, where he is commemorated by a bust by Sir Francis Chantrey.

tower arch, is a memorial plaque with a splendid bust by Sir Francis Chantrey.

On the south wall of St John the Baptist church in Eltham is a wooden plaque marking the approximate burial place of the actor-manager **Thomas Doggett** (c. 1670–1721). Doggett was one of the most popular comedy actors in London, with many roles specially written for him, but he is now remembered for instigating the annual Doggett's Coat and Badge race on the Thames to mark the second anniversary of the accession of George I. Organised every July by the Worshipful Company of Fishmongers, it claims to be oldest rowing race in the world.

LONDON BOROUGH OF BROMLEY

Beckenham Crematorium and Cemetery, in Elmers End Road SE20, contains four interesting graves, all in the older northern section. Turn right past the lodge, and after the path curves to the left by the railway line, take the path which forks to the left, and you will soon find the grave of **Frederick York Wolseley** (1837–99), who in 1895 produced the Wolseley motor car, the first to be made in England. What is less well known is that, while living in Australia, he invented a sheep-shearing machine, which revolutionised wool production. The black marble headstone was put up in 1988 by Wolseley enthusiasts. Nearby is the last resting place of **William Gilbert (W. G.) Grace** (1848–1915), the most famous cricketer of his generation, and still considered to be a giant of the sport. He excelled as both batsman and bowler, and his portly, bearded figure is instantly recognizable. He played for

Gloucestershire as well as England, which he captained many times, and he was also a qualified doctor. In 1898 he moved to London, where he played for the London County team in Crystal Palace and also for Eltham. His grave has a white marble cross and a plaque with cricket bat, ball and stumps. Return to the main path, and turn left, where about 60 yards on the left is the white marble tomb of **Thomas Crapper** (1836–1910), a plumber who improved the design of the water closet at a time when demand for them was high due to the building of the new London sewers. He built a showroom advertising his wares in Chelsea, and supplied the Prince of Wales at Sandringham. Crapper retired to Anerley, which is why he was buried here. Continue along this path, and on the left just after

The grave of the famous cricketer W. G. Grace in Beckenham Cemetery.

Sir Malcolm Campbell, who broke many land and water speed records, is buried in St Nicholas churchyard in Chislehurst.

The great tenor William Heddle Nash is buried in Chislehurst Cemetery.

the third junction is the grave, marked by a stone cross, of **William Walker** (1869–1918), a deep-sea diver who is famous for saving Winchester Cathedral. The cathedral needed underpinning, but the high water table made work difficult. For five years Walker worked under water and in almost complete darkness, laying bags of concrete to seal the inflow of water so that it could be pumped out, allowing the work of underpinning to start. He lived in South Norwood, and returned there every weekend.

In the churchyard of St Nicholas, Church Lane, Chislehurst, to the south of the tower and close to the gate, is a Celtic cross marking the grave of the Campbell family, including **Sir Malcolm Campbell**

(1885–1948), the celebrated sportsman who broke many speed records on both land and water. He called his cars and speedboats *Bluebird* after the symbol of the unattainable in Maeterlinck's play of the same name. He was the first man to achieve 300mph on land, at Bonneville Flats, Utah, in 1935, and reached 141.74mph on Coniston Water in 1939. His son, Donald, followed in his footsteps, breaking many world records before he was killed in another attempt at Coniston Water. In the south-east corner of the churchyard is the grave, with a stone cross, of **William Willett** (1856–1915), a successful builder who is best remembered as a promoter of 'daylight saving', inspired, he said, by the sight of drawn blinds on summer mornings. Several attempts were made to get the Daylight Saving Bill through Parliament, but he didn't live long enough to see it become law.

In Chislehurst Cemetery, in Beaverwood Road, BR7 6HF, is the grave of the great tenor **William Heddle Nash** (1894–1961). To find his grave, a simple stone cross with his name on the crossbar, take the central path behind the lodge to the central roundabout. The grave is on the right hand side. Heddle Nash was the leading lyric tenor of his generation, singing the great roles of Italian and French opera as well as performing in oratorios such as Handel's *Messiah*. He was chosen by Elgar to sing the title role in *The Dream of Gerontius*, and on his grave is a line from *Gerontius*, 'I went to sleep and now I am refreshed'.

On the south side of the churchyard of St Giles the Abbot in Church Road, Farnborough, is a tall Celtic cross to the Lubbock family, including **Sir John Lubbock** (1834–1913). Lubbock ran the family bank, but also had an interest in natural history, having been tutored by Charles Darwin, a family friend. He later became an MP, and can be thanked for introducing the Bank Holiday Bill, creating the first non-religious holidays in Britain. They are still often referred to as St Lubbock's Days. On the cross are carved

The grave of Sir John Lubbock, the banker who introduced bank holidays, is marked by an impressive obelisk in the graveyard of St Giles the Abbot in Farnborough.

a beehive (a symbol for industry), and a dolmen, which relates to his bill to preserve ancient monuments.

WEST NORWOOD CEMETERY

WEST NORWOOD CEMETERY, in Norwood Road SE27, was the second of the 'Magnificent Seven' cemeteries to be built, opening in 1836. It was developed by the South Metropolitan Cemetery Company and designed in the Gothic Revival style by Sir William Tite, who is buried there. Set in an elevated location and beautifully landscaped, it soon attracted many wealthy Londoners. The cemetery is now run by Lambeth Council, and the Friends of West Norwood Cemetery run regular tours, publish various guides and raise funds for conservation work. Details can be found on their website: www.fownc.org.

On the right a few yards inside the cemetery is the rather severe grey headstone of **Sir Hiram Maxim** (1840–1916), the American-born engineer who developed the automatic gun that bears his name. It was the first fully automatic machine gun and was used on many early-twentieth-century battlefields. The British version, the Vickers machine gun, remained in use until 1963. In the centre of the open area to the right is the grave

of **Eric Morley** (1918–2000), the creator of *Come Dancing* and founder of the Miss World beauty contest. The marble scroll-shaped headstone is accompanied by a dove. A short distance further along the main path, on the left, is a granite pedestal topped by a draped urn that commemorates **Thomas (Tom) King** (1835–88), the great bare-knuckle fighter, who was both British and American champion in a sport which was then illegal.

Take the right fork and turn left into the road to the Crematorium. On the right is the squat, railed monument

The grave of Sir Hiram Maxim, the inventor of the machine gun.

Opposite: The terracotta mausoleum of Sir Henry Doulton (see page 224), who ran the famous Lambeth pottery business.

The grave of palaeontologist Gideon Mantell, with its prehistoric tree.

to **Gideon Mantell** (1790–1852), the palaeontologist who discovered the *Iguanadon* and various other dinosaurs. He sold his extensive fossil collection to the British Museum (now the Natural History Museum). His grave was damaged in the 1987 hurricane, and when it was restored in 1992 a gingko, a prehistoric tree, was planted inside the railings. Return to the main path, turn left and about 50 yards up the hill on the right is the large vault of the Jerrold family. Buried here are father and son **Douglas William Jerrold** (1803– 57) and **(William) Blanchard Jerrold** (1826–84), both writers. Douglas was a radical journalist who wrote satirical articles for *Punch* and was also a prolific playwright, his most successful play being the melodrama *Black-Eyed Susan*. Huge crowds attended his funeral and Dickens and Thackeray were pallbearers. His son Blanchard wrote for the *Illustrated London News* and for Dickens' *Household Words*, but he is best known for his collaboration with the French artist Gustave Doré on the book *London: A Pilgrimage*, which exposed the underbelly of Victorian society. The tomb was destroyed in the 1987 hurricane but was restored in 2004. Further up the hill, on the left and on the edge of the trees, is the grave of **Charles Alcock** (1842–1907), the sporting pioneer. He founded the FA Challenge Cup, the first final in 1872 being won by the Wanderers, captained by Alcock himself. He also organised the first test match against the Australians in 1880 at the Oval, home of the Surrey County Cricket Club, of which he was secretary. His grave was adopted by the Football Association in 1992, recognising Alcock as the 'forgotten father of English sport'. The simple white cross was restored in 1999 with the help of the FA and Surrey CCC, when a carving of the FA Cup was added.

Walk back down the hill and turn right onto Ship Path where, on the left, is the grave of the engineer **Sir Henry Bessemer** (1813–98), a pink coped granite ledger with a headstone. The invention of a cheap bronze powder used in gold paint made his fortune, but his reputation is based on the Bessemer converter, which offered a new way of producing good quality steel much more cheaply than had previously been possible. Continue up Ship Path, where on the left is the tomb of **Sir Horace Jones** (1819–87) the architect and surveyor to the City of London. He designed Smithfield, Billingsgate and Leadenhall markets, but his most iconic structure was Tower Bridge, which he didn't live to see finished. The tomb is a granite sarcophagus resting, unusually, on four stone balls. Continue up this path and turn left at the next path. On the right is the modest grave of **Isabella Mary Beeton** (1836–65). She was the nineteenth century's 'domestic goddess', writing for and editing magazines aimed at a middle-class female audience. She is best known for *Beeton's Book of Household Management*, which combined recipes with household tips, and is still in print today.

Retrace your steps and continue along this path until you reach the paved road and turn left. Almost immediately on your left is the badly eroded memorial to **Thomas Winter** (1795–1851), the bare-knuckle champion known as Tom Spring. He didn't have strong hands but won his fights using tactics rather than heavy hitting, which led to his opponents giving him nicknames such as 'The Light Tapper' and 'Lady's Maid'. He had a fine physique and as a young man was a model at the Royal Academy. His Cotswold stone monument originally bore a portrait of Winter and below is a sculpture of a lion and a lamb,

The white marble cross marking the grave of sporting pioneer Charles Alcock.

The tomb of Sir Horace Jones, the architect who designed Tower Bridge.

now almost unrecognisable. A little further on the left is a large slab marking the grave of **Richard Bentley** (1794–1871), the printer who published the works of many celebrated authors. Dickens worked for him as editor of his monthly magazine, *Bentley's Miscellany*, and his novel *Oliver Twist* appeared in the magazine. On the right is a scaffolding-clad building which houses the catacombs. The chapel that stood above them was destroyed by bombing in the Second World War, and the catacombs are not open to the public. In the catacombs is buried **Sir William Tite** (1798–1873), the architect who designed the cemetery buildings. He was a prolific architect and worked in several styles. While Norwood Cemetery is neo-Gothic, his Mill Hill

School was severely classical, as is his best-known building, the Royal Exchange in the City. At the right hand end of the building is the grave of **William Marsden** (1796–1867), a surgeon who changed the way hospitals operated. After failing to gain admission to a hospital for a girl he found seriously ill on the steps of St Andrew's church in Holborn, he opened a dispensary of his own. He was later responsible for the establishment of the Royal Free and Royal Marsden Hospitals. The tomb is in the form of a column on a plinth, but the urn which stood on top is now lost.

Turn back and left onto St-Mary-at-Hill Path, and about 10 yards on the right in the eighth row is the grave, with a headstone and a footstone, of **Samuel Prout**

(1783–1852), the celebrated watercolour artist who specialised in topographical views. Continue along St Mary-at-Hill Path, where on the left is a massive stone slab surrounded by a holly hedge. This is the family vault of the Cubitt family, including **Thomas Cubitt** (1788–1855), who was the greatest speculative builder of the nineteenth century, developing Belgravia and Pimlico as well as large parts of Bloomsbury and Clapham. He also built Osborne House on the Isle of Wight to Prince Albert's designs, and he later built the east wing of Buckingham Palace. His most important legacy is Pimlico, which even during his own lifetime was often referred to as 'Mr Cubitt's District'.

Continue along this path and turn left onto Doulton Path. Turn left off the path at the Sturdy tomb to find the family grave of **Thomas Letts** (1803–73), a limestone pedestal with rams' heads at the four corners. Letts was a stationer who specialised in printing diaries and calendars at a factory in New Cross, and the name lives on. In front of the Letts tomb is a large ledger stone marking the grave of **William Wyon** (1795–1851), a member of the famous family of engravers. He worked at the Royal Mint, where he made dies for the coins of George III, William IV and Queen Victoria as well as many medals. The first adhesive postage stamps such as the 'penny black' used the head of the queen from Wyon's Coronation medal. About ten yards behind is the grave of **William Burges** (1827–81), the eccentric architect and designer who

The modest grave of Mrs Beeton, whose book *Beeton's Book of Household Management* is still in print.

The memorial to William Marsden, the surgeon who founded two London hospitals and improved the way hospitals were run.

The grave of the architect William Burges, who specialised in Gothic buildings with highly colourful interiors.

The simple headstone of the important topographical artist David Roberts.

worked exclusively in the Gothic style. He is best known for his work on Cardiff Castle and Castell Coch, and his own home, Tower House in Kensington, is a unique medieval fantasy. His tomb, which he designed for his mother, is more restrained and bears an elaborate foliated cross carved on its lid. Return to the Doulton Path and take the next path on the left, where straight ahead is the large headstone to **George Jennings** (1810–82), the sanitary engineer who provided the public toilets at the Crystal Palace in 1851, for which the charge was one penny, giving us the expression 'to spend a penny'. He later recommended building underground public toilets in the City, but the proposal was rejected by the Corporation, and the first were built a few years after his death.

At the end of the Doulton Path is the splendid terracotta mausoleum of **Sir Henry Doulton** (1820–97) (see page 218). Henry developed his family's pottery business in Lambeth, working with the Lambeth School of Art to create colourful, glazed earthenware pottery, which came to be known as Doulton Ware. Harold Peto designed the family mausoleum using terracotta from the Doulton factory, including sculptural panels on the gables. It has fine wrought iron doors and the interior has a highly decorated ceiling. On the slope behind is the simple grave of the engineer **Sir William Cubitt** (1785–1861), a plain slab with an inscription. He was involved in the construction of the Crystal Palace, for which he was knighted. Early in his career he invented the treadmill, using human

The terracotta mausoleum of Sir Henry Tate, the sugar magnate whose art collection is the nucleus of Tate Britain.

The City solicitor, Charles Pearson, who was instrumental in the creation of the London Underground, is buried in his son-in-law's tomb.

instead of animal power to grind corn, and the invention was later used in prisons as a form of punishment. He is not related to Thomas Cubitt mentioned above.

At the end of Doulton Path go straight ahead by the side of the crematorium. A few yards on the left is the simple headstone marking the last resting place of the Scottish artist **David Roberts** (1796–1864), who began his career as a theatrical scene-painter before turning to the topographical paintings that were to make his name. He travelled extensively in Europe and the Middle East, and the pictures inspired by his travels proved very popular. He also produced a number of paintings of London from the Thames. A little further on is the impressive terracotta mausoleum of **Sir Henry Tate** (1819–99),

the sugar magnate. It was designed by Harold Peto, and the interior contains some splendid mosaics. The Lancashire-born sugar refiner built a massive refinery by the Thames in Silvertown, and it was here that he produced sugar in cubes for the first time. He was an avid collector of modern British art, including the Pre-Raphaelites, and he left his collection to the nation, which is now housed in Tate Britain. Just round the corner is the tomb of the Baptist preacher **Charles Haddon Spurgeon** (1834–92) with a relief portrait. He gave his first sermon at the age of 17, and soon became something of a celebrity. In 1861 he opened the Metropolitan Tabernacle at the Elephant and Castle, of which he was pastor for 38 years. The building, rebuilt after a fire in 1898, is still a local landmark.

This elegant little cross marks the grave of John Henry Pepper, the scientist who invented the 'Pepper's Ghost' illusion.

The memorial to Paul Julius Baron de Reuter, who founded the eponymous news agency.

At the end of this path is the family tomb of Sir Thomas Gabriel, in which is buried **Charles Pearson** (1793–1862), whose daughter had married Gabriel. Pearson was the City Solicitor from 1839, and his lasting legacy is that he campaigned for an underground railway to improve London's transport system, though he did not live long enough to see his plans come to fruition.

Retrace your steps and turn left down the slope. On the right, set back from the path, is an elegant little white marble cross to **John Henry Pepper** (1821–1900), a scientist who gave popular lectures using magic lanterns and illusions. He is most famous for the illusion known as 'Pepper's ghost', using hidden mirrors, which was used in many theatres. A few yards further down is the pink granite pedestal with a large urn on top, the grave of **Paul Julius Baron de Reuter** (1816–99), who founded the famous news agency which still carries his name. Starting in a small way using racing pigeons in France, he moved to London, where he offered a news service using new cable lines. He was soon able to offer the fast transmission of news and economic data, something taken for granted in the twenty-first century.

Return to the main path and go down the hill to the Greek Orthodox

The grave of Henry Greathead, who designed the shield that allowed for tunnelling through London's clay to build the Underground railway.

Necropolis, which is full of the flamboyant tombs of wealthy merchants, including a replica of the Parthenon. Just inside the gate is a heavily carved tomb chest with a mourning female figure. Here is buried **Maria Zambaco** (1843–1914), an artist and model who was painted by Dante Gabriel Rossetti, Whistler and Edward Burne-Jones, with whom she had an affair. She was the daughter of a Greek merchant, Demetrios Cassavetti, and is buried in the family tomb. Continue on this path, which curves round to the left, and on the right at the next junction is a tall pink granite monument, topped off with a cross, to **Paul Cinquevalli** (1859–1918), the celebrated

The last resting place of Paul Cinquevalli, renowned juggler and star of the music hall.

228

Maria Zambaco, the artist's model and lover of Edward Burne-Jones, is buried with her family in the Greek Necropolis.

juggler. He performed all over the world, but his greatest successes were in London, where he performed for royalty as well as in the music halls and in pantomime. He had amazing strength and dexterity, and could juggle with almost anything. Perhaps his greatest trick was juggling balls while holding in his mouth a man sitting in a chair. About 40 yards further along, over to the right by the wall, is the tomb of **James Henry Greathead** (1844–96), a simple ledger stone with a cross carved on the top, overlooked by the angel of an adjacent grave. Greathead was an inventor and civil engineer who designed a shield that allowed workmen to tunnel through London's clay to build many of London's underground railway lines.

SOUTH-WEST LONDON

LONDON BOROUGH OF RICHMOND

Barnes Common Cemetery, off Rocks Lane, opened in 1854 as a new cemetery for the parish church, but was closed to burials in 1954. It has been declared a nature reserve, and the tombstones are now somewhat lost among the undergrowth. The best access is from Mill Hill Road. Look for the sign to the Barnes Common Local Nature Reserve and walk straight up the right-hand path. The first tomb, just outside the trees, is the grey granite ledger of **Ebenezer Cobb Morley** (1831–1924), the lawyer and sportsman who was instrumental in setting up the Football Association and drafting the first rules of the game, making him an influential figure in the history of the game. His grave was restored in 2013 and a wreath was laid here to commemorate the FA's 150th anniversary. Just inside the main part of the cemetery, to the right near a headless angel, is the grave of **Francis Turner Palgrave** (1824–97), with a lamb in the centre of the cross. Palgrave was a poet, but his best-known work is *The Golden*

Opposite: The grave of Howard Carter, the archaeologist who discovered the tomb of Tutankhamun, in Putney Vale Cemetery (see page 247).

Treasury, an anthology of English lyric poetry and songs.

Richmond and East Sheen Cemetery is an amalgamation of two cemeteries, Richmond Cemetery, which opened in 1853, and East Sheen in 1906. The main entrance is in Sheen Road, via a private road, Kings Ride Gate. Just past the office on the right is the grave of the popular actor **Roy Kinnear** (1934–88), who appeared in many films but is perhaps best known for his regular appearances on the satirical television programme, *That Was The Week That Was*. He died after a fall from a horse while filming *The Return of the Musketeers* in Spain. In the top right hand corner of this block is the tomb of the cemetery's most exotic resident, **William Ellsworth Robinson** (1861–1918), an American magician working in England using the stage name **Chung Ling Soo**. He didn't speak a word of Chinese but kept up the pretence off stage, even speaking through an interpreter, and his true identity only came out after his death. His most famous trick was catching a bullet in his teeth, but one night at the Wood Green Empire the trick went horribly wrong, and he was seriously wounded, dying in hospital the following day. The grave is surmounted by an angel, making it very prominent.

The grave of Ebenezer Cobb Morley, the little known sportsman who helped found the Football Association, is buried in Barnes Common Cemetery.

Walking up the main path towards the chapel, take the next path on the right, where on the right beside the path is the family grave of **Archibald Leitch** (1865–1939), the Glasgow-born architect and engineer who specialised in designing football stadia, his speciality being grandstands. He built more than 30 football stadia all over the country, including Chelsea's at Stamford Bridge and Fulham's ground at Craven Cottage. His designs survived into the 1970s, but after the Hillsborough disaster most of his stands were demolished, though the Craven Cottage pavilion at Fulham's ground has been listed. Continue up the central path, and behind the chapel to the left is the grave of the actor **Fulton Mackay** (1922–87), who is best known as the self-important prison warder Mr Mackay in the television series *Porridge* with Ronnie Barker.

Go through into the old Richmond cemetery to find, in section M, the grave of the popular novelist **Mary Elizabeth Braddon** (1835–1915), a solid, four-square granite chest tomb. She wrote over 80 novels, the most famous of which was *Lady Audley's Secret*, a supreme example of the popular 'sensation fiction' of its time. Her own life reflected the themes of her novels, as she lived for many years with her publisher, John Maxwell, bearing him six children, but was unable to marry him until 1874, as his wife was in a mental institution. The inscription gives her married name, with her maiden name in brackets. In section E is the grave of the Polish-born composer and conductor

The headstone of actor Roy Kinnear in Richmond and East Sheen Cemetery bears the masks of Comedy and Tragedy.

An angel marks the last resting place of William Ellsworth Robinson, the American magician who pretended to be Chinese, performing as Chung Ling Soo.

Sir Andrzej Panufnik (1914–91), with a beautifully cut inscription by Richard Kindersley. To escape the oppressive communist regime, he defected in 1954 and spent the rest of his life in England, becoming a British citizen in 1961. His music was banned for many years in Poland, but with the fall of communism he returned in triumph to conduct his music in Warsaw.

Walk back up the central path and go through the gates and turn left into section W where, in the third row, is the simple grave of the Pre-Raphaelite painter **Arthur Hughes** (1832–1915), with no headstone, just an inscription round the kerbstone. His best-known painting, *April Love*, is in the Tate. He was also an important book illustrator, supplying designs for Thomas Hughes' *Tom Brown's Schooldays*. In section 14 is the grave of sculptor **William McMillan** (1887–1977). His sculpture was full of variety, and his London commissions include the statues of George VI overlooking the Mall, and Alcock and Brown at Heathrow. He worked from a studio in Chelsea, but died in hospital in Richmond.

In the graveyard of St Mary the Virgin, Mortlake, in Mortlake High Street SW14,

The chest tomb of Mary Elizabeth Braddon, the prolific writer of sensational novels, in Richmond and East Sheen Cemetery. The Latin quotation from one of Horace's Odes says 'Exegi monumentum aere perennius' (I have raised a monument more permanent than bronze), predicting her eternal fame.

The grave of the Polish composer Sir Andrzej Panufnik, with its curious design, in Richmond and East Sheen Cemetery.

is the grave of the statesman **Henry Addington, Viscount Sidmouth** (1757–1844). He was an effective Speaker of the Commons, and later a reactionary Home Secretary for 11 years, but his four years as prime minister were not considered to be his finest hour. The unusual chest tomb is south of the chancel, and there is a fine wall memorial in the north aisle of the church. **John Dee** (1527–1609) is buried beneath the chancel of the church, though his grave is unmarked. Dee has long had a reputation as a magician or wizard and he did practise alchemy, but he was a major scholar of his day, and his vast collection of books was far greater than any library in the Oxford or Cambridge colleges. He was also astrologer to Elizabeth I, who visited him at his house in Mortlake, which backed on to the churchyard. A simple

The sculptor William McMillan is buried in Richmond and East Sheen Cemetery.

Near this place lie the remains of
JOHN DEE MA
CLERK IN HOLY ORDERS
1527 ~ 1609
Astronomer, Geographer
Mathematician
Adviser to Queen Elizabeth I

John Dee, the Elizabethan astrologer and scholar, lived in Mortlake and was buried under the chancel of St Mary the Virgin.

plaque was erected on the south wall of the church in 2013.

In 1854 the churchyard closed for new burials, and what is now known as the Old Mortlake Burial Ground opened in South Worple Way SW14. To the right of the path is the plain slab marking the grave of **Sir Edwin Chadwick** (1800–90), the social reformer best remembered for his pioneering work in health reform and improving London's sanitation. Some of his recommendations, rejected at the time, are considered to be predecessors of the welfare state. Nearby, next to the path, is the tomb of **Georgina Hogarth** (1827–1917), Dickens's sister-in-law, who for many years ran his household and was with him when he died. Close by is the grave of

Charles Dickens the Younger (1837–96), the eldest son of novelist Charles Dickens. He edited his father's magazine *All the Year Round*, and wrote several guidebooks, including *Dickens's Dictionary of London*. Close to the southern gate a Celtic cross marks the burial site of the composer **Sir Arthur Edward Drummond Bliss** (1891–1975), who produced orchestral and chamber music as well as film music and ballet scores, most notably *Checkmate*. He was appointed Master of the Queen's Music in 1953 and composed music for the investiture of the Prince of Wales in 1969.

Mortlake Roman Catholic Cemetery in North Worple Way is behind St Mary Magdalen RC church. Here is one of London's most spectacular and original

Sir Edwin Chadwick, the great Victorian reformer, is buried in Old Mortlake Burial Ground under a plain ledger.

tombs, that of the explorer **Sir Richard Burton** (1821–90). Burton was one of the most colourful characters of his time, an army officer, explorer, diplomat and best-selling author. An extraordinary linguist, he learnt over 40 different languages, which allowed him to move among natives in disguise, most famously making the pilgrimage to Mecca dressed as a sheikh. He wrote many books about his travels, as well as translations of erotic books such as the *Kama Sutra* and the *Arabian Nights*. His tomb, which also contains his wife, is made in the form of a desert tent, based on one he used in Syria, and is made of sandstone from the Forest of Dean. At the rear a ladder allows you to look in through a window to see the two gilded coffins. Buried to the north of the church is the architect **John Francis Bentley** (1839–1902). Bentley built several churches in London, but his masterpiece is the Roman Catholic Westminster Cathedral, which he designed in the Byzantine style. His tomb is simple but elegant, in the form of a coffin with a wreath carved on top.

The small churchyard of St Anne, Kew contains a number of interesting graves.

Sir Arthur Bliss, the composer and Master of the Queen's Music, is buried in Old Mortlake Burial Ground.

Buried to the south of the church, under a raised ledger, is the great artist **Thomas Gainsborough** (1727–88), who was one of the best portrait painters of his time, and a serious rival to Sir Joshua Reynolds. He was a founder member of the Royal Academy, though he later fell out with them over the way his paintings were hung. He was particularly famed for his elegant poses and bravura brushwork. He often visited his friend, the artist **Joshua Kirby** (1716–74), who lived in Kew and worked as drawing

Opposite: The unique tomb of explorer Sir Richard Burton, in the form of a desert tent, in the graveyard of St Mary Magdalen church in Mortlake.

The squat chest tomb of artist Thomas Gainsborough, who is buried in St Anne's graveyard at Kew.

Johan Zoffany spent his last three decades at Strand on the Green and is buried at Kew.

master to the royal family, and is buried close to him in a fairly modest tomb. Also interred here in a large chest tomb is the artist **Johan Zoffany** (1733–1810). The German-born Zoffany made his name in London painting portraits and conversation pieces. He was much sought after by the top actors of the day to paint them in their major roles, offering us a vivid depiction of them in action. He became a member of the Royal Academy, and painted the famous portrait of its founding members. In 1780 he moved to Strand on the Green, just across the river from Kew.

At the east end of the graveyard is a chest tomb with a brick base; buried here are two famous botanists who both became directors of nearby Kew Gardens. **Sir William Jackson Hooker** (1785–1865) was interested in botany from an early age, and became an expert in mosses and ferns. In 1841 he became the first full-time director at Kew, which he enlarged and improved, attracting many new visitors. He also increased the propagation of plants, including *Chinchona*, which were sent to India to provide a cure for malaria, and plane trees, which were planted throughout

London. He was succeeded by his son **Sir Joseph Dalton Hooker** (1817–1911), who had travelled to the Antarctic and the Himalayas collecting plants, including a new species of rhododendron, which became popular with British gardeners. Under his directorship of Kew, rubber trees were taken, without permission, from Brazil to British colonies in the East.

In the south-west corner of St Mary Magdalene church in Richmond is a stone plaque marking the last resting place of the great Shakespearean actor **Edmund Kean** (1787–1833). There is a memorial to him in the north-west corner, with a relief portrait between a pair of curtains. Kean rose from humble beginnings to become a star of the London stage, making a celebrated debut as Shylock at Drury Lane in 1814. He excelled in tragic roles such as Lear and Othello, and had considerable success touring America, but a life of whoring and drinking took its toll, and he was later unable to learn new roles. In 1831 he moved to Richmond, where he ran the King's Theatre until his death. He was buried here because Westminster Abbey refused to bury him next to David Garrick. Buried in the north-

The great Shakespearean actor, Edmund Kean, was buried in St Mary Magdalene in Richmond.

Thomas Twining, who founded the famous tea company, has a memorial on the exterior wall of St Mary's Twickenham.

west corner of the church is the Scottish poet **James Thomson** (1700–48), who lived in Richmond in his later years. His most important work is *The Seasons*, but he is best known as the author of *Rule Britannia*, which was set to music by Thomas Arne. The fine brass plaque on the west wall was added in 1792.

St Mary Twickenham contains the tombs of several important eighteenth-century figures. The poet **Alexander Pope** (1688–1744) is buried with his parents in front of the chancel step, marked by a simple stone with a P carved in it. A brass plaque was installed alongside it in 1962 by members of the English faculty of Yale University. In the north gallery is a larger memorial with a portrait medallion, erected by Bishop Warburton in 1761. Despite suffering from very poor health throughout his life, and being Catholic, Pope became hugely successful. He translated Homer and edited Shakespeare, but he is best known for his epic satires *The Rape of the Lock* and *The Dunciad*. In 1719 he had a villa built by the Thames in Twickenham, along with its famous grotto, and he lived there for the rest of his life.

Also buried in the church is **Sir Godfrey Kneller** (1646–1723), the portrait painter. Born in Germany as Gottfried Kniller, he studied in Amsterdam with Rembrandt and in Rome with Bernini, before arriving in London in 1676, where he

The memorial to the poet Alexander Pope in St Mary's church in Twickenham, where he lived for much of his life.

The portrait artist Sir Godfrey Kneller is buried in St Mary's Twickenham, with no memorial, but over his grave is a stained glass window with his coat of arms.

soon established himself, painting portraits of the king and his court in the style of Van Dyck. In 1709 he built a villa in Whitton, near Twickenham, which after his death was re-named Kneller Hall, and a new building on the site now houses the Royal School of Military Music. Kneller is buried in the north-east corner of the church, under a window which bears his coat of arms. There is no monument to him, and his memorial, by Rysbrack, is in Westminster Abbey, which would have upset the artist, as he said that 'they do bury fools there'.

On the outside wall of the church, at the east end, is a memorial to **Thomas Twining** (1675–1741), an East India merchant who bought up Tom's Coffee House, later introducing tea, setting up the famous Twining tea company, which still has a shop in the Strand. Close by is a memorial to the actress **Catherine (Kitty) Clive** (1711–85), who lived in Twickenham for over 40 years and was buried in the churchyard. She was one of the most popular actresses of her time, and worked with all the top actors and authors, including David Garrick. Her first major part was Polly in *The Beggar's Opera*, which she continued to play for many years. Also buried here, but with no memorial, is the great Shakespearean actress **Hannah Pritchard** (1709–68),

The baroque cartouche to the celebrated actress Peg Woffington in St Mary with St Alban in Teddington makes no mention of her celebrity as an actress.

In the church of St Mary with St Alban in Ferry Road, Teddington, is buried the famous Irish actress **Margaret (Peg) Woffington** (1720–60). She had a very wide repertoire of roles, but excelled in high comedy, and was particularly successful in breeches roles. She had a long partnership with David Garrick, both on and offstage. She bought a home in Teddington in the 1740s, and was buried in the parish church where she has a memorial on the north wall of the chancel. Curiously, she is referred to as 'spinster', but there is no mention of her stage career. On the west wall of the church is a neo-classical tablet to **Henry Flitcroft** (1697–1769), the architect who designed St Giles-in-the-Fields, the first Palladian church in London, and built the west wing of Woburn Abbey. Under the west tower of the church are two memorials to **Stephen Hales** (1677–1761), who was curate here for 51 years. He is buried beneath the tower, whose construction he paid for. As well as a rector, he was an important amateur scientist, and is sometimes compared to Isaac Newton. He carried out experiments on such matters as ventilation and kidney stones, and even experimented on animals. His portrait appears in the east window.

In Teddington Cemetery, in Shacklegate Lane, is the grave of the novelist **Richard Doddridge Blackmore** (1825–1900). Blackmore trained as a lawyer, but after a short spell teaching in Twickenham settled in Teddington and became a market gardener. He wrote poetry and historical novels, the most famous of which was *Lorna Doone*, set in seventeenth-century Exmoor. The grave, of pink granite, is on the left of the main path, shortly before the chapel.

the greatest Lady Macbeth of the day, a part she played many times with David Garrick. She was buried in Twickenham because she owned property there, but her memorial was erected in Westminster Abbey.

The explorer, George Vancouver, died in Petersham and is buried in St Peter's churchyard.

The grave of Sir Richard Owen, the palaeontologist who coined the word 'dinosaur', at St Andrew's Ham.

On the south side of the graveyard of St Peter's church, Petersham, is the grave of **George Vancouver** (1757–98), the explorer who sailed twice with Captain Cook before being sent to survey the north-west coast of north America. The island and city of Vancouver are both named after him, as are a number of geographical features. He settled in Petersham to write up his journal, but became ill and died aged only 40. The grave, of white stone, was restored in the 1960s and is now Grade II listed. In the centre of the graveyard is the pink granite tomb of **Glyn Francis Warren Philpot** (1884–1937), who was a hugely successful portrait painter in the 1920s and

'30s. His star waned after his death, but his work has been through a long overdue re-evaluation in recent years.

On the south side of St Andrew's church, in Church Road, Ham, is the pink granite tomb of **Sir Richard Owen** (1804–92), the palaeontologist who coined the word 'dinosaur'. He began his career cataloguing specimens at the Hunterian Museum before going on to run the natural history section of the British Museum (now the Natural History Museum). He was a major scientific figure, but his reputation suffered after he openly criticised Darwin's *Origin of Species*. The Natural History Museum, which he proposed and carried through to its completion, is his greatest legacy.

LONDON BOROUGH OF WANDSWORTH
Lambeth Cemetery in Blackshaw Road, Tooting, SW17, is the last resting place of **George Galvin** (1860–1904), the music hall star better known as **Dan Leno**. His grave, a white marble cross, can be found just inside the entrance to the right of the path leading to the left-hand chapel. He began his career at the age of four as

the 'Infant Wonder', and was famous for comedy routines in which he told stories of ordinary everyday life accompanied by a wide range of facial expressions. He appeared for many years in the Drury Lane pantomime as the dame. He was so popular that thousands of people lined the streets to watch his funeral procession.

Putney Vale Cemetery, alongside the busy A3, opened in 1891, with the crematorium opening in 1938. Turn right up Richards Way, and right at the top in the corner by the roundabout is the curious grave of **Joseph Bruce Ismay** (1862–1937), head of the White Star Line shipping company, which built the *Titanic*. He was on board when the ship sank in 1912, and survived amid considerable controversy. Although he was seen to help women and children into the lifeboats and was later cleared of blame at the enquiry, he had been responsible for the decision to provide an inadequate number of lifeboats. His and his wife's ashes are buried in a tomb that is one of the most unusual and eccentric in London. It consists of four elements: a central chest tomb with carvings of sailing ships on all four sides, a ledger, a carved seat and an upright stone with a biblical text on one side and unusual carvings on the other. To the left of the roundabout is the grave of **Vladek Sheybal** (1923–92), the Polish actor who escaped to England in 1958 and carved out a successful career in television and film, mostly playing villains. He appeared in several Ken Russell films and *From Russia with Love*.

A short way along Alexander Way, on the right, is the pink granite grave of **Sir Peirson Frank** (1881–1951), an engineer who was a forgotten hero of the Second

The great music hall entertainer, Dan Leno, is buried in Lambeth Cemetery.

World War. As chief engineer at the London County Council he ran the rapid response unit that repaired bomb damage to the river walls, and has been justly called 'the man who saved London from drowning'. He also worked on the demolition of the old Waterloo Bridge and construction of its replacement, and built Wandsworth Bridge. Just before the next junction, by the wall on the right, is the appropriately craggy block of stone that marks the grave of the sculptor **Sir Jacob Epstein** (1880–1959). The American-born sculptor studied in Paris before arriving in London, where he soon became a controversial figure. The leading British avant-garde sculptor of his day, his work was often called ugly, and *Rima*, his

In a corner of Putney Vale Cemetery, this unusual chest tomb, with carvings of sailing ships, is only one element of the monument to Joseph Bruce Ismay, owner of the White Star Line, who survived the sinking of the *Titanic*.

memorial to W. H. Hudson in Hyde Park, was vandalised on several occasions. His reputation as a major artist is now secure, and several important works can be seen in London, including a *Madonna & Child* in Cavendish Square and the statue of Jan Christiaan Smuts in Parliament Square.

About 20 yards further on, by the path, a simple headstone marks the grave of Belfast-born artist **Sir John Lavery** (1856–1941). He trained in Glasgow and became a popular painter of genre pictures, and was a member of the group known as the Glasgow Boys. He moved to London where he gained a reputation as a portrait painter, including formal portraits of the royal family, and later lived in America, where he painted portraits of various Hollywood stars. Turn sharp left and about 40 yards on the left you will find the grave

of **Sandy Denny** (1947–78), the singer and songwriter who is considered to be a founder of folk rock. She is best known for her work with Fairport Convention, and her best known song is the sad *Who Knows Where the Time Goes?* Her short life ended with addictions to drugs and alcohol and she died after a fall.

The grave of Sir Peirson Frank in Putney Vale Cemetery, a forgotten hero of the Second World War.

The suitably rugged memorial to the sculptor Jacob Epstein in Putney Vale Cemetery.

Retrace your steps to find, on a corner plot on the left, the black marble grave of **Vesta Tilley** (1864–1952), the famous music hall artist. Born Matilda Alice Powles, she began performing at the age of five, and at eight was working in London as the Great Little Tilley. She changed her name to Vesta after the famous brand of matches, and was promoted as 'a bright spark'. She often performed in drag, most famously as Burlington Bertie. In 1890 she married Walter de Frece, and the headstone gives her name as Lady Matilda Alice de Frece. Continue along Alexander Way and a short way further along, on the right, are two white marble graves with Russian crosses. They are to members of the Kerensky family, including

Alexander Kerensky (1881–1970), who was prime minister of the Russian Provisional Government that was overthrown by the Bolsheviks in 1917. He spent the rest of his life in exile and died in New York, but the Russian churches there refused to bury him, so his body was flown to London to be buried here. A few yards further on, on the left, is the grave of the popular broadcaster **Roy Plomley** (1914–85), best known as the creator and for over 40 years the presenter of the popular radio programme *Desert Island Discs*. The original series was to consist of only eight programmes, but he was an excellent interviewer and he recorded 1,791 programmes, and more than 70 years later the programme is still going strong, making it the longest-running British radio programme of all time.

A short distance on the right is the classical mausoleum of the Sainsbury family,

The grave of folk rock singer Sandy Denny in Putney Vale Cemetery.

The tomb of the great music hall star Vesta Tilley in Putney Vale Cemetery.

The popular radio presenter, Roy Plomley, is buried in Putney Vale Cemetery.

who ran the grocery business that grew into the supermarket chain bearing their name. The first to be buried here was **John James Sainsbury** (1844–1928), who opened the first shop in Drury Lane in 1869 before opening up branches in the suburbs. It was very much a family business, and his son

John Benjamin Sainsbury (1871–1956) took over the reins on his father's death, and his ashes too were interred in the mausoleum. Turn left down Schofield Road and take the next right, where on the left is the rough block of stone that is the appropriate grave marker of the famous strongman **Eugen Sandow** (1867–1925), who is considered to be the founder of modern body-building. The Prussian-born Sandow had a magnificent physique and became a celebrated music hall performer in London, and he also had successful tours in America working in vaudeville and circuses. He had been unfaithful to his wife, who didn't erect anything to mark his grave. In 2002 a traditional grave was created, but it was replaced in 2009 by the present marker, which was erected by his great-great-grandson. Continue along this path and turn right. Just before the main path, on the right, is the modest headstone to **Richard John Beattie (Dick) Seaman** (1913–39), who was considered to be one of the greatest pre-war racing drivers. Against his father's wishes, but with financial help from his mother, he began to compete so successfully that in 1936 Mercedes offered him a place in their team. In 1938 he won the German Grand Prix at the Nürburgring, but in the following year he crashed during the Belgian Grand Prix and died of his injuries. Hitler sent a large and rather flashy wreath to his funeral.

Turn left into Alexander Way and continue along this road, which curves round to the left. Turn right at the crossroads before the chapel and at the back is the grave of **Jennifer Paterson** (1928–99), the celebrity chef best known for the television series *Two Fat Ladies*, which

This rough-hewn block marks the grave of body-builder Eugen Sandow in Putney Vale Cemetery.

The grave, in Putney Vale Cemetery, of Sir William Orpen, the celebrated portrait painter.

she co-presented with Clarissa Dickson Wright. Further along this path, also at the back on the right, is the double grave of **Sir Owen Seaman** (1861–1936) and his parents. He was a celebrated literary satirist, writing parodies of Tennyson and Kipling, and was editor of *Punch* from 1906 to 1932. During his tenure the circulation went up, but it became a rather staid, conservative publication. A. A. Milne was a contributor to the magazine, and it is said that he based his miserable character Eyore on Seaman. Walk round the chapel and turn left along Central Drive. At the roundabout turn left up Schofield Road, and to the left of the path in the second block, in the second row, is the modest headstone to the artist **Sir William Orpen** (1878–1931). Orpen studied at the Slade in London, where his enormous natural talent

was recognised, and he went on to become a highly successful portrait painter. He was an official war artist during the First World War, painting both official portraits and haunting scenes of the battlefields; many of these paintings are now in the Imperial War Museum.

Take the next left and after the next crossing, on the left, is the last resting place of **Howard Carter** (1874–1939), the archaeologist who discovered the tomb of Tutankhamun (see page 230). His interest in archaeology was kindled when he worked in Egypt as an artist with W. M. Flinders Petrie, and he worked for several years for the antiquities service there. In 1922, working with Lord Carnarvon, he located the tomb, a discovery that hit the headlines worldwide and made his reputation. His grave was until recently in a rather poor condition, with an almost illegible inscription, but the British Museum contributed to its renovation so that it now looks brand new. Continue on this path and at the end, turn left; towards the end of the block, on the left, is the grave of **Francis Durbridge** (1912–98), the crime writer. His Paul Temple plays appeared on radio and television, and for over 20 years his *Francis Durbridge Presents* dramas were the must-see programmes of the time.

Many famous people have been cremated at the Putney Vale Crematorium, but most have had their ashes scattered elsewhere. Two who were scattered here, in the Garden of Remembrance, are the popular comedy actresses **Joan Sims** (1930–2001) and **Hattie Jacques** (1922–80), who are best remembered for their performances in the *Carry On* films.

LONDON BOROUGH OF MERTON

The churchyard of St Mary's Wimbledon contains the fine neo-classical mausoleum of **Sir Joseph William Bazalgette** (1819–91), the great nineteenth-century engineer, who spent his last years in Wimbledon. He created London's sewer system, built three of its bridges, and also constructed the Victoria, Albert and Chelsea embankments. He was also involved in easing traffic congestion by building new streets, such as Shaftesbury Avenue and Northumberland Avenue. Also buried in the churchyard is the political economist **Arnold Toynbee** (1852–83). He was also a social reformer and carried out social work in London's East End. Toynbee Hall, a university settlement in Whitechapel, was named after him and opened the year after his death. His tomb,

The magnificent mausoleum of Sir Joseph Bazalgette, the great engineer who built London's sewer system, in St Mary's graveyard in Wimbledon.

a raised cruciform ledger which has lost its inscription, is by the northern wall of the graveyard.

One of Britain's greatest tennis players, **Frederick (Fred) Perry** (1909–95), has a statue by David Wynne at the All England Lawn Tennis Club at Wimbledon, which was erected in 1984. When he died, his ashes were interred beneath the statue. He won the Wimbledon singles title in 1934, 1935 and 1936, and it was another 77 years before another Briton, Andy Murray, won there in 2013.

Streatham Park Cemetery, in Rowan Road, SW6, is the last resting place of a number of popular entertainers. Go down the main path beyond the office, where on the right is the grave, with an Art Deco cross, of **Ernest Augustus (Gus) Elen**

The ashes of the great tennis player, Fred Perry, have been interred in the base of his statue at the All England Lawn Tennis Club in Wimbledon.

Lupino Lane, the cockney comedian and film star, is buried in Streatham Park Cemetery.

(1862–1940), the popular singer who became one of music-hall's biggest stars, specialising in 'coster' songs. One of his best-known songs was *'If it wasn't for the 'ouses in between'*. At the end of the main drive is the white marble grave of the comic actor **William Thomson (Will) Hay** (1888–1949). He developed his main character, the bumbling schoolteacher, in the music hall, but it transferred successfully to radio and film. He made 17 films, including *Oh, Mr Porter!* in which he played an incompetent stationmaster. About 40 yards behind is the simple grave of **Ben Warriss** (1909–93), a comedian famous as part of a double act with his cousin, Jimmy Jewel. They had many successes on television and appeared seven times at the Royal Variety Performance. Returning to the path, turn right and on the left is the grave of **Lupino Lane**

(1892–1959), the cockney comedian who appeared in many silent movies in Britain and Hollywood. He greatest success was playing the part of Bill Snibson in *Me and my Girl*, as well as creating the routine for *The Lambeth Walk*. He had begun his career using the name Nipper Lane, or Nip, and this nickname appears on his grave.

On the other side of the path is a group of black marble box tombs. In the last row is the grave of **Desmond Dekker** (1941–2006), the reggae singer who was very popular in the 1960s and is best known for his big hit *Israelites*, which topped the UK singles chart. Return to the path and turn right. Take the next right, then left past the Jewish cemetery, right again and then take the next path on the left to find the grave of the popular singer **Dorothy Squires** (1915–98). Almost at the end of the path, her simple grave marker is about 10 yards to the right. She was once the most successful British female singer, with a career spanning more than three decades, but in her later years she was involved in over 30 court cases, eventually being banned from the High Court as a 'vexatious litigant'.

LONDON BOROUGH OF SUTTON

In Bandon Hill Cemetery, in Plough Lane, Wallington, is the grave of the composer **Samuel Coleridge-Taylor** (1875–1912). It can be found just inside the main gate and over to the right. Samuel was of mixed race, and was brought up by his English mother in Croydon, where he was based for the rest of his short life. His work *The Song of Hiawatha* became a major success, although he sold the copyright so that he never received any royalties. He composed much orchestral and chamber music as well as songs, many of which were inspired by Negro spirituals. He died aged only 37, and thousands of people attended

The composer Samuel Coleridge-Taylor, whose music is finding a new audience after many years of obscurity, is buried in Bandon Hill Cemetery.

his funeral. The headstone carries a poem by his friend, Alfred Noyes, which includes the line, 'He lives while music lives', and a line of music from *Hiawatha* has been carved along the bottom.

FURTHER READING

Arnold, Catharine, *Necropolis – London and its Dead*, Simon & Schuster, 2006

Barnes, Richard, *The Art of Memory – Sculpture in the Cemeteries of London*, Frontier, 2016.

Curl, James Stevens, *The Victorian Celebration of Death*, Sutton Publishing, 2000.

Jackson, Lee, *Dirty Old London*, Yale, 2014.

Johnson, Malcolm, *Crypts of London*, The History Press, 2013.

Meller, Hugh and Parsons, Brian, *London's Cemeteries*, The History Press, 2011.

I have also found helpful the many books and pamphlets published by, or in conjunction with, the individual cemeteries.

GLOSSARY OF TERMS

Broken Column: Usually denotes a life cut short, or someone who died in the prime of life.

Cartouche: An oval-shaped wall memorial, often elaborately carved.

Catacomb: Underground burial place with galleries of recesses, or 'loculi', for storing coffins.

Celtic Cross: A cross set within a circle, often with interlace decoration on the shaft. Originally used by the early Celtic Christians for high crosses, they became popular in the nineteenth century as grave markers in graveyards and cemeteries.

Cenotaph: An empty tomb, often a memorial to someone buried elsewhere.

Chest tomb: A large tomb shaped like a box or chest.

Coffin tomb: A tomb shaped like a coffin.

Columbarium: Space with niches for storing cremated remains, looking like the inside of a dovecote. The word comes from the Latin *columba* for dove.

Common Graves: Places in a cemetery where unrelated people are buried, often with only a simple marker or none at all.

Coped Ledger: A ledger stone with a gabled top.

Crypt: An underground space beneath a church, often used as a burial space.

Deadboard or **Graveboard:** A grave marker in the form of a wooden rail supported by two posts, one at each end.

Epitaph: Words inscribed on a tomb or gravestone, with details of the deceased, often including their achievements.

Footstone: A stone which marks the foot of a grave, which might have the deceased's initials or information not on the headstone.

Headstone: A stone marker at the head of a grave, which carries the inscription, and often some carved decoration.

Ledger: A large flat horizontal stone slab. The heavy slabs were thought to be a deterrent against body snatchers. Sometimes they are raised on a low plinth.

Mausoleum: A grand, free-standing, structure, built to hold coffins of several generations of a family. The word comes from the tomb of Mausolus, which was one of the Seven Wonders of the World.

Necropolis: Sometimes used to describe modern cemeteries, the word is Greek for a City of the Dead, a cemetery built outside the city walls.

Obelisk: A tall four-sided pillar, tapering to a pyramid top. They became very popular in the nineteenth century, following contemporary discoveries in Egypt.

Pedestal Tomb: Similar to a chest tomb, but taller and narrower.

Sarcophagus: A box-shaped coffin, usually above ground. They are often covered in decorative carvings, in imitation of the classical originals.

Table tomb: Rather like a chest tomb, with a ledger stone on four corner columns, and no side panels.

Vault: A large underground stone structure containing a number of coffins, usually built for a family, and marked by a stone slab with the family name.

Weepers: Mourning figures carved on the side of tombs in churches, often the deceased's children.

INDEX OF NAMES